Rock & Roll Recollections:

A Journalist's 50-Year Diary

Rock & Roll Recollections:

A Journalist's 50-Year Diary

By William R. Chemerka

Rock and Roll Recollections
© 2014 William R. Chemerka. All Rights Reserved.

All illustrations are copyright of their respective owners, and are also reproduced here in the spirit of publicity. Whilst we have made every effort to acknowledge specific credits whenever possible, we apologize for any omissions, and will undertake every effort to make any appropriate changes in future editions of this book if necessary.

No part of this book may be reproduced in any form or by any means, electronic, mechanical, digital, photocopying or recording, except for the inclusion in a review, without permission in writing from the publisher.

Published in the USA by:
BearManor Media
P O Box 71426
Albany, Georgia 31708
www.bearmanormedia.com

ISBN   978-1-59393-765-2 (paperback)

Printed in the United States of America.

Book & cover design by Darlene and Dan Swanson of Van-garde Imagery, Inc.

Contents

	Dedication vii
	Acknowledgements ix
	Foreword xiii
	Author's Introduction xvii
Chapter 1:	The Beach Boys 1
Chapter 2:	John Beland 15
Chapter 3:	Phil Collins. 35
Chapter 4:	Peter Criss 49
Chapter 5:	Danny and the Juniors. .63
Chapter 6:	Judas Priest. 87
Chapter 7:	Meat Loaf. 101
Chapter 8:	Motörhead 115
Chapter 9:	Peter Noone of Herman's Hermits 129
Chapter 10:	Platinum Hook 143
Chapter 11:	The Ramones 165
Chapter 12:	Van Halen. 179
Chapter 13:	Stevie Ray Vaughan 203
Chapter 14:	The Who 217
Chapter 15:	The Young Rascals 235
Chapter 16:	ZZ Top. 249
Chapter 17:	Notes and Quotes. 261
	The Beatles 261
	Richard Blake. 262
	Rick Nielsen of Cheap Trick. 263
	Phil Collen of Def Leppard. 264

Larry Graham 264
Steve Howe of Yes 265
Jermaine Jackson 266
Joan Jett 267
Brian Johsnon of AC/DC 268
Kentucky Headhunters 269
Phil Lynott of Thin Lizzy 270
John Mellencamp 270
Righteous Brothers 271
Dee Snider of Twisted Sister 272
Ian Stewart of The Rolling Stones 273
Edgar Winter 274

Index 277

Dedication

To the talented members of the first two bands I was part of: The Abstractions and The Soul Dukes.

The Abstractions were Mike Byrne (drums), Eddie DeRosa (guitar and vocals), Greg Lebed (guitar and vocals), George Johnston (keyboards), and Sam Wilezol (guitar).

The Soul Dukes were Stephen Daniels (drums and vocals), Glynn Nesbitt (guitar), Richard Nesbitt (trumpet), William "Stag" Ford (saxophone and vocals), John Alston (saxophone and vocals), Larry Williams (keyboards), and Charlie Daniels (congas and vocals).

Acknowledgments

Thanks to all the musicians and singers who were kind enough to be interviewed by me over the span of nearly fifty years. Included in this book are contributions from Joey Ramone and Johnny Ramone of The Ramones; Stephen Daniels and Robin Corley of The Soul Dukes and Platinum Hook; John Alston of The Soul Dukes; Glynn Nesbitt and Larry Williams of The Soul Dukes and Parkway North; Danny Rapp, Joe Terranova, David White, Bill Carlucci, Frank Maffei, and Bobby Maffei of Danny and the Juniors; Kaye (McCool) Krebs of The Pixies Three; Meat Loaf; David Lee Roth, Eddie Van Halen, Michael Anthony, and Alex Van Halen of Van Halen; Peter Noone of Herman's Hermits; Mike Love, Dennis Wilson, Bruce Johnston, Carl Wilson, and Al Jardine of The Beach Boys; Stevie Ray Vaughan; Rob Halford, Glen Tipton, and K. K. Downing of Judas Priest; Lemmy Kilmister of Motörhead; Kim McAuliffe of Girlschool; Billy Gibbons, Dusty Hill, and Frank Beard of ZZ Top; Felix Cavaliere, Eddie Brigati, Gene Cornish, and Dino Danelli of The Young Rascals; Peter Criss of Kiss; Phil Collen of Def Leppard; Joan Jett; Larry Graham; Ellen Foley; John Mellencamp; Dee Snider of Twisted Sister; Phil Lynott of Thin Lizzy; Jerry Garcia; Bobby Hatfield and Bill Medley of The Righteous Brothers; Fred Young and Richard Young of The Kentucky Headhunters; Jermaine Jackson; Rick Nielsen of Cheap Trick;

Brian Johnson of AC/DC; Edgar Winter; Steve Howe of Yes; Rich Blake; John Beland, and Phil Collins.

It was enjoyable to communicate with a number of the artists who brought me up to date with their careers in 2014: Phil Collins, Peter Noone, Felix Cavaliere, John Beland, Kaye (McCool) Krebs, Rich Blake, and members of The Soul Dukes, Platinum Hook, and Danny and the Juniors.

I value the the contributions of John Madara, David Zucker, Floyd Vivino, Jim "J. B." Burlage, Cutter Brandenburg, Ed Anderson, Kenny Laguna, Dick Duryea, Nancy Grossi, Bill Jentz, Dave Lowrey, Richard Luce, Bill Groneman, Mark "Twig" Greenburg, Tony Pasqua, Mrs. Sheketa M. Daniels, Paul (Pauly D) DeLorenzo, and Jon and Stefanie Serpico.

Thanks to Diane Casazza, publisher of *The Aquarian Weekly*, for allowing me to utilize some quoted remarks from a number of my articles that I wrote over the years. I also appreciate the instrumental fellowship provided by *Aquarian* staffers Marc Sceurman, Nic Luciano, and Mike Greenblatt in the publication's houseband: Late For Press. And thanks to photographer Mark Weiss and *Aquarian* photographers Bob Sorce and Cathy Miller, who accompanied me on many of my interviews and concert review assignments.

A fond thank you to the JBT: Kathy Mager, Anne Marie Mager, and Karen Riley. Thanks also to Abstractions roadies Walter Mager and George Coppola.

I am indebted to the following hard-core Beatlemaniacs for their friendship: Linda Zarro, Diana Zarro, Carla Zarro, Karen Pagowski, Nancy Eckert, June Welebir, Valerie Ziegler, and Georgette Turpak. And thanks for the additional Beatles memories from Jo Anne Carpenito, Joanne Senneca, Roberta Ciccarella, Kathy Addonizio, Carol Vitale, Kathy Tremper, Valerie Hrooshkin, Donna Toth, Patty Vastano, and Barbara Willson.

Acknowledgements

I am grateful for my "oldies but goodies" college classmates, especially Tom Basnight, Gary Wilson, Tom Buro, Judy Samson, Nina Eisenberg, and Maria Muzyka.

A special "thank you" to my fellow bandmates over the years in The Abstractions; The Soul Dukes; Garden State Express; Emerson, Electric, and DeStefano; Late For Press; The Edukatorz; The R.P.S. Band; Triple Play; The Alamo Blues Band; Justify; Canebrake 7; Yankee Blue; The Undercover Blues Band; and Midnight Chill.

I am grateful to Michael Boldt of Dez Manku who invited me to play on a couple of tracks from his band's debut album, *Welcome to the Big Time*. Michael organized a number of images for this book and suggested the cover idea. Brian Pearce was also helpful with image selections.

Of course, thanks to my wife, Debbie, for her assistance and encouragement.

As always, I appreciate the support of Ben Omart and the rest of the BearManor Media staff.

Thanks also to Darlene and Dan Swanson of Van-garde Imagery, Inc.

And thanks to metal man, Eddie Trunk!

Foreword

As a student at Madison High School in Madison, New Jersey where I grew up, I was somewhat of an outcast in many ways. I rarely drank, never did a drug in my life, sucked at sports, and never cared about fitting in with the hip scene. There were so many kids that I saw fake it; others pretended they liked certain music that they really didn't enjoy. Some wore clothes that they really didn't want to wear, and others acted in ways just to get an invitation to the parties on the weekend and be in the "in" crowd.

I was not one of those people. You see, I liked hard Rock and Metal music. More specifically, I liked Kiss, and for me to identify myself as a member of the Kiss Army from 1979-1982, well that's a whole different story! We are talking about Kiss at the most ridiculed time of the band's career – *Dynasty, Unmasked, Music from "The Elder."* I was verbally abused for being a Kiss fan and often maintain that if I wasn't a pretty big kid I would have had my ass kicked on a regular basis at Madison High School. I found very few students who could relate to my passion for Kiss and hard Rock in general, but oddly I found someone and it was one of the teachers! That teacher would be William Chemerka, author of this very book, and known to all simply as "Mr. C."

As I went through those four years of school struggling to find a connection with someone who shared a similar passion for Rock music as I did, Mr. C became my beacon. I mean, how insanely cool is it that the economics and history teacher would catch me in the hall and talk about an emerging new band he just saw and interviewed called Van Halen! Now in my younger years, every other band that wasn't Kiss was a threat to Kiss. But I matured as I went into my junior and senior years and opened up much more to other bands. Mr. C was there to engage, discuss, and debate all. I can't begin to tell you how important this was to me as a young kid trying to find my way and be encouraged to chase my passion for music.

Mr. C wrote music reviews that I read. In turn, that inspired me to write the school newspaper's music column called "Sharps & Flats." I'd also catch him from time to time on local cable TV talking music. I mean, who ever had a teacher that would debate Aerosmith, write a story on Peter Criss in the local paper, and be seen on TV at night covering music?

Despite my relatively poor grades due to my only interest being Rock music, I truly looked forward to school for one reason: to catch a couple minutes with Mr. C. It was at this time that I also first discovered broadcasting, and I went to one of the local colleges over the summer to be a part of its radio station (predictably my only college experience!). To have a teacher who "got it" was hugely important to me at the time. He also had my back. I'll never forget an exchange student from the Netherlands (Mr. C can tell you better because he *still* talks about it!) named Kate. While waiting for class to start, she would just start in on me. She used to say, "Kiss sucks!" I'll never forget the grin on Chemerka's face as he relished the anger it got out of me. He eventually stepped in to apply some logic to a debate where there was actually very little.

It's important to note that although Mr. C had a huge impact on me I was far from the only one. He had an amazing ability to relate to all the kids at school. No matter what you were into or what your scene was, you loved Mr. C and hoped like hell you would get into his classes. You knew it would be different, engaging, fun, and oh yeah, educational. Simply put he was the cool teacher and everyone wanted to be around him. He's pretty much the only teacher in my life I have maintained a friendship with and think of often. I'm thrilled he has taken the time to tell some of his stories in this book. He has many sides to him so I'm sure this is just scratching the surface, but this book is a great read nonetheless. Although my scope of interest falls more to the hard Rock stuff, I also found some new and interesting information out in these pages that would have surely "stumped the Trunk" had I not read it. For example, who knew Phil Collins was into the Alamo?

Thirty-two years after my graduation, Mr. C is still teaching, and that's a good thing! I was honored to be asked to contribute to this book and I hope through reading it you get not only some great music tales but also a sense of the special person who has written them. I'm grateful for his friendship, support and encouragement then and now.

    Eddie Trunk
    Host/Co-Producer *That Metal Show* VH1 Classic
    Eddie Trunk Show Q104.3 FM NYC
    Eddie Trunk Live SiriusXM

Author's Introduction

Music has been part of my life for as long as I can remember.

My parents were fans of the big bands that dominated the Popular music scene of the 1930s and 1940s, especially the orchestras led by Count Basie and Jimmie Lunceford. Our home was constantly filled with the sounds of swinging instrumentals spinning from 78-rpm records. And my folks loved to dance to those uptempo tunes. Mom also played piano and the vibes, although she never had a formal music lesson. My parents also appreciated Frank Sinatra, Joe Williams, and Ella Fitzgerald, who were masters of vocal phrasing. As I grew older, my folks hoped that I would one day share their passion for Jazz. Alas, that was not to be because my puberty coincided with the early development of Rock and Roll.

When Bill Haley and His Comets reached the top of the charts with "Rock Around the Clock" in 1955, I stopped singing "The Ballad of Davy Crockett" in the school yard and began humming lyrics that I could barely understand. Surprisingly, that Western Swing-flavored beat of Bill Haley and His Comets was ironically similar to the rhythmic punch that characterized some of my parents' favorite tunes. I may not have become the Jazz fan that they had hoped for but my appreciation for Rhythm and Blues music originated with their precious record collection.

Then along came Elvis Presley. Credit my best friend, Lenny Hekel, and his two older teenage sisters, Patty and Lillian, for playing Elvis records every time I went to their apartment. That's where my Rock and Roll indoctrination began: the Hekel's place on 24th Street in Union City, New Jersey.

I remember seeing Elvis for the first time in 1956 – on the Dorsey Brothers' TV program, *Stage Show*. Despite that grainy black and white image on the small screen, Elvis projected a clear, raw, and untamed talent that was unlike any of the other popular singers who came before him. But Presley and his peers – from Little Richard and Gene Vincent to Fats Domino and Carl Perkins – were making more than musical noise. These artists were speaking to a new generation, and those in that young demographic group were listening intently. Maybe Patty and Lillian were on to something. However, my parents thought I was on the wrong cultural path, a dangerous road filled with social unrest. And warnings were everywhere. For example, the Newark *Star-Ledger* newspaper reported on July 10, 1956: "Jersey City officials yesterday flatly rejected plans to stage a Rock 'n' roll concert here Friday night because, they said, of teenage riots which have erupted at similar programs in other cities." Despite the warning, Rock and Roll was here to stay.

Dick Clark's Philadelphia-based *American Bandstand* went national on August 5, 1957, and Lenny's sisters had the afternoon program on their television every time I stopped by. Clark played the hits and the kids danced. It was a simple but effective concept – and my indoctrination continued.

Young Ricky Nelson was soon singing on TV's *The Adventures of Ozzie and Harriet*. In the early autumn of 1957, with leftover birthday money, I purchased my first 45-rpm single: Nelson's "Be-Bop Baby." The acquisition of additional vinyl discs soon followed. Of course, I had to use my parents' record player, a device which had only been christened with Jazz discs. My parents – God bless 'em – allowed me to enjoy my music without any interference or criticism.

Author's Introduction

By the end of the year, I added several singles to my growing collection: Sam Cooke's "You Send Me," Buddy Holly's "Peggy Sue," The Everly Brothers' "Wake Up Little Susie," The Rays' "Silhouettes," Larry Williams' "Bony Maronie," Chuck Berry's "Rock and Roll Music," Bill Justis' "Raunchy," and Jerry Lee Lewis' "Great Balls of Fire." And then I heard Danny and the Juniors' "At The Hop" played on *American Bandstand* – 2:31 of upbeat, bopping, sing-a-long perfection that eventually went to the top of the music charts in early 1958. It became my favorite song, and it remains so to this day.

My interest in popular music continued throughout the late 1950s and early 1960s. I enjoyed everything from the classic vocal groups (also favorites of one of my best school chums, Frank Ferina), instrumentals by Duane Eddy, the Ventures, and Johnny and the Hurricanes (my neighborhood friends and classmates, John Cogan and Jeff O'Connell, were major fans of instrumental bands) to early James Brown tunes and hits by such Motown performers as The Miracles and The Marvelettes (my good friend, Charles Cusamano, was always listening to Rhythm and Blues performers).

My pocket transistor radio was tuned in all the time to New York City's big three Rock and Roll radio stations – WINS, WABC, and WMCA – and Newark, New Jersey's Rhythm and Blues station, WNJR. Furthermore, my parents used to take me with them to see free summer Jazz concerts in the park during my junior high school years. It was music, seemingly all the time.

But to my ears, Rock and Roll's early energy and unique style was being replaced by a pervasive tameness in the early 1960s, characterized by the carefully produced tunes of such "teen idols" as Bobby Vee, Bobby Vinton, and Bobby Rydell. The excitement that was Rock and Roll in the 1950s had nearly evaporated. Even Elvis had seemingly lost his mojo after he returned home from his stint in the U. S. Army.

However, the Pop music landscape wasn't totally bland at that time. There were some solid tunes released like "Shop Around" by The Miracles, "Quarter to Three" by Gary U. S. Bonds, "Peppermint Twist" by Joey Dee and the Starliters, and "Up on the Roof" by The Drifters. But those recordings were exceptions to the rule. Even among chart topping singles, for every "Please Mr. Postman" by The Marvellettes there was a "Go Away Little Girl" by Steve Lawrence and a "Sukiyaki" by Kyu Sakamoto. For every "Sherry" by The Four Seasons there was an "I'm Leaving It Up To You" by Dale and Grace and a "Dominique" by The Singing Nun. Fortunately, the musical times were about to be "a-Changin', as Bob Dylan wrote in his "The Times They Are 'a-Changin'" song and album (1964).

My pop musical interests shifted to something new: the Folk music revival that was captivating college campus audiences and the urban beat generation. Soon, the Rock and Roll beat was no longer in fashion; the musical *message* was. The creative efforts of many groups contributed to my growing appreciation of acoustic music, contemplative lyrics, and socio-economic awareness, particularly Bob Dylan; Peter, Paul and Mary; Bud and Travis; Joan Baez; The Kingston Trio; and Pete Seeger.

In the summer of 1963, I attended my first Folk concert: Peter, Paul and Mary. It was thoroughly enjoyable to see the talented trio perform – and in the round, no less – at the now long-gone Gladiator's Arena in Totowa, New Jersey. The group provided the audience with a meaningful set of tunes that entertained and, more importantly, enlightened.

Bob Dylan, of course, was something else. The singer-songwriter delivered compositions that were thought provoking and occasional explosive. In particular, Dylan's "The Lonesome Death of Hattie Carroll," which was recorded in 1963, was the most powerfully moving song I ever heard about injustice.

However, my musical world got pleasantly turned upside down with the arrival of The Beatles. Of course, I wasn't alone. I was hooked from the first few measures of the band's "I Want to Hold Your Hand," which was broadcast in December 1963 on various New York radio stations. The song was upbeat, guitar-driven Pop, and it shared the energy of Rock and Roll's early years. Yet, it was something new, something bright, and exciting. After I witnessed a brief film clip of a Beatles performance that was featured on *The Jack Paar Program* on January 3, 1964, I caught a dose of Beatlemania. My Folk music albums started to collect dust.

The Beatles' arrival in the United States and the foursome's appearance on *The Ed Sullivan Show* on February 9, 1964 was a momentous event in Pop music history. The Beatles even helped end the period of mourning that followed in the wake of President Kennedy's assassination. On November 23, 1963, a day after Kennedy's death, I remember seeing a chalk-written message on a nearby playground's basketball court that read: "Lee Harvey Oswald sucks." About six weeks later on that same playground's handball court wall, I noticed a chalk-drawn heart with the words "I Love Paul" written in it. I wondered if the two messages had been written by the same person, but it really didn't really matter who wrote them. The two messages were so strikingly different in tone and yet they were both connected by different strands of emotion. It seemed as if the nation's period of sorrow had ended with a resounding "yeah, yeah, yeah."

Documenting the so-called "British Invasion" became the task of *Beatles Unlimited*, a newsletter published by mop top fans in Connecticut. After someone gave me a copy of the humble publication, I contacted its publisher and offered my writing services. My Rock and Roll journalism sojourn was about to begin.

By the summer of 1964, I was sporting a Beatles haircut and managed to be among the first teens to purchase advance tickets to the band's debut film, *A Hard Day's Night,* when they went on sale early in the morning on July 22 at the Loews Theater in Newark. A *Newark Evening News* article and photograph captured the event. I saw The Beatles in concert for the first time at Atlantic City's Convention Hall on August 30 (I went with Linda Zarro, whom I had met in line for *A Hard Day's Night* tickets).

The next month, I joined a panel of fellow teenagers on David Susskind's *Open End* TV show in New York City. During the taped program, "The Beatles and the Beatlemaniacs," Susskind probed us with numerous questions and we responded with a collective defense of the four music makers from Liverpool. All of us tried to be as mature and responsible as possible with our remarks, but I blurted out that I disliked buses, one of George Harrison's pet peeves. It was an awkward response, but I couldn't afford a car at the time and it was meaningful to me that somebody else – a Beatle, no less – loathed bus transportation, too. The two-hour program aired on Sunday night, September 27, 1964.

Brian Epstein, The Beatles' manager, was informed about the program. Weeks later, Beatles Press Officer Derek Taylor sent me a letter from NEMS Enterprises in London. Dated October 16, 1964, it read: "The Beatles are most grateful to you for the skill and understanding with which you discussed Beatlemania on the 'Open End Show' on September 27th. We understood it was an excellent discussion. Very many thanks." In a postscript, Taylor noted: "The Beatles send this picture with their best wishes." The black and white glossy photo was signed in pen by all four band members! I still have that precious letter and photo. And, no, it's not for sale.

Of course, I wasn't satisfied listening to The Beatles or defending them on television: I wanted to be a Beatle – or at least a reasonable facsimile. To be sure, 10 million other young guys wanted the same dream. By 1966, I was playing electric bass in my first band, The Abstractions. We played cover tunes (mostly American and British Rhythm and Blues hits) and performed at bars (our first gig: Augie's Tavern in West Orange, New Jersey), high schools, church-sponsored functions, college dances, private parties, and outdoor events. Our claim to fame was that we never lost a battle-of-the bands competition, and every one of those competitions was on some other band's turf. We had business cards made up, but under my name were printed the words "base" guitar! Among the bassists who influenced me were Donald "Duck" Dunn of Booker T & the M.G.'s, Motown Funk Brothers James Jamerson and Bob Babbitt, Bill Wyman of The Rolling Stones, and Paul McCartney.

Our garage band made some money and we had lots of fun being the Abstractions, "the Masters of the Beat." We were good but not quite good enough to be full-time professionals, and we soon went our separate non-musical ways. However, every guy in the band has been my friend ever since.

While taking my first courses at Bloomfield College, I met fellow freshman Mark "Twig" Greenberg, who played drums in another local band. We shared a common interest in British groups and somehow he always managed to secure copies of *New Musical Express*, *Melody Maker*, and hard-to-get British singles and EPs. He later left college to join Richard and the Young Lions, an interesting garage band that had cracked the *Billboard* Hot 100 in 1966 with "Open Up Your Door."

Looking to expand my musical horizons, I left The Abstractions and successfully auditioned for The Soul Dukes. After I joined the group, it was later described by the New Jersey Historical Society as one "of the first integrated Soul bands." [For more on both bands go to: http://www.60sgaragebands.com/abstractions.html] It was a special experience to be the only White guy in a Black band, and I became a better person because of it. While touring with The Soul Dukes (we performed everywhere from Small's Paradise in Harlem on the so-called "chitlin circuit" to major venues like Shea Stadium!), I had the opportunity to meet many other band members who I became friends with, especially those in The Commodores, the Brooklyn Bridge, the Magnificent Men, and the Age of Reason.

In 1966, I sent in a critical letter about popular music to the *New-*

ark Evening News*, New Jersey's largest daily newspaper at the time. The publication had printed a number of factual errors about contemporary musical performers and songs, and I brought it to the attention of its editors. No big deal, I thought. A week later, I received a phone call from one of the editors who invited me to write a weekly music column titled "On the Record." To me, this *was* a big deal. It was a great opportunity to be able to write about popular music and get paid for it. I did that for two years, writing record reviews and book reviews, providing music news, and conducting interviews. My first interview was in 1967 with The Beach Boys and their supporting act, The Buckinghams. It was a great first interview assignment. And playing in a Rock band gave me insights to the artists I interviewed and wrote about.

However, an active duty stint at Fort Dix, New Jersey and Fort Knox, Kentucky put my music and journalism activities on hold. During my subsequent undergraduate years, I edited music articles for the campus newspaper, hosted *The Oldies Show with Emerson* on WBCR-FM radio, and sang doo-wop tunes at frat parties with fellow classmates Tom Basnight, Gary Wilson, and Tom Buro. Furthermore, the beginning of a teaching career interrupted my professional journalism work for a several years.

While I was dating my future wife, Debbie, I also got involved in musical theater in the early seventies, appearing in productions of *Jesus Christ Superstar*, *South Pacific*, and *The Wizard of Oz*, among others. *Jesus Christ Superstar* was the most enjoyable because of its Rock score. Cast as Herod, I had the opportunity to sing "Herod's Song (Try It and See)."

By the mid-1970s, I was back in the writing groove, joining the staff of *Entertainment Spectrum*, where I teamed up with a former college classmate, George Dassinger, in the publication's music department. Before the decade was over, I was employed at *The Aquarian Weekly*, (which later transformed into *East Coast Rocker* before returing to its original name years later), where I remained until the early 1990s. I also wrote occasional articles for *Relix* magazine and other publications, and during those years I interviewed/reviewed nearly every major act from Abba to ZZ Top and hundreds of local bands. Asbury Park, New Jersey's Convention Hall, was the site of many of my favorite interviews. I was also responsible for organizing regional and national record sales charts, a statistical interest that has never ceased to fascinate me. As a result, record chart information punctuates the forthcoming chapters of this volume.

The staff of *The Aquarian Weekly* included a number of musicians, and in time the publication formed its own band, Late For Press. We played at our annual end-of-year parties and even managed to perform at the Dirt club, one of the New York metro area's most important venues for independent and alternative artists.

In November 1981, *The Aquarian Weekly* and Suburban Cablevision, New Jersey's largest cable network at the time, co-produced the *Night Owl Special*, which I wrote and co-hosted. The program covered the current trends in popular music, and the production's success led to a monthly concert series, *The Night Owl Concert*, that featured up and coming bands in the New York metro area. I also hosted or co-hosted the *Aquarian's* "Nights of Rock and Roll" and "Nights of Original Music" at New York metro area clubs. One memorable night on March 25, 1981 at New Jersey's Dirt club featured the Smithereens, a promising band at the time. On another night, Blondie's Clem Burke stopped by the club and we talked about the contemporary music scene, a discussion that went on for quite some time. The 1980s was a particularly busy time for me, and I was doing all of these music-related activities while I was teaching.

As an educator, I taught a unit on "The Economics of the Music Industry" in the Introduction to Economics elective at Madison High School in New Jersey. The students enjoyed the class and appreciated the break they got from the more basic elements of the so-called dismal science. It was a break for me, too.

In my Economics II elective, one of the books I assigned was *Apple to the Core*, a book written by Peter McCabe and Robert D. Schonfeld in 1972, which traced the rise and fall of The Beatles' artistic and commercial conglomerate, Apple Corps. It was important for my students to know that popular music and the study of the allocation of scare means among competing ends were inextricably connected. In 1975 and in 1989, the Joint Council on Economic Education acknowledged the unit in its National Awards Program for the Teaching of Economics (Honorable Mention, Senior High Level).

In 1980 and 1981, I taught an inter-term course at Bloomfield College, my alma mater, titled "An Examination of the Socio-Economic Trends in Pop/Rock music, 1954-1980."

My high school students also enjoyed reading my articles and interviews about some of their favorite performers. On a couple of occasions, I provided the school newspaper, *The Dodger*, with "exclusive" information. For example, during a backstage interview in Philadelphia, David Lee Roth of Van Halen sported a pair of athletic socks that featured a trim of maroon and gold, which were also the school colors of Madison High. I asked Roth to pose – not a difficult task – and point to his socks. I photographed the singer and later gave a copy of the photo to *The Dodger*, which subsequently printed the image with an accompanying story. Understandably, the photo was well received by the students; however, most faculty members didn't quite get it.

Above all, my Rock and Roll journalistic efforts helped me to establish a better professional relationship with my students. And my students kept me informed on what *they* liked, not what the mainstream Rock and Roll press preferred. Indirectly, Rock and Roll helped me to increase the probability of learning – and that's what teaching is all about.

One of my students, Eddie Trunk, went on to be the leading proponent of Hard Rock and Heavy Metal, courtesy of his various radio DJ gigs, his interesting books, and the popular VH1 Classic television program, *That Metal Show*. He was kind enough to mention my Van Halen proselytizing in *Eddie Trunk's Essential Hard Rock And Heavy Metal*.

Sometimes, though, Rock music challenged the learning process and the relationship between teacher and student. Pink Floyd's chant, "we don't need no education," from "Another Brick in the Wall (Part 2)" in 1979; The Ramones' remonstration, "well I don't care about history," from "Rock 'n' Roll High School" in 1979; and Nirvana's command, "here we are now, entertain us," from "Smells Like Teen Spirit" in 1991, signified a distinct change from "Be True to You School," The Beach Boys' 1963 chart hit.

In 1997, I authored "Beatlemania in New Jersey" in *Teenage New Jersey: 1941-1975*, a book that was originally published by the New Jersey Historical Society and later reprinted by Rutgers University Press. The book coincided with the historical society's exhibit about "Teenage New Jersey," which featured a number of items related to The Soul Dukes including the Gibson electric bass that I played. In 1998, the entire exhibit was shipped to the Newcastle Discovery Museum in Great Britain and renamed "Born in the USA: Stateside to Tyneside Teenagers, 1941-1975." And, for some reason, the visual centerpiece of the exhibit was my bass guitar. It was a pleasant surprise.

A good friend, Allen J. Wiener, and I teamed up to write *Music of the Alamo* in 2008. Phil Collins was kind enough to write the introduction, and Fess Parker, TV's "Davy Crockett," penned the foreword. Readers were surprised to discover that artists like Donovan, The Rolling Stones, Johnny Cash, Peter and Gordon, Billy Joel, and Tom Petty and the Heartbreakers had recorded songs about the Alamo and its most famous defender, Davy Crockett.

In the early twenty-first century, I wrote occasional music-related articles for such diverse publications as *The Aquarian Weekly*; *Roundup* magazine, the official publication of the Western Writers of America; New Jersey's *Star-Ledger* newspaper (some local bands and other personal profiles in the "In The Towns" and "A Place in History" sections); and *The Alamo Journal*, the official publication of The Alamo Society (several rockers are big Alamo buffs, as readers will soon discover). And every now and then, I joined a band or provided some bass lines and lyrics to a fellow musician's CD.

Music! For me, there's something about driving on an interstate late at night when the Doors' "Light My Fire" comes on the radio, and the excitement is instantaneous when I hear the first chord of "A Hard Day's Night." I appreciate the rhythmic groove that drives James Brown's "Cold Sweat," the harmonic spirituality that pervades The Beach Boys' "God Only Knows," the chant-a-long power of Kiss' live recording "Rock and Roll All Nite," the pulsating infectiousness of Sam the Sham and the Pharaohs' "Wooly Bully," the vocal joy of The Drifters' "Up On The Roof," the silky smoothness of Smokey Robinson & The Miracles' "Ooo Baby Baby," the machine-gun intensity of Green Day's "Basket Case," the irresistible union of Carlos Santana and Michelle Branch on "The Game of Love," the powerful complexity of Led Zeppelin's "Ramble On," the rocking exuberance of Bruce Springsteen's "Tunnel of Love," the soulful brilliance of El Chicano's "What's Going On," the romantic intoxication of Meat Loaf's "It's All Coming Back to Me Now," and the Rock and Roll purity of Eddie Cochrane's "Somethin' Else." And those are just a few of the songs that continue to stir my spirit.

As I wrote this book, I rediscovered many interesting interconnections between the artists I had met and interviewed. Some of the artists had shared the same stage over the years, sometimes in awkward concert lineups. A few performers commented on their contemporaries and rivals, and not always in a flattering manner. Others performed as members of Ringo Starr's All-Starr Band, and several shared a common non-musical historical interest: the Alamo. Besides music videos, a number of artists appeared in motion pictures and television productions, and three bands showed up as cartoon characters on *The Simp-*

Author's Introduction

sons. Some of the performers regularly contributed to charity benefits and a few established foundations which provided opportunities for youngsters. All the bands, except one, suffered from internal problems, death, and lineup changes. And a number of the artists ended up in the Rock and Roll Hall of Fame.

From my first article in *Beatles Unlimited* in 1964 to my most recent interview with Felix Cavaliere of The Young Rascals in 2014, it's been about fifty years of Rock and Roll journalism. The following essays and the abbreviated Notes & Quotes section are not intended to serve as comprehensive biographical histories of various performers; rather, the following recollections provide insights to musical personalities at particular times in their careers when they crossed my path. Some stories are funny, some are serious – but all are memorable in one way or another. I hope you enjoy the musical ride down memory lane.

Please press the "play" button and rock on!

William R. Chemerka
Summer 2014

Chapter 1

The Beach Boys

"Good Vibrations"

The Beach Boys.

The group's name conjures up images of a seemingly endless summer, a season filled with memories of sun, surf, and sing-a-long tunes that reflect the joys of youthful exuberance.

I was fortunate that my first professional interview assignment for the *Newark Evening News* was The Beach Boys, America's best-known band at the time. The popular California-based group was scheduled to perform at Newark's Symphony Hall on April 29, 1967. The Buckinghams, who scored on the charts with the year's first #1 single, "Kind of a Drag," were slated to open the show.

The Beach Boys lineup had undergone a major change since the band last performed at the Newark venue on February 15, 1965. Brian Wilson, the group's primary writer, arranger, and bassist, had left the touring band in order to remain in the studio as a producer. However, he was also suffering from mental problems at the time but few knew of his condition except members of the band, his family, some close friends, and several business associates. The band leader's condition would not be made public until years later. Brian's place was taken initially by Glen Campbell and later by Bruce Johnston. Nevertheless, Brian occasionally returned to the lineup during the band's 1965 concert tour, which featured the basic lineup of Carl Wilson (guitar and vocals), Mike Love (vocals), Al Jardine (guitar and vocals), Dennis Wilson (drums and vocals), and Johnston (bass and vocals).

By the time of the Newark concert, The Beach Boys had established themselves as one of the most successful music acts in the world. The brothers Wilson – Brian, Carl, and Dennis – joined forces with Mike Love, a cousin, and high school classmate Al Jardine in 1961. The group's first single, "Surfin,'" barely dented the record charts but the band managed a Top 20 hit the following year with "Surfin' Safari." Young David Marks had replaced Jardine in early 1962 and remained with the band until late 1963 when Jardine returned.

In 1963, The Beach Boys scored their first Top 5 hit with "Surfin' U. S. A." The song, instrumentally based on Chuck Berry's "Sweet Little Sixteen," was an aquatic salute to over a dozen California surf locations, as well as spots in Hawaii and Australia. And the single's flip side, "Shut Down," was a catchy ode to a drag race between a Corvette Stingray and a Superstock Dodge.

From then on, it was hit after hit. Songs about girls ("Help Me, Rhonda"), cars ("Little Deuce Coup"), school spirit ("Be True to Your School"), and more girls ("Fun, Fun, Fun") reinforced the band's status as the kings of so-called "surf Rock." But the quintet was more than just another surf band: The Beach Boys blended wonderful harmonies, catchy rhythms, hook-laden arrangements, and superb production techniques into a qualitative, assembly-line hit making machine.

The Beach Boys scored their first #1 one song in the summer of 1964 with "I Get Around," an optimistic tune about social mobility and self-respect. The flip side, "Don't Worry Baby," a lush harmony-driven restrained rocker about peer pressure, confidence, and love, was carried by Brian Wilson's comfortable falsetto lead. The two-sided hit (the B-side, "Don't Worry Baby," reached #24 on the *Billboard* Hot 100) marked another step in the West Coast band's ascent to overtake the Four Seasons as America's most popular recording group at the time. The New Jersey-based Four Seasons, though, bumped "I Get Around" from the top of the charts with "Rag Doll" in mid-July. It marked the East Coast group's fourth #1 single.

1964 was also the year of The Beatles-led British Invasion. By April, The Beatles held the top two positions on the LP charts and the top five singles on the *Billboard* Hot 100 (the Liverpool-based quartet placed an additional nine singles on the chart). Many American acts struggled under the tidal wave of British musical exports, but The Beach Boys held strong in 1964 with their *All Summer Long* album, which rose to #4, and the chart topping *Beach Boys Concert* live LP.

Coincidentally, Beach Boys and Beatles records were distributed by Capitol Records in the United States. Both bands competed for a larger share of the fan base while respecting the other's music, and they developed a friendly rivalry. In particular, Paul McCartney and Brian Wilson initiated a spirited competitiveness that resulted in both songwriters penning some of the best music in Rock history. Eventually, members of both bands crossed paths. On August 22, 1965, Carl Wilson and Mike Love visited The Beatles in their dressing room at the Portland Coliseum, marking the first time that any of The Beatles and The Beach Boys had met each other.

The Beach Boys hit-making offensive continued. The band's three 1965 album releases – *The Beach Boys Today!*, *Summer Days (And Summer Nights!!)*, and *Beach Boys' Party!* – reached the top six on the LP charts. And the band also scored with four hit singles including the memorable "California Girls" and "Help Me, Rhonda," which went to #1.

More hit singles charted the following year, including "Barbara Ann," a casual, live remake of the Regents' 1961 blast, and "Sloop John B." *Best of The Beach Boys* became a best selling LP, too.

By the time I first met them, The Beach Boys had cranked out twenty-one Top 40 singles, including the brilliant two-sided hit "Wouldn't It Be Nice" and "God Only Knows," and the memorable masterpiece "Good Vibrations," which became the band's third #1 hit. The singles and the albums – particularly 1966's *Pet Sounds* – added up to about 20 million retail sales units at that particular juncture. Paul McCartney would later claim that "God Only Knows" was his favorite Beach Boys song, and at a benefit thirty-five years later, he and Brian Wilson sang the song together.

The Beach Boys' songs were not only vinyl offerings to the record-buying public: they delivered inviting images of surfing to the land-locked American heartland; they elevated souped-up cars and hot rods into chariots of asphalt royalty; and they expressed the common emotions of teenagers, from loneliness and heartbreak to camaraderie and confidence. Other artists had communicated similar feelings and experiences, but none had articulated them so effortlessly and with such harmonic elegance.

But to some, the all-American appearance and sound of The Beach Boys was looking somewhat dated by mid-1967. Since few band members in other groups were dressing alike by the summer of love, The Beach Boys' clean-cut wardrobe seemed "out." In the world of Rock, uniformity was out; individuality was in.

The contemporary music scene was also filled with vibrant new music, from Psychedelic and Garage Rock to Memphis Soul and Folk Rock. And a second wave of British Invasion bands added to the eclectic Pop mix. Furthermore, The Beach Boys' home state had become the epicenter for a host of emerging bands, such as the Doors, Jefferson Airplane, The Grateful Dead, Moby Grape, Big Brother and the Holding Company, The Beau Brummels, and The Strawberry Alarm Clock, among others. It was, to be sure, a transitional challenging time for The Beach Boys as they traveled to Newark for their concert.

The Beach Boys were helping to set up their own equipment at the center of the Symphony Hall stage by the time I arrived. Dick Duryea, their road manager, introduced me to the band members. They were already dressed for the show, all five wearing white slacks and striped shirts, which helped reinforce – for better or worse – their classic identity. They were all friendly and polite, but Johnston was the most outgoing. Initially, Dennis Wilson was the most reserved, although he became quite animated and quite a bit cocky when he described a recent car accident he had experienced on his own private drag strip. "I almost broke my two-hundred-mile-per-hour record in my Cobra," he explained with a confident smile from his elevated drum seat. "But my safety parachute broke and I cracked up." He promptly grabbed his drum sticks and did a quick roll on his snare as if he was providing a percussive shot to a stand-up comedian's punch line.

When asked about the band's popularity on both sides of the Atlantic, Jardine confidently replied: "Our music speaks for itself." In fact, the previous year, Great Britain's *New Musical Express* poll named The Beach Boys as the most popular "vocal group" in Rock music, breaking a three-run that The Beatles had held. The Beatles, though, won the poll category the next three years.

Dennis Wilson acknowledged that some of the band's inspiration came from its competition. "The Beatles *Rubber Soul* [album] jolted Brian up into the hills, and he's never come down," he said.

The Beach Boys also utilized various musical genres to expand their style. "The spiritual concept of happiness is extremely important to the lyrics of our songs," explained Carl Wilson. "And some of the better church music is contained within some of our new work."

At the time, Brian Wilson was working on a new album, *Smiley Smile*, a vinyl substitute of sorts for the *Smile* LP, which had not been completed due, in part, to his emotional problems. Wilson's loyal band members only spoke of him in short, polite, descriptive phrases and preferred to talk instead about their new songs. "Our music is coming along," said Love. "It's really encompassing of all areas."

In the studio, Brian Wilson was utilizing more musicians than just the other Beach Boys. "Now we have five people singing and nine people playing, with the addition of four musicians," said Johnston. "We can do much more if we have to while performing, almost like our records."

Symphony Hall's front doors opened and The Beach Boys promptly disappeared into their dressing room and waited. The fans poured in the theater and within an hour, the curtain opened as the Buckinghams began performing "Don't You Care," their most recent Top 10 hit. Ironically, by the end of the year, the Buckinghams placed four Top 12 songs in *Billboard's* Hot 100, including the #1 hit, "Kind Of A Drag." And in December the Chicago-based group released the single "Susan," which would reach #11 in early 1968. In 1967, The Beach Boys had only two new Top 40 hits; however, the Buckinghams never again broke the Top 40.

Following the Buckinghams' set, The Beach Boys walked onstage and were enthusiastically greeted by the near sold out audience of approximately 2,700, which was composed primarily of teenage girls. The group energetically played most of their hits, from "Surfer Girl" and "I Get Around" to "God Only Knows" and "Wouldn't It Be Nice," and the crowd approved with appreciative screams and cheers. On "California Girls," the crowd went wild when Mike Love sang the lyrical line "East Coast girls are hip/I really dig those styles they wear." Smiles came across the faces of The Beach Boys as they exchanged glances. "The boys must really be enjoying themselves," Duryea told me from the side of the stage.

When the show ended, Duryea told me that The Beach Boys were headed for Europe. But before they left Symphony Hall, a few members of the band commented about the expectation of being far away from home.

"I'll really miss California," said Carl Wilson.

"Yeah, and all the girls," added Love with a grin.

"I'm going to miss the East Coast," remarked Dennis Wilson. "I love it very much."

The band was soon on its way across the Atlantic. The Beach Boys opened their European tour on May 2 in Dublin and then moved on to shows held at various venues in England and Scotland.

On December 16, 1967, The Beach Boys performed at a UNICEF (United Nations International Children's Emergency Fund) concert in Paris. Among those in attendance were John Lennon and his wife, Cynthia, and George Harrison and his wife, Pattie.

Also while in Europe in late 1967, during the group's promotion of its *Wild Honey* LP, The Beach Boys crossed paths with the Maharishi Mahesh Yogi, a champion of Transcendental Meditation (TM), whom The Beatles had met earlier. Love became very interested in all aspects of TM, and the next year he traveled to India and joined the popular guru at his retreat. The band's next album, *Friends*, reflected the band's association with the Indian mystic with such tracks as "Anna Lee, the Healer" and "Transcendental Meditation." Among the album's liner notes, Brian Wilson acknowledged the "bad things that had happened to" him. It was an interesting confession, to say the least.

Friends, though, was a chart failure in the United States, and *Best of The Beach Boys Vol. 2* only reached #50. Despite the band's expanding style (Brian Wilson was still its primary creative force), many American music fans perceived the quintet as an anachronistic surf band that had little relevance to a world punctuated by the Vietnam War, campus unrest, urban rioting, political assassinations, and more sophisticated musical acts. *Best of The Beach Boys Vol. 3* in 1968 barely dented the album charts. The band's popularity reached new lows.

In 1968, Brian and his wife, Marilyn, became parents with the birth of a daughter, Carnie. A year later, Wendy was born. Decades later, the two siblings would join Chynna Phillips, the daughter of John and Michelle Phillips of The Mamas and the Papas, in the successful Pop vocal group Wilson Phillips.

In 1969, The Beach Boys released *20/20*, which included the Top 40 hit, "I Can Hear Music." But the album struggled to #68 on the LP charts, and the hit single would be the band's last until five years later.

A handful of relatively unsuccessful albums followed in the early 1970s; however, *Endless Summer*, a best-of collection in 1974, went to #1, and 1976's *15 Big Ones*, which was heavy on nostalgic re-workings of select oldies but goodies, like Chuck Berry's "Rock and Roll Music," managed to break the Top 10 and revive the band's popularity. But the group's 1977 follow-up, *Love You*, was only a minor album hit.

In June 1978, I had a conversation with Love about the band's status during the age of Disco, Punk, and Heavy Metal. It was eleven years after my first interview with The Beach Boys. At the time, the band had been recording its next LP, the *M. I. U. Album*, a musical tribute of sorts to Iowa's Maharishi International University, an educational center dedicated to the teachings of the Eastern mystic.

"Transcendental Meditation, or TM, attempts to make the mind and body function more efficiently," said Love. "We met the Maharishi Mahesh Yogi in December 1967, when we did a United Nations show in Paris. The whole group now meditates, and Al Jardine and I are now teachers."

Love explained that TM helped maintain his long-time association with his fellow musicians. "Any group is only as strong as its members," he pointed out. "I don't think I'd be in the group if it wasn't for meditation. It raises your toleration to tension and stress. It helps against the fatiguing effects of physical and mental activity."

During the interview, Love sounded as if he were attempting to recruit me to join his fellow TM practitioners. "We don't proselytize," assured Love. "People can find what we stand for in our music. It reflects the value of the heart rather than the intellectual side of what we are all about."

But he quickly noted TM's growing influence. "TM's 13,000 teachers agree that all is not right with the world," explained Love. "But rather than drop out [of society], TM allows one to extend one's I.Q. By increasing the number of TM's students and TM's ability to grow, the world can be altered. If two percent of the world actively meditated, we could end all major wars. And if we could get only five percent of the world to meditate we could end world starvation."

However, Love never explained how those two goals could be achieved. But he did say how TM affected his creativity. "I took a six-month course in TM from January to July last year [1977], and in that time period I wrote fifty songs."

Love also viewed the band differently from its Surf-Rock days. "We see ourselves today as modern, middle-class Folk singers," he said. "In the future, I'm sure people will study our music as a relevant part of what the music was at the time."

He boldly predicted that the band would still be performing many years in the future. "I can still see us playing then," said Love. "Not as active as now, but I can see a limited summer engagement with a tour with the London or New York Symphony Orchestra, even joined by the Soviet Red Army choir. They would do a symphonic medley of tunes and then we would come on and perform. There is no limit to what we can do."

Love's optimistic spirit seemed to underscore The Beach Boys' career. In 1979, the band had a Top 40 hit with "Good Timin,'" a song with lush harmonies that were as splendid as any previous Beach Boys tune. The recording marked the band's thirtieth Top 40 score, which topped the Four Seasons' total of twenty-nine American hits at the time.

The Beach Boys continued their musical journey into the 1980s, but Dennis Wilson drowned while diving at the Marina del Ray in Los Angeles on December 28, 1983. The thirty-nine-year-old musician was later buried at sea.

The following year, the group teamed up with its American rival, the Four Seasons, on the single "East Meets West," but the recording failed to chart. The Beach Boys continued to perform and their July 4 concerts became memorable events, especially the 1985 show in Philadelphia where approximately 1 million people attended.

The Beach Boys were inducted into the Rock and Roll Hall of Fame in 1988, and scored a #1 hit that same year with "Kokomo," marking over twenty-one years since its last chart topper – "Good Vibrations." The gap of twenty-one years and two months between #1 singles was a record that stood until Cher broke it in 1999 with "Believe," which came nearly twenty-five years after her "Dark Lady" hit. "Kokomo," which was also featured on the *Cocktail* film soundtrack, was The Beach Boys' thirty-fifth chart hit and fourth #1 single. The Four Seasons, though, netted five #1 hits during their career (not counting two additional solo chart toppers for lead singer Frankie Valli). However, The Supremes generated more #1 hits than both The Beach Boys and Four Seasons combined: twelve.

In 1989, the group followed up with the fairly successful *Still Cruisin'* LP, which was a mix of new compositions and classic Beach Boys' tunes used in such various motion pictures as *Lethal Weapon 2, Good Morning Vietnam,* and *Troop Beverly Hills,* among others. The album reached #46 on the charts and was certified platinum by the Recording Industry Asociation of America (RIAA).

The next year, The Beach Boys were indirectly connected to one of the hottest acts in Pop when Brian Wilson's daughters in Wilson Phillips scored with a self-titled multi-platinum album and three #1 singles: "Hold On," "Release Me" and "You're in Love."

However, by the early 1990s, The Beach Boys were surviving on their name and past glories. Gone were the imaginative recording sessions and catchy compositions. The group tried to avoid being labeled as just another oldies group by releasing *Summer in Paradise* in 1992. The album was a tribute to summer, featuring some originals, a reworked version of "Surfin,'" and such non-Beach Boys' chestnuts as "Remember (Walking in the Sand)" and "Hot Fun in the Summertime." Although four of The Beach Boys sang on the album (Brian did not participate due to a legal dispute at the time) only Bruce Johnston contributed instrumentation; electronic tracks and other musicians filled in the gaps. *Summer in Paradise* bombed; as a matter of fact, it was the poorest selling recording in the band's history: it supposedly sold fewer than 10,000 CD copies.

The Beach Boys rebounded four years later with *Stars and Stripes Vol. 1*, essentially a collection of the band's memorable tunes performed primarily by various country artists, including Lorrie Morgan ("Don't Worry Baby"), Toby Keith ("Be True to Your School") and Sawyer Brown ("I Get Around"). Brian Wilson rejoined the lineup and co-produced the album with Joe Thomas. The album easily surpassed the dismal sales of *Summer in Paradise* but only managed to reach #101 on the *Billboard* roster. There would never be a volume two.

Brian teamed up with his daughters in 1997 to record *The Wilsons*. The Beach Boys' leader wrote "Til I Die," co-wrote two songs, and sang on several others but the album and its single release, "Monday Without You," were commercial disappointments.

Internal band struggles, Brian's periodic medical ups and downs, and the death of Carl Wilson from cancer in 1998, resulted in two different Beach Boys lineups: one with Jardine and the other with the remaining members, sans Brian. Jardine even teamed up with Brian's daughters for an extended series of concerts and an album, *Live in Las Vegas*. Jardine's lineup also included his two sons, Matt and Adam. Legal hassles among the band members continued through the early years of the new century.

However, in 2006 the remaining band members reunited and were joined by David Marks to commemorate the fortieth anniversary of *Pet Sounds*.

Finally, the unfinished *Smile* album was completed and resurrected as *The Smile Sessions* in late 2011. The Capitol Records release was a critical and commercial success (the album broke the Top 30 in both the United States and Great Britain), although it failed to generate precious metal status from the RIAA. The album in its Deluxe Box Set format later won the Best Historical Album Grammy Award.

Brian Wilson rejoined The Beach Boys in a live performance at the Grammy Awards ceremony on February 12, 2012. The band, along with guest performers from Maroon Five and Foster the People, delivered a spirited version of "Good Vibrations." It marked the first time in six years since Wilson had performed live with his bandmates.

The Beach Boys – original members Brian Wilson, Mike Love, Al Jardine, David Marks, and veteran member Bruce Johnston – took to the road with two musical directors and nine additional musicians in a nostalgic salute to its 50th Anniversary. The band also released a successful new album, *That's Why God Made the Radio*, and a title-track Top 40 hit. Another hit album, *Fifty Big Ones*, a greatest hits collection, followed in October. The Beach Boys were back yet again but the "good vibrations" would soon end.

Mike Love issued a public statement that he and Johnston would be returning to the road without Wilson, Jardine, and Marks. "This tour was always envisioned as a limited run," noted Love. "None of us wanted to do a 50th Anniversary tour that lasted ten years. Like any good party, no one wanted it to end. However, that was impossible, given that we had already set up shows in smaller cities with a different configuration of the band – the configuration that had been touring together every year for the last thirteen years."

Wilson responded in a press release. "What's confusing is that by Mike not wanting or letting Al, David and me tour with the band, it sort of feels like we're being fired," stated Wilson.

Once again, The Beach Boys split into two separate identities but the group would be united in a new album release.

In May 2013, Capitol Records released the celebratory *Live – The 50th Anniversary Tour*, a forty-one track collection that included nearly every Beach Boys chart hit. The CD cover featured a photo of the band members holding hands in unison as they faced an adoring concert audience. For yet another moment, harmony ruled among the ranks of the group.

Brian Wilson later teamed up with guitarist Jeff Beck on a new album (Wilson's first since *That Lucky Old Sun* in 2008) that included contributions from his fellow Beach Boys.

In 2014, The Beach Boys celebrated the 50th Anniversary of their first #1 single, "I Get Around," and both incarnations of the group hit the road. On March 15, Love, the oldest Beach Boy, turned seventy-three and he was still singing "Fun, Fun, Fun" as if was yesterday.

After twenty-nine studio albums, nearly three dozen compilation albums (mostly greatest hits collections), and over eighty American singles, The Beach Boys remain the most prolific and successful American band in Rock history.

Chapter 2

John Beland

"Back on the Road Again"

For over forty years, guitarist-singer-songwriter-arranger-producer John Beland has been on the road traveling to nearly every place on the globe. Over the years, the Texan has also contributed his multi-talented musical skills to such performers as Rick Nelson, Linda Ronstadt, Garth Brooks, Dolly Parton, Merle Haggard, Kris Kristofferson, Johnny Cash, The Bellamy Brothers, Kim Carnes, and The Flying Burrito Brothers, to name a few.

Yet, Beland isn't a household name – except to those knowledgeable fans that have a genuine appreciation for rockdom's unheralded heroes. He doesn't seem to mind, though. Although Beland is content to have supported other artists on stage and in the studio for most of his career, he is much more than a superb sideman.

As a youngster living in Hometown, Illinois, Beland got caught up in the Davy Crockett Craze in the 1950s and its popular anthem, "The Ballad of Davy Crockett." He also became interested in the Alamo, where Crockett died in 1836. "The perception of the Alamo, especially to kids my age, came from the story Disney painted," recalled Beland.

"But it was *The Last Command* [in 1955] that started my fascination with the Alamo."

Beland had an inspirational musical moment during the summer of 1957. "It's when I heard the electric guitar on Dale Hawkins' 'Susie-Q,'" he explained. "That really got my attention. Ironically, it was played by a fourteen-year-old James Burton who later went out to California where he became the famous guitarist for Ricky Nelson and Elvis."

Beland spent most of his free time learning how to play the guitar, and he quickly became proficient. As a teenager, he played with local bands, delivering diverse guitar licks in a number of styles.

In the mid-1960s, Beland and his family moved from Illinois to Los Angeles where he joined the embryonic Country-Rock music scene. One night at the legendary Troubador club in Hollywood his instrumental and vocal skills helped him secure a recording contract with Ranwood Records, which was formed by producer Randy Wood, the founder of Dot Records, and TV band leader Lawrence Welk.

"I had a minor hit in 1969 with 'Baby You Come Rolling Cross My Mind' which featured banjo player Bernie Leadon, who later was a member of the Eagles," remarked Beland. "The song was originally recorded by a group called The Peppermint Trolley Company. Dan Dalton, who produced my version of the song, also had The Peppermint Trolley Company under contract. Dan had already made the agreement with ABC Television for the group to sing the theme song for a new TV sitcom but the band wanted no part of it and split up. So, I was hired to sing it, under The Peppermint Trolley Company name. I sang the song along with Dan's wife and singer Paul Parrish. The TV show: *The Brady Bunch!*"

Beland put the bubblegum Rock episode behind him and sought something more substantial. "In 1968, I answered an ad in the *Hollywood Reporter* placed by a group that needed a guitarist who could sing high harmonies," said Beland. "The band was Spanky and Our Gang of 'Sunday Will Never Be the Same' fame. However, since Spanky had left, they were now going to call the band One Man's Family and pursue a more Country-Pop direction which was right up my alley. At the time, I still had my own solo deal with Ranwood Records and was playing around Los Angeles with Glenn Frey and J. D. Souther who were performing as Longbranch Pennywhistle. I went to the audition and met Spanky and Our Gang members Nigel Pickering and Kenny Hodges. I sang and played and, to my surprise, landed the gig."

Beland's association with Pickering and company eventually led to another musical relationship. "The guys lived and rehearsed in Topangana Canyon, north of Los Angeles, where a lot of big musical acts and actors lived," said Beland. "Nigel's neighbor was none other than Linda Ronstadt, the beauty of the Troubador. But she was still not nationally known at the time. Linda would stop by and hear us rehearse. She was a fan of our complex five-part harmonies and country arrangements. One of those songs was the Everly Brothers' 'When Will I Be Loved.' Much later, Linda would have a hit with that song – using *our* old arrangement!"

Offstage, Beland recalled Pickering's matchmaking efforts. "Nigel dated Linda's beautiful roommate, Brook," explained Beland. "One day, we were invited to Rock photographer Henry Diltz's house for a party and a guitar session. Nigel told me he was going to fix me up with Brook's roommate for the night. I was unaware it was Linda until I got to the door. Then I asked Nigel who my date was. He told me as he knocked on the door. I almost fainted from nerves. I wanted to run down the hills but I pulled myself together. Linda and Brook came out and we were on our way. From the very beginning, Linda and I connected. At the party we became very close and she asked me if I wanted to play guitar for her in the new band she was putting together for her solo career. All the while, Nigel kept whispering in my ear to say 'yes' because it was a 'sure thing' I could land her in the sack if I did. I told Nigel to shut up and mind his own business. Besides, I was doing well without his tips."

When pressed about his evening with the singer, Beland responded in a gentlemanly manner. "Let's just say, it was a great date," he noted.

Twenty four hours later, the situation changed. "The next day, I told Linda that I couldn't take her offer because I had already committed to a tour with One Man's Family," said Beland. "She was very nice about it and told me that if I ever should leave the group, I would have a gig with her anytime."

Beland and One Man's Family hit the road. "We toured the country playing with the Hollies, the Byrds, Steppenwolf, and other big acts on the concert trail," said Beland. "We were playing a unique style of Country and Pop with tight harmonies, some comedy. It was fabulous. I loved the band and learned a wealth of stuff from vets like Nigel and Kenny, who were about twenty years older than I was."

Beland returned to Illinois. "While in Chicago, we did a series at the Aragon Ballroom with the Byrds and the Second City improvisational comedy group," said Beland. "The Byrds were great and I became acquainted with their guitarist, the legendary Clarence White. We later became great friends."

But One Man's Family disbanded. "Unfortunately, Nigel fell in love with a local girl, and before we knew it the band broke up," stated Beland. "I was shattered because we were close to a major record deal in Los Angeles and I knew the band would be a hit. I immediately called Linda. She said the gig with her was still mine if I wanted it, so I got back to Los Angeles as soon as possible."

Beland promptly journeyed back to the West Coast. "On the ride home from Chicago, we were reading a review in *Billboard* about our last show with the Byrds," recalled Beland. "Here's what the review said: 'One man's Family (formerly Spanky & Our Gang) wowed the crowd with their tight harmonies and solid song selections. Looks like these guys are going to be around a long time.'"

Linda Ronstadt and the Stone Poneys scored a Top 20 hit with "Different Drum" in early 1968, but the band soon broke up. She recorded her first solo album, *Hand Sown ... Home Grown*, a year later, but utilized a cadre of studio musicians to make the record. She didn't have her own band until she recruited a collection of musicians (including Beland) who played a wide range of styles – from Country and Folk to Cajun and Rock and Roll. "Swampwater was formed after we were all hired to be her band," explained Beland.

Swampwater's Cajun fiddler, Gib Guilbeau, and Beland soon became close friends as they toured the nation at such diverse venues as the Hollywood Bowl, the Fillmore West, and the Grand Ole Opry. Swampwater later left Ronstadt and became Arlo Guthrie's backing band. Ronstadt recruited a new band which eventually went out on its own as The Eagles.

Swampwater released a pair of albums: a self-titled effort in 1970 on the King label and another similarly named LP on RCA in 1971. "Nashville Lady," a Beland-penned tune from the first album, was later recorded by mainstream vocalist Englebert Humperdinck. It was a mixed blessing.

"I was shocked, having it been the first song I ever had published as well as not too thrilled about," said Beland. "It was also performed on *The Lawrence Welk Show*, sung by Guy Hovis, and recorded by Swampwater. Humperdink was hot that year and sold many albums. It was a slight windfall for me, especially at nineteen years old."

But Swampwater failed to generate any kind of widespread commercial success. During his tenure with the band, Beland performed on his first movie soundtrack when he played the dobro for musical director Quincy Jones on *Honky*, a 1971 film about an interracial romance.

A brief stint backing Kris Kristofferson took him to San Antonio in 1973. "I was thrilled that we were playing in San Antonio because I could finally see the Alamo in person!" remarked Beland. "But the show schedule was tight and we zipped in and out of San Antonio in the blink of an eye. I never saw the Alamo. As I rode to the airport in the limo the following morning, I asked the driver how far away our hotel was from the Alamo. He said, 'Are you kidding? You were staying right next door to it.' In fact, we had been staying at the Crockett Hotel!"

Two years later, Beland left Swampwater and joined Johnny Tillotson, a Pop singer who had placed fourteen Top 40 hits – including "Poetry in Motion," a #2 smash – on the *Billboard* Hot 100 between 1960 and 1965. For the next two years, Beland and Tillotson toured extensively.

"We played theaters in the United States and the United Kingdom," said Beland. "We played packaged bills with Bobby Vee and Del Shannon; military bases throughout Germany and England; Las Vegas – the Golden Nugget, the Sahara, and the Hilton; telethons around the country; nightclubs through the South, and lots of TV."

While in England, Tillotson gave Apple Records A&R head Tony King a copy of one of Beland's demo tapes. King shared the tape with Ringo Starr who recommended that Beland be signed to Apple, The Beatles' record company.

"It was utter shock and disbelief," explained Beland, who was thrilled to be professionally associated with The Beatles. "Ringo was a terrific, fabulous, and friendly guy."

But another shock was on the way. Beland recorded the *John Edward Beland* album but developing financial problems at Apple resulted in a cancellation of the recording. "When Apple folded unexpectedly, my manager, Mort Downey, secured a release from Apple and went to Florence Greenberg at Scepter Records who made my original label offer prior to Apple," said Beland. His self-titled, eleven-track collection debuted in 1973. A single, "Banjo Man" and "A Place to Rest My Head," was released but it failed to chart.

After his initial associations with Tillotson and Apple Records, Beland was invited by singer-songwriter Kris Kristofferson to join him and his wife, Rita Coolidge, on tour and in the studio in 1974. Beland played on Kristofferson's *Spooky Lady's Sideshow* in 1974 and a follow-up LP that was not released.

In 1976, the "King" called.

Beland was invited to replace Elvis Presley's guitarist James Burton who was leaving to join Emmylou Harris's band. But at the last moment, Burton changed his mind and remained with Presley.

"I felt very bad because I had already informed family and friends about the gig," said Beland, who had met Elvis backstage in Augusta, Georgia the year before. "And the money would have been top dollar: $1,250 a week. That said, I had other offers on the table from other acts at the time, so I wasn't caught with my pants down."

Surprisingly, Beland and Burton crossed paths a number of times during the next decade. The pair usually ended up together in a recording studio delivering guitar tracks for everything from Mazda car commercials to the motion picture soundtrack of *Brubaker*.

During the remainder of the 1970s, Beland was busy performing with a number of diverse artists including Dolly Parton and Mac Davis. At times, Beland worked simultaneously with a few artists, bouncing back and forth between assorted tours and recording dates.

"I did a lot of session work in Los Angeles at that time, everything from commercials, TV soundtracks, and recording," explained Beland, who also played bass guitar, mandolin, and keyboards. "I was also signed to Screen Gems in Nashville as a staff writer and shuttled quite frequently between Los Angeles and Nashville."

Following his association with Kristofferson, Beland joined The Bellamy Brothers of "Let Your Love Flow" fame. He later contributed guitar work for the group's 1977 album, *Plain & Fancy*, and joined the band on tour.

At about the same time, Beland became part of Kim Carnes' band and contributed to three of the singer's albums: *Sailin'* in 1976, *St. Vincent's Court* in 1979, and *Romance Dance* in 1980.

Of all the artists Beland played for at this time in his career, one stood out. "I first joined Rick Nelson in 1978, after working with Dolly Parton," noted Beland. "I knew Rick from a number of TV shows we did together when I was with Linda Ronstadt. I was a huge fan of his. I think I knew more about his records than he did, and my guitar style was very similar to that of his old guitarist, James Burton, who was a key element in Rick's biggest hits. Right from the start, we hit it off. It was as if I had known him for years. He was funny and kind and very humble. He was simply a fabulous guy to work for."

Beland was concerned that Rick Nelson wasn't following the best career path at the time. Nelson, one of the most popular artists during Rock and Roll's first decade, had over thirty Top 40 hits from 1957 to 1964, including two chart toppers, "Poor Little Fool" in 1958 and "Travelin' Man" in 1961, but The Beatles-led British Invasion, psychedelic Rock, Motown, and Folk Rock edged Nelson into the oldies but goodies category. He made a brief comeback with the autobiographical "Garden Party" in 1972, but additional chart hits did not follow.

"When I got to Rick, the first thing I noticed was the total lack of direction he seemed to have going on in his career," Beland pointed out. "He had just brought on a new manager, Greg McDonald, who was also aware of it. For years, Rick surrounded himself with band members and producers who convinced him that his old records were 'dated' and not 'hip' any longer. This resulted in Rick forming the Stone Canyon Band and pursuing a more country direction, which I believe was a terrible mistake. His records weren't selling any longer, although he did have a new record deal with CBS when I came along."

One Rick Nelson album that Beland played on was particularly forgetful. "I played on an album he was recording called *Return to Vienna*, produced by Al Kooper," said Beland. "Every big-shot musician was on the date, from Michael McDonald to Dr. John. But the material was crap and the sessions were disorganized with no focus on Rick, who mostly stayed in the vocal booth while Kooper ran the show. Well, CBS finally woke up and cancelled the release of the album and fired Kooper. Then they flew Rick to Memphis along with me and manager Greg McDonald. Together, we cornered Rick and decided to cut an album of songs in the old Rick Nelson Rockabilly style. Larry Rogers produced it and recorded us in a little house in Memphis on a sixteen-track machine, using a local rhythm section from Rogers' studio band called Shilo."

Nelson and Beland worked closely together on the album. "Rick and I selected and arranged the material," said Beland. "The album was called *The Memphis Sessions* and it brought back Rick's old love for Rock and Roll. It was great and yielded his last chart hit, 'Dream Lover,' which I arranged."

Nelson, Beland, and the rest of the band went out on tour. "Working with Rick was incredible," said Beland. "All of our shows were fantastic. We scrapped the steel guitar-Stone Canyon crap and replaced it with a tight rocking band like his old TV show band. And we went back doing all his hits. Rick's bookings skyrocketed back up. We did tons of TV, including him hosting *Saturday Night Live* on February 17, 1979, where we performed 'Hello Mary Lou,' 'Travelin' Man,' and 'Fools Rush In.' And we closed the show with 'Dream Lover.'"

Beland stayed with Nelson for another two years. "In 1980, I had an offer to join the rag-tag Flying Burrito Brothers," said Beland. "It meant leaving Rick, but I had to do it because it offered me the position of producer and main writer. I hated leaving Rick but he was supportive and he encouraged me to do it. I never wanted to make a lifelong career playing back up with anyone. I was a writer, producer, and arranger first and foremost, and Rick understood that. So, in 1981, reluctantly and sadly, we went our separate ways. I started demo recording with The Flying Burrito Brothers 'unofficially' in 1980 during my time off with Rick. I officially joined them in 1981."

The Flying Burrito Brothers band, formed by ex-Byrds Gram Parsons and Chris Hillman in 1968, was an early proponent of Country Rock. Parsons, though, died of a drug overdose in 1973. His body was going to be flown to Louisiana for burial. Later, two friends stole Parsons' coffin at Los Angeles International Airport and transported it to Joshua Tree, California, where they cremated it according to the performer's wishes. The body-snatching episode advanced Parson's legacy.

"I had been approached to join The Flying Burrito Brothers earlier but had no interest in it," explained Beland. "At that time, they were reduced to playing small clubs and had lost their CBS deal. I had worked with various Flying Burrito Brothers alumni over the years like Bernie Leadon, Chris Ethridge, and Sneaky Pete [Kleinow], so joining in 1980 wasn't any great change for me. We all knew each other well. But the first lineup I joined was very undisciplined and extremely loose. The 1980 Flying Burrito Brothers were old, stale, and boring. What made me stay in the band was the prospect of taking it over and aiming it towards a more contemporary Country direction, namely towards making 'hits.' Together with Gib Guilbeau, we co-wrote a bunch of great commercial country songs and systematically started firing weak players like bassist Skip Battin."

As a result of a further reduction in the band's lineup and a record deal with Curb Records, Beland, and Guilbeau reformed the group. "I always felt bad and very guilty about being in The Flying Burrito Brothers," admitted Beland. "I was never a fan of Gram Parsons or the band's music after their first album, which I liked. I hated being associated with that legacy. I always felt that Parson's legacy was overblown because of the nature of his death. I knew Gram from my association with Clarence White and always found Parsons as a troubled, stoned, very average singer. But when I joined, the press had elevated Parsons' status to that of the 'Savior of Country Rock,' which was all bullshit. When we had hits as The Flying Burrito Brothers, I hated responding to questions relating to how Gram might have felt seeing our chart success. I wanted to change our name to the Guilbeau/Beland Band, but my partner, Gib, was firmly planted in the whole Flying Burrito Brothers history."

In early 1981, the Michael Lloyd-produced Curb Records album, *Hearts on the Line*, was released. The LP generated a couple of Top 40 Country hits: "Does She Wish She Was Single Again" and "She Belongs to Everyone But Me." *Billboard* recognized The Flying Burrito Brothers as the best "Crossover" performers of the year, and *Record World* magazine named them the "Best New Vocal Group."

The following year, Lloyd produced the band's *Sunset Sundown*, which included three more Top 40 Country tunes: "If Something Should Come Between Us (Let It Be Love)," "Closer To You," and "I'm Drinking Canada Dry." But Kleinhow left the band, leaving Beland and Guilbeau to carry on as a duo.

"Being in The Flying Burrito Brothers was a double-edged sword," acknowledged Beland. "The success was great and exciting, but the ties to past members and being stuck in Gram's over-hyped importance was a drag for me."

Curb records brought in Randy Scruggs to produce the group's next album, *Our Roots Are Country Music*. "The album was never released, although a single, 'Blue and Broken Hearted Me,' was released," noted Beland.

More big hits didn't follow, and The Flying Burrito Brothers folded in 1985. "I was glad when the duo ended," declared Beland. "Gib and I were miles apart vision-wise. By that time, we were recording very sub-standard songs, mostly written by Guilbeau and his son, Ronnie. I wanted to get out and pursue production, which I finally did."

Beland and Rick Nelson almost joined forces again. "In 1985, I was asked to rejoin Rick because his guitarist, Bobby Neil – who replaced me and played acoustic guitar on *The Memphis Sessions* – was leaving Rick to go back home to his wife and family in Memphis. Bobby and

Rick called me from the road and asked if I wanted my old job back. I jumped at the chance! The Flying Burrito Brothers had broken up and I was sour with Nashville where I was living. I was supposed to join Rick right after his New Year's Eve gig in Texas."

On December 31, 1985, Nelson's leased DC-3 aircraft departed from Guntersville, Alabama, where he had performed the previous day. The singer's destination was Dallas, Texas, where he was going to perform at the end-of-year event. But the plane crashed a few miles from its destination. Only the two injured pilots survived; Nelson and six others perished.

"The crash changed all of that," said Beland. "They all died – everyone I knew, including Rick and his girlfriend, in the very plane I would have soon been on. I was devastated and traumatized. For years, I couldn't get the news images of the flaming plane out of my head, or the imaginary images of my friends burning up in the plane. To this day, I still have trouble with it and still miss Rick tremendously. He was more than just a boss: he was a dear friend. And working with him was the greatest thrill of my career."

Beland kept busy. He played with Nicolette Larson and Garth Brooks, wrote distinctive tunes for the likes of The Whites and Mark Farner, and penned the intro of *The Ricky Nelson Story*, a biography that was published in Great Britain in 1988.

At the end of the decade, The Flying Burrito Brothers were resurrected in a new lineup that included Beland, Guilbeau, Kleinow, and two other musicians. An album, *The Flying Burrito Brothers: Encore – Live in Europe in 1990*, was released at about the same time that Beland was working again with the Bellamy Brothers. "Cowboy Beat," which was co-penned by Beland and the band, became a Top 40 Country hit in 1992.

The next year, The Flying Burrito Brothers, with its ever changing lineup, released a new album, *Eye of a Hurricane*. The song collection – primarily written or co-written by Beland – wasn't a big hit in the United

States but it helped promote the band's popularity in Europe, where a large fan base embraced American Country Rock. The group subsequently toured Western Europe, where it was enthusiastically received.

Beland continued his international sojourn by teaming up with artists from China and Australia before returning to the United States where The Flying Burrito Brothers released *California Jukebox* in 1997. The band – minus Guilbeau – followed up with a new album: *Sons of the Golden West*.

"My favorite recordings were the last two albums The Flying Burrito Brothers did: *California Jukebox* and *Sons of the Golden West*," said Beland. "Those albums reflected what I originally envisioned for the band when I first joined them. I felt as if I had more creative control over the direction of the music when we did those last two CDs. Before that, I was at odds with Guilbeau's choices of material and I wanted to go to a harder sound than the softer Country stuff we did in the eighties."

Beland explained that he did not appreciate the production on the earlier albums. "I absolutely hated the production of Michael Lloyd on our hits, and was equally not happy with Randy Scruggs either," said Beland. "I thought that they missed the boat on what California Country Rock should sound like. Lloyd was a fluff Pop producer and Scruggs was mainstream Country. I suggested we use Jimmy Bowen, whom I had a close working relationship with, but Curb turned him down. I also suggested Ken Mansfield, who did the legendary Outlaws album and with whom I had a long working relationship with. But he, too, was turned down."

Beland emphasized that he did not become a member of The Flying Burrito Brothers only to perform. "My sole intent, from the very beginning when I was asked to join the band, was to produce the act, but Curb fought it and assigned others to produce us," he pointed out. "The result was that our records sounded lightweight and nowhere near as strong as the original demos we did ourselves. Furthermore, Lloyd was using the same musicians and studio on our records as he was using on The Bellamy Brothers' records, which he also produced. The result was that our records sounded like theirs. I raised a fit about it, but could not convince Curb to let Lloyd go. When they finally did, they assigned Randy Scruggs, whose production direction was again lightweight and light years away from how I saw us as an act."

Beland was convinced that had he played a more important role in the band's production process, the group would have been more successful. "The last two albums were produced by me, and I believe they had the most solid sound ever in the bands recorded history," stated Beland. "Larry Patton was a different kind of vocalist with a good edge and a nice departure from Gib's soft Country sound. Yes, we had hits, but they were not the kind of strong edgy records we could have made had I been at the helm. I played a strong role in the arrangements and played on every one of our hit records, but in the end, Lloyd and Scruggs were *not* the right producers for us. I never listen to those early eighties records because they sound so soft and lightweight. The songs were real good and they scored great on the charts; however, I never liked the final results of those hits."

On the eve of the new century, Beland spent most of his creative time on production. He supervised and fine-tuned albums by Australian artists Lee Conway and Tamika Kellehear, and also toured Down Under with a new incarnation of The Flying Burrito Brothers. And Beland produced Merle Haggard's "Mama's Hungry Eyes" in 1998. "To sit behind the board and produce a session on Merle was a dream come true," remarked Beland.

In 2001, Beland produced and released *Burrito Works*, a fourteen-song collection of some of the performer's favorite compositions. Working with the latest incarnation of The Flying Burrito Brothers, Beland received musical contributions from the likes of Buck Owens, Ricky Skaggs, Alison Krauss, and other notable country artists.

That same year, Beland released a solo album, *Bare Bones*, in which he played all the instruments. "Although I can hold my own on guitar in the studio or on tour, I consider myself, first and foremost, a songwriter," stated Beland. "I was taught by the best: Larry Murray, Freddy Weller, Dewayne Blackwell, Austin Roberts, Brian Cadd, Paul Parrish, Bobby Fischer, and other great hit tunesmiths. *Bare Bones* is a collection of some of the best songs I have ever written."

In 2002, Beland produced and released *The Very Best of John Beland*, which included contributions from some of his former Flying Burrito Brothers bandmates, country notables Buck Owens and Ricky Skaggs, and others.

He moved to Texas in 2004. "Prior to that I lived in Brisbane, Australia for a short spell," said Beland. "And prior to that, I was in Napa, California; before that, Nashville."

Over the next few years, Beland kept active. He toured the British Isles; supported Rick Nelson's sons, Gunnar and Matthew, in concert; released *Silverado Morning*, an instrumental album; produced other artists; released *Big Guitars – Volume I*, a tribute to such classic tunes as "Perfidia" and "Cry For a Shadow;" released *Christmas At Baxters*, *Easy To Be Free: The Songs of Rick Nelson*, and *Cast Your Fate to the Wind*; toured Canada and Scandinavia; and produced *John Beland: The Flying Burrito Brothers Years*.

Beland finally visited the Alamo in 2007. "The Alamo means a lot to me, now being a Texan myself and living so close to where it all happened in 1836," he said. "I don't think I'll ever grow tired of reading about the Alamo. Like my fellow musicians and Alamo buffs Dusty Hill and Phil Collins, it's pretty imbedded in me and I wouldn't want it any other way."

In 2010, Beland released *Big Guitars – Volume II*. Two years later, he teamed up again with Larry Patton on *Patton & Beland: Reach For The Sky!* The duo toured Denmark and Norway. "It was fun working with

Larry but eventually I wanted to continue off on my own," said Beland. "My being in bands or duos had taken up a lot of my years and I felt the need to finally put that to an end."

Beland soon established a Scandinavian connection of sorts with The Southern Girls, a vocal trio from Kristiansand, Norway. "They met with me in Mandal, Norway in 2012, and expressed a desire to record a contemporary Country album with an American producer," explained Beland. "When I heard their vocals, I was floored. They had that harmony sound that spelled 'hit' all over it. Fortunately for me, they allowed me complete creative control over the project, which made things go exactly the direction I wanted to take with them, which was a cross between the 'Trio' – Emmylou Harris, Linda Ronstadt, and Dolly Parton – and Abba. I specifically geared their sound towards European radio instead of the USA. The girls were incredible in the studio and needed little direction from me. I believe they are going to be a smash act."

The result of the recording session was *A Little Bit of This – A Little Bit of That*. Beland played all of the instruments on the album except one. "The drums were played by ace Florida session man Frank Basile," said Beland. "The music was recorded here at my place in Texas and Florida. All vocals were done in Kristiansand, Norway."

In early 2013, Beland produced, arranged, and performed all the tracks on *Outside The Alamo: Songs of Ned Huthmacher*, a twelve-song indie CD. "These songs of Ned's are bits of poetry, sentiment, history, and music woven into an unusual, but beautiful tapestry," wrote Beland in the liner notes.

On August 23, 2013, the *USA Today* reported that Linda Ronstadt was suffering with Parkinson's Disease. The newspaper noted that during an interview with the AARP about her forthcoming memoir, *Simple Dreams*, Ronstadt explained that the illness also prevented her from ever singing again.

Beland was devastated by the news. The next day, he posted the following message on his Facebook page: "It's with tremendous sadness that I learned the news of my dear friend Linda Ronstadt's battle with Parkinson's Disease. In a way, I owe a major part of my career in music to Linda, who opened so many doors for me when she took me on as her guitarist many years ago. But more than that, I had a terrific personal relationship with Linda and she was truly a sweetheart to know and work for. I wish her only the best. My prayers and continued admiration and undying friendship go with her as she fights this."

On the following day, Beland added some additional thoughts about Ronstadt. "Even in my naive youth, twenty years old, up onstage living my Illinois dream of one day being a big shot guitarist, I still could sense something seriously historical was going on around me. I felt this whenever I played the Troubadour with Linda. Just a fleeting sensation that would hit me somewhere in the show, and when it did, I realized right at that moment that I was participating in something historic, something people would remember years from that night. I knew how great she was; it didn't take a rocket scientist to figure out that she was the best. Onstage we shared a confidence in our music: we knew that nobody could follow us; nobody could follow 'her.' Every night was an explosion of talent that tore through every audience we played for. I recall the pounding on the tables and shouts for 'more' erupting long after we had left the stage and were sitting in the dressing room. We were like a combat unit: an elite, tight, well-rehearsed band of musicians fronted by the greatest singer in Rock and Roll. Nobody played what we played. How could they? It was to be experienced. You just had to have been there, watching it happen. And for all her greatness and importance she was one of us. She was just Linda – funny, sweet, and painfully insecure in her ability. All of us who shared that stage with her, who toured with her, who were traveled with her, loved her. What a ride we all took – on her tremendous coat tails."

Beland was more upbeat after she was inducted in the Rock and

Roll Hall of Fame in 2014. "I believe that Linda's induction into the Rock and Roll Hall Of Fame has been long overdue," he stated. "Her importance in the formation of what is now termed 'Country Rock' far surpasses that of bands like The Eagles, Poco, or anyone else, including my own band, The Flying Burrito Brothers. It was Linda who broke ranks with Pop music's guidelines by single-handedly merging Rock with traditional Country instruments, back when steel guitars and fiddles were taboo in Pop music. She built the bridge between Country and Rock for all of the early L.A. bands to cross over. She made it 'cool' to like Country. I'm happy for her. She deserves her place with the greats of Rock."

Beland was moved by her induction ceremony. "Witnessing Linda Ronstadt get inducted was emotional," he noted. "I choked up a bit as I watched Glenn Frey make an eliquent speech and it stirred up so many memories as I listened. Glenn looked pretty choked up too!"

Also in 2014, Beland sojourned back to Scandanavia where he played guitar for Bright Owe Ognedal. "He is a fabulous Norwegian Country-Blues Rocker with a killer band," said Beland, who was on the road again.

"These days my time is mostly spent recording abroad, primarily in Australia and Norway," noted Beland. "Both countries have been havens for Country Rock fans for many years. Because of this, I have been called to tour and record in both countries for many years, building up an audience and creating a good reputation both live and in the studio. It's refreshing to go abroad and be appreciated for recorded work you did decades earlier. For that, I'm extremely blessed."

A relatively secret part of Beland's past emerged when a long-lost member of his family recently surfaced: his son, Chris, who is also a musician. And this personal story of family heartache and reconciliation will be documented in a motion picture titled *Becoming Beland*.

"It's a film based upon the true story of my son, Chris, finding his real father, me," stated Beland. "The film will focus on Chris' life and struggle to find himself, his music, and his family while at the same time discovering who his real father is. We're all thrilled over the project, to say the least. It's an amazing, heartfelt and true story. But I don't want to get into too much about the film before it comes out."

After performing for over fifty years, Beland remains focused, confident, and content about his career. "So the road goes on, with a few detours along the way, but still filled with many adventures and fabulous music," said Beland. "How lucky am I?"

Chapter 3

Phil Collins

"Against All Odds"

In 2012, Phil Collins, the mega-selling singer-songwriter-drummer, produced a new creative work – a book – and it surprised most of the Rock and Roll Hall of Fame member's fans and contemporaries because it wasn't about music; it was about the Alamo, the famous mission-fortress that served as the place where Davy Crockett, William B. Travis, Jim Bowie, and an undersized garrison of Texians and Tejanos fought to the death against General Antonio López de Santa Anna's Mexican Army in 1836.

Although I had reviewed a number of Collins' videos and albums in the 1980s, it wasn't until he joined The Alamo Society that we finally met.

Collins invited me to be among a handful of Alamo historians to pen a few words about his *The Alamo and Beyond: A Collector's Journey*. I wrote the following on the volume's dust jacket: "Phil Collins' *The Alamo and Beyond: A Collector's Journey* is more than just a stunning presentation of impressive primary source documents and artifacts from the Texas Revolution: it is an important research source which helps us better understand the life and times of those who helped create the

Texas Republic." His volume was a first-class effort, and it was enjoyable to sing his literary praises.

In a way, the origin of my association with Collins goes back further than a few years ago; in fact, it began in the mid-1950s when as youngsters Collins and I viewed Walt Disney's *Davy Crockett* series, which starred Fess Parker, from opposite sides of the Atlantic Ocean

The final episode of the Disney trilogy, "Davy Crockett at the Alamo," left an indelible impression on both of us. "Timing in life is everything and the timing of the Disney series seemed to be crucial," said Collins. "Even Crockett's clothes looked cool! I went searching for a suede-fringe coat way into the sixties. David Crosby had one, too. Certainly with the Alamo-related Crockett story, there was a huge romantic edge: doing the right thing, no matter what. That certainly appealed to me. To know what awaits you, yet you still stay. That was courage personified."

Collins vividly recalled Fess Parker's final moments on screen. "I do remember that it didn't show him die and that he went down fighting," he remarked. "Of course, that last scene summed up the way Crockett was presented to us."

Collins also remembered "The Ballad of Davy Crockett," which was a huge chart hit in many countries, especially in the United States and the United Kingdom. "I won a few talent competitions singing that song when I was six or so," he declared. "I have an original copy of the music framed in my basement."

Collins' interest in the Alamo increased after he saw John Wayne's *The Alamo* in 1961. "This, if anything, was *the* pivotal moment for me," he said. "I thought the casting was spectacular, the music fantastic. Obviously, we now know it was an over-romanticized version of the story, but it was a great movie that was made by Wayne with loving care."

Besides the Alamo and Davy Crockett, Collins developed a keen interest in music. Like so many musicians, Collins was influenced by The

Beatles; as a matter of fact, as a thirteen-year-old he was a television audience extra in the 1964 film *A Hard Day's Night*. He was soon acting on stage and in film, but quickly shifted his focus to music.

"The sixties was a fantastic time to grow up in musically," he said. "I took it all in: Motown, Stax, Atlantic Soul, The Beatles, Count Basie – so many things that formed the base of my musical influences."

He joined a local band (he had been playing drums since he was a child) and the group, Flaming Youth, released an album, *Ark 2*, in 1969; however, the group disbanded.

Collins successfully auditioned for the progressive Rock band, Genesis – which included original members Peter Gabriel (vocals), Tony Banks (keyboards), and Mike Rutherford (bass) – in 1970. He debuted his musical skills on the imaginative *Nursery Cryme* in 1971. For the next few years, he served the band primarily as its drummer but occasionally provided lead vocals. Gabriel, however, was the focal point of the band. Gabriel handled most of the lead singing responsibilities while frequently costumed in outrageous outfits, some of which completely shrouded his identity.

While he was with Genesis, Collins made his first pilgrimage to the Alamo in 1973. "Genesis was out on our first USA tour," he said. "Peter Gabriel, our tour manager, and I had three days off. We decided that each of us would choose a place to visit. Peter chose Hot Springs, Arkansas; Richard, our tour man, chose the Grand Canyon; and I chose the Alamo. Obviously, I was in awe of being in this place that had played such a huge part of my life. But I was also surprised that there was so little to see. We're still paying the price for the politicians and the 'mover' in the past that for some reason decided to tear most of it down. I know the Mexican Army destroyed a lot of it when they left after the battle, but they also left a lot standing. In my wildest dreams, I imagine a time when some of the walls could be replaced, but then a reconstruction is not the same thing either."

Early in his music career, Collins was unaware that outside of museums, historical documents and movie collectibles relating to the Alamo were available to purchase. "I didn't have the money to buy memorabilia nor did I think it existed," explained Collins. "Only in the eighties did I come across an old Crockett letter and that turned me around. I didn't get the letter; it was too expensive at the time, though not by today's standards. Now I'm an avid collector. I've made some great friends at the Alamo, with the Daughters of the Republic of Texas and with Texas historians. I'm not a 'Pop star' when I'm there; I'm an Alamo buff who wants to *know* and wants to *learn*. It's incredibly interesting."

The Genesis lineup with Gabriel lasted until 1974 with the release of *The Lamb Lies Down on Broadway,* one of Collins' favorite albums with the band. After Gabriel left the group a year later to go solo, Collins assumed the former singer's role, minus his former bandmate's outlandish costuming. Collins' sincere and passionate vocal style, which frequently reflected personal issues in his life, became a familiar and accessible sound on FM radio for years. That same year, Collins married Andrea Bertorelli, who gave birth to a son, Simon, in 1976. However, the couple divorced five years later.

Following the departure of guitarist Steve Hackett (he joined after Collins had been added to the lineup), Genesis remained as a trio and produced a string of commercial best-selling albums including 1978's *...And Then There Were Three...,* the band's first American platinum album; the multi-platinum *Abacab* in 1981; *Genesis* in 1983; and *Invisible Touch* in 1986, which produced five American Top 4 singles including the chart-topping title track.

Collins was involved with other musical projects besides those with Genesis. His first solo album, *Face Value,* in 1981, a collection of original compositions (except for The Beatles' "Tomorrow Never Knows"), included the Top 20 hit "In The Air Tonight." The LP, which featured the musicianship of guitarist Daryl Stuermer, who had played with Genesis on past tours, went to the top of the British charts and was a Top 10, multi-platinum success in the United States.

Their best-selling hit albums and singles followed throughout the 1980s. *Hello, I Must Be Going* in 1982 spawned his successful version of The Supremes' "You Can't Hurry Love," a preview of his 2010 tribute to Motown CD. His recording of the title track from the 1984 film *Against All Odds* became his first single to top the American charts. The tune also received an Oscar nomination but Collins wasn't extended an invitation to perform the song at the 57th Academy Awards ceremony; as a matter of fact, he was the only nominee not given the opportunity to sing. Instead, Broadway performer Ann Reinking was recruited to sing the song while Collins sat in the audience. It was an awkward situation, but Collins dismissed the snub with characteristic charm and wit. However, Stevie Wonder won the golden statuette for "I Just Called to Say I Love You" from *The Woman in Red*. Also in 1984, Collins married Jill Tavelman. The couple became parents in 1989 with the birth of a daughter, Lilly.

The next year, Collins released the most successful album of his career: *No Jacket Required*. Collins co-produced the recording with Hugh Padgham, and the pair recruited a talented lineup of musicians including bassist Leland Sklar. The ten-song collection of Collins' originals went to #1 in ten countries, sold over 12 million copies in the United States, and generated four Top 10 American singles including two #1 hits: "Sussudio" and "One More Night."

"The 'No Jacket Required' title came from two places around the same time," explained Collins. "Both 1984-ish. Firstly, I was on tour with with ex-Led Zeppelin front man Robert Plant on his first solo tour. I'd played drums on his first two CDs – 1982's *Pictures at Eleven* and 1983's *The Principle of Moments* – and he asked me to tour with him. We stayed at the Ambassador East Hotel in Chicago and we both went to the bar – he in a very loud suit; me in a brand new, smart and expensive leather jacket and pants. I was denied entry, but he was admitted. Go figure. Secondly, I was on holiday in the Virgin Islands and was stopped from entering the hotel restaurant because I didn't have a jacket and tie. The couple behind me – who became life-long friends, and they came from Dallas – joked about 'no jacket required' or something like that. So when I had to come with an album title, I grabbed the opportunity to retaliate in some way! Eventually on David Letterman and the old Johnny Carson show, I told everyone the Chicago story. The hotel finally sent me a jacket with paint all over it saying: 'You can even wear this, just stop talking about the story!'"

Collins dropped a hint about his Alamo interest in the 1985 video "Don't Lose My Number" in which he mentions *The Alamo* and John Wayne to an actor who portrays Peter, the video's director.

"That was one of those improvised sketches for the video," noted Collins. "We made a lot of stuff as we went along. Some of Peter's lines were written, but I was asked to add my replies. *The Alamo* and John Wayne were always at the top of the heap for me. My passion for the Alamo and its story had evolved long before then, but this was an easy way to use the 'power of suggestion.'"

On July 13, 1985, Collins had the distinction of being the only musical artist to perform at the Live Aid benefit concert for Ethiopian famine relief at both Great Britain's Wembley Stadium and Philadelphia's John F. Kennedy Stadium. Collins flew to the United States via the Concorde following his appearance at Wembley Stadium.

At Wembley Stadium, Collins joined Sting for a seven-song set that concluded with "Every Breath You Take," which had earned The Police a 1984 Grammy Award for Song of the Year. Collins shared a funny story with my wife, Debbie, and me in Texas several years ago about his collaboration with The Police's front man. "I always a stickler for lyrics and always made sure I'd memorize them, especially if I was working with someone else's song or with another performer," said Collins with a smile. "When I was informed that I would be singing 'Every Breath You Take' with Sting, I made it a point to study and learn those lyrics. Well, I studied them and had them down pat. But when it got time to perform the song, Sting was the one who messed up. Although I was singing the correct lyrics it sounded as if I was the one who was making the mistake. And some critic accused *me* of messing up the song!"

Collins took a brief break from the world of music and returning to acting. On December 13, 1985 Collins portrayed Phil Mayhew, a British con man, in a *Miami Vice* episode titled "Phil the Shill." Three years later, he starred in the title role of *Buster*, a British film based on the 1963 Great Train Robbery. Two songs from the film's soundtrack album topped the American charts: a reworking of The Mindbenders' 1965 hit, "A Groovy Kind of Love," and "Two Hearts."

In 1989, Collins released *...But Seriously*, which included the arresting "Another Day In Paradise," a composition that addressed the issue of homelessness. The album, which also reflected other socio-political concerns, went to #1 in several nations and achieved multi-platinum status in 1990.

A year later, Collins was back with Genesis. The band released the multi-platinum *We Can't Dance*, which was followed by a successful world tour. In 1993, Genesis was regarded as one of rockdom's most popular bands; in fact, the group received an American Music Award as the industry's top Pop/Rock unit. Collins' next solo LP, *Both Sides*, released later in the year, was not that successful, at least compared to the artist's previous track record. Still, the album went platinum and one of the collection's singles, "Both Sides of the Story," was a Top 10 hit.

The demands of singing lengthy sets night after night in venues around the world proved to be a challenge, but Collins developed a unique way to keep his lungs and vocals chords in top shape. "I learned how to play the bagpipes," he said. "I 'learned' how to play in 1994 with [Scots Guard Pipe-Major] Jim Banks as my tutor. I used to play every day before the show to open up my lungs. It drove everyone crazy, though. It's a strange thing about the bagpipes; you either love them or hate them."

Genesis' 1996's *Dance Into The Night* only managed to reach gold status, and soon thereafter Collins left the band, although he performed several of his former group's songs with his new lineup, the Phil Collins Big Band. That same year, he divorced his second wife.

In 1998, his *...Hits* album went multi-platinum and his interpretation of Cyndi Lauper's "True Colors" became a Top 40 hit. A year later, Collins married Orianne Cevey. The Collins family grew with the birth of two boys, Nicholas and Mathew.

The next year, he released his soundtrack album from the Walt Disney animated motion picture *Tarzan*. The album's most popular track, "You'll Be in My Heart," was rewarded with an Oscar at the 72nd Academy Awards in 2000 for Best Original Song. This time, Collins performed his own song at the ceremony.

In 2000, Collins and his wife established the Little Dreams Foundation (LDF) which was designed to "help kids in their pursuit of excellence in art, music or sports." Once accepted in the program, the children are assisted by a number of individuals including LDF "godparents." Among those who have served in that capacity are Natalie Cole, Frida Lyngstad of Abba, and Collins.

His next album, *Testify*, in 2002, featured a diverse range of compositions, from the reflective "Wake Up Call" to the heartfelt "Come With Me." However, the recording stalled at #30 on the American album chart. Still, *Testify* managed to produce the adult contemporary hit "Can't Stop Loving You," which was originally recorded by Leo Sayer in 1978. The following year, Collins was inducted into the Songwriters Hall of Fame.

Collins remained active in the new century's first decade. He wrote nine new songs for the Broadway production of *Tarzan*, which opened in 2006, and reunited with Tony Banks and Mike Rutherford for a Genesis world tour in 2007. But during the tour, he dislocated one of the vertebrae in his neck which affected his ability to grip the drum sticks. Unfortunately, a subsequent operation didn't eradicate the problem with his hands.

When I became aware of Collins' interest in the Alamo, I contacted him and asked if he would be interested in writing the introduction to a book that fellow Alamo Society member Allen Wiener and I were writing: *Music of the Alamo: From 19th Century Ballads to Big-Screen Soundtracks*. He enthusiastically agreed and his generous comments were included in the volume upon its release in 2008.

"I consider myself a lifelong Alamo 'freak,'" he wrote in the introduction. "By that I mean that I have been living the story since I was a child of six. Reason being: I happened to grow up at a time when Walt Disney's 'Davy Crockett' movies, starring Fess Parker, were out and I became that character. I became Davy Crockett. I thought I was the only one. Wrong! I even won a few talent contests singing 'The Ballad of Davy Crockett.'"

Collins and his third wife divorced in 2008.

He became quite active in various Alamo-related projects and events. In March 2009, Collins appeared at the annual Alamo Society symposium and attended an Alamo ceremony hosted by the Daughters of the Republic of Texas. He participated in a March 6, 2009 dawn ceremony on Alamo Plaza and addressed the Alamo Defenders Descendants Association (ADDA) at a ceremony inside the Alamo. "These men, your ancestors, died fighting for what they believed to be right," said Collins at the ADDA event. "So I stand here in awe of you. To be here at fifty-eight years old and to be able to talk to the descendants of those brave men who have influenced my life since I was barely six years old is beyond comprehension."

He also became co-owner of the History Shop, which is located across the street from the Alamo. Collins also participated in an archeological dig at the shop's site. "We found a huge amount of horseshoes and quite a few fire pits plus the usual things like buttons, buckles, lance heads, flints, musket balls, and pieces of iron used as cannon fodder," explained Collins. "We also found a flattened cannonball with pieces of wall embedded in it. Clearly, it had been fired, hit the Alamo wall and rebounded. As an exercise it was stimulating, plus I have some very cool new stuff at home in my collection." His home is in Switzerland but he has an apartment in New York City.

Several years ago, Collins invited me to his Manhattan apartment where photos of his children filled his living room. One prominent wall featured a painting of the Alamo and a photo of the famous mission-fortress. However, nowhere in his residence's largest room were any noticeable mementos from his illustrious and award-winning music career. I had to go to his office and look carefully behind the windowed door of bookcase to see a row of Grammy Awards and his Oscar for "You'll Be in My Heart." A bathroom wall, of all places, features additional music awards and related material, and an adjacent hallway's walls are replete with gold records and photos of musical celebrities. It's all so very low key for such an accomplished artist; however, among the assorted images and awards is a photo of Collins with Queen Elizabeth II. After all, he is a Lieutenant of the Royal Victorian Order. While we chatted, his girlfriend, Dana Tyler, the charming and talented Emmy Award-winning WCBS-TV news anchor and reporter, prepared some snacks and served us each a glass of Guiness for lunch. "Only one glass for me," he quipped. "It's too early in the day."

Later, I conducted a series of interviews with him for *The Alamo Journal*, the official publication of The Alamo Society. He restated how Fess Parker's characterization of Davy Crockett inspired him as a boy and explained that he was especially interested in one of the Alamo's couriers.

"I have a fascination with John W. Smith in particular," said Collins.

"One of the first historical documents I bought was the receipt for the sale of his saddle. The receipt is dated April 1836, just before the Battle of San Jacinto. It is one of my most prized possessions. He was one of the last messengers out of the Alamo and after the battle became mayor of San Antonio. Yet, I believe there are no photos or images of him. There are images of his wife, but not him. If anyone out there has an image of Smith, please pass it on!"

A color reproduction of Smith's receipt and its transcript was included with other items from Collins' impressive collection in his book, *The Alamo and Beyond: A Collector's Journey*. "This story of the Alamo has touched many more people than one would think," he wrote in his dedication. "So, I would like to pay my respects to those men on both sides of the walls in those months of February and March 1836."

In 2010, Collins shared his passion for American Soul music when he released *Going Back*, an Atlantic CD collection of eighteen Motown tracks that included such classic tracks as "(Love Is Like A) Heat Wave," "Papa Was A Rolling Stone," "Something About You," and "Standing in the Shadows of Love."

"My aim in finally making this record was to see if it was possible for me to recapture the sound and the feelings that I got from listening to these songs the first time around," wrote Collins in the CD's liner notes booklet. In order to make his recordings as genuine as possible, he recruited several of the Funk Brothers – the name given to Motown's incredibly talented staff of veteran session musicians. Collins secured the unique services of guitarists Eddie Willis and Ray Monette, and bassist Bob Babbitt. And legendary Motown songwriter Lamont Dozier added some liner notes, thanking Collins for recording "In My Lonely Room," one of the Detroit-based tunesmith's favorites.

Collins wasn't content to just release a CD: he took *Going Back* on the road – and with the Funk Brothers! He kicked off a limited American tour on June 20, 2010 in Philadelphia where he was joined onstage by a full lineup of musicians and background vocalists. Collins sang but did not play drums. At that point in his illustrious career, he didn't need to tour or prove anything; he just wanted to perform some of his favorite music and share it with appreciative audiences. Enthusiastic crowds were glad to witness the superstar musician, especially since he is one of three performers – Paul McCartney and Michael Jackson are the other two – who have sold over 100 million recordings with their respective bands and over 100 million recordings as solo performers. It's a staggering accomplishment, to say the least.

He invited Debbie and me to be his guests at his second concert in Philadelphia at the Electric Factory on June 21. Always generous, he provided us with special tickets and all-access passes to the show. After the well-received concert, we were escorted backstage where Collins and Dana Tyler awaited us in the main dressing room. Outside the room, he asked what we thought of the concert and we immediately responded with positive comments. I told him that it was wonderful and noted that in a way it was like overhearing someone sing in the shower. He looked at me with a puzzled smile. I quickly explained that when someone sings his or her favorite songs in the privacy of their own home, it marks highest level of personal enthusiasm and passion for a particular piece of music – at least according to my shower-stall perspective. He chuckled at my pseudo-intellectual reply and invited us into his dressing room for some Alamo talk and wine.

Collins knew of my appreciation for Bob Babbitt and he introduced me to the legendary four-string master. "I'm just a pawn in this," he exclaimed with a broad grin as Babbitt and I conversed. Collins stood back and said nothing as the legendary Motown bassist and I chatted. He was content to introduce two people who shared mutual interests to each other, and I appreciated his gesture very much.

Also backstage was one of Collins' background singers, Terron Brooks, who played Eddie Kendricks in the 1998 TV movie *The Tempta-*

tions. Veteran session bassist Leland Sklar also showed up with camera in hand. He was eager to take personal photos of nearly everyone "flipping the bird" at him – at his request! It was a wonderful night. Sadly, Bob Babbitt died two years later on July 16, 2012.

In 2013, Collins stated that he had "finally" retired from performing and recording. He was seemingly content to spend time with his children and Dana Tyler.

However, his so called retirement would last a year. In early 2014, various media reports noted that a Genesis reunion was in the works and that Collins was going to team up with Adele, the captivating British songstress whose two first albums, *19* in 2008 and *21* in 2011, dominated the charts in the United States and Europe and earned eight Grammy Awards. However, the collobaration stalled in April. "Nothing much is happening," explained Collins. "Adele has fallen quiet as she's 'not feeling creative' right now and is moving house."

Still, the Genesis project was progessing. "Been busy with the kids and a Genesis TV special for the UK," he remarked. "However, no Genesis reunion plans, and not much going on with me!"

Collins announced in June that he was donating his multi-million-dollar collection of Texas Revolution artifacts and documents to the Alamo, and on June 26 he took part in a presentation program and press conference in front of the historic mission's church building. Collins explained that at his age, sixty-three, he wondered about the fate of his collection. He also said that he wanted his extensive home collection to be shared by many more people. "I look at it every day, but nobody else was enjoying it," he noted. But he said that he would still keep collecting and donating to the Alamo.

So much had gone on in his career. It appeared that Collins was finally retiring from the music business. But then again, as an artist, his creativity may manifest itself yet again.

Chapter 4

Peter Criss

"Hooked On Rock And Roll"

Peter Criss made a name for himself in Rock history, of course, as the drummer of Kiss, the legendary band that pledged to "Rock and Roll all night and party every day." Joining with Paul Stanley (guitar and vocals), Gene Simmons (bass and vocals), and Ace Frehley (guitar and vocals), Criss added his percussion skills and occasional vocals to such memorable, megawatt hard Rock albums as *Destroyer*, *Alive!*, and *Love Gun*, to name a few.

Criss was born George Peter John Criscuola in Brooklyn, New York on December 20, 1945, four months after the end of World War II and less than two weeks from the "official" beginning of the Baby Boom.

He grew up listening to Jazz (drummer Gene Krupa was his favorite musician, and he later took lessons from the legendary performer) and Rock and Roll. Following The Beatles-led British Invasion in 1964, Criss started playing drums in local bands. One group, Chelsea, managed to secure an album deal with Decca Records, but the band's self-titled LP in 1970 (the same year he married Lydia Di Leonardo) failed to generate attention from critics or the public.

The next year, Chelsea reformed as Lips; however, the band soon folded and Criss looked elsewhere to display his musical chops. He didn't have to wait too long.

In late 1972, Criss joined forces with Gene Simmons and Paul Stanley, formerly of Wicked Lester, and formed Kiss; the next year, Ace Frehley completed the lineup. As 1973 progressed, the band's members developed their unique make-up styles (Criss became the Catman) and recorded their self-titled debut album on the newly formed Casablanca Records. *Kiss* contained a number of tracks that would become essential songs in the band's catalog: "Strutter," "Nothin' to Lose," "Cold Gin," "Deuce," and "Black Diamond," which featured Criss on lead vocals. But *Kiss* and its 1974 follow-up, *Hotter Than Hell*, failed to make a significant impact on the LP charts; the first recording reached #87 on the *Billboard* charts and the second release stalled at #100.

Kiss took to the streets. The band toured extensively, delivering its mega-decibel show with theatrical flair and a fan-friendly attitude. The quartet's concerts were complemented with staged actions that ranged from Simmons' "blood" spitting and pyrotechnic antics to Frehley's fireworks-loaded guitar work. As the group gained in popularity, its stage show got bigger, flashier, and louder, and the band's hard work paid off with better LP sales.

The next album, *Dressed to Kill*, which included the quartet's signature anthem, "Rock and Roll All Nite," made it to #32, but the label's bottom line was bleeding more red ink than Simmons' stage blood supply.

Fortunately, the *Alive!* LP hit the retail store racks in 1975. The LP, which captured the exhuberant spirit of the band in concert, helped elevate Kiss to the Top 10 of the *Billboard* charts. It was just the beginning of the band's glory days. Over the next few years, the band released such platinum best sellers as *Destroyer*, *Rock and Roll Over*, *Love Gun*, *Alive II*, and *Double Platinum*, a greatest hits package.

Among its single releases, the highest chart-tracking Kiss single was "Beth," a ballad from *Destroyer*, sung by Criss which reached #7 on the *Billboard* Hot 100 chart. "Beth" became the highest-charting single in the history of the band and was a frequent concert encore tune for the group. On *Rock And Roll Over*, the drummer comfortably performed "Hard Luck Woman," a mid-tempo rocker that reached #15 on the singles chart.

A 1977 Gallup Poll identified Kiss as the most popular Rock band in the world among American fans; however, the foursome was regularly panned by many music critics, who preferred artists that specialized in lyrical social consciousness and assorted artsy-related themes. Furthermore, the band's makeup and stage antics were generally frowned upon as meaningless adornments by the fourth estate. But the members of Kiss were having the time of their lives and ignored the critics.

When he wasn't rock and rolling all night, Criss was experiencing a second childhood. He devoted some of his time to racing cars and collecting antique toys and various Baby Boomer collectibles – from Mickey Mouse and Flash Gordon items to Hopalong Cassidy and Howdy Doody creations.

Kiss' Alive II Tour in 1977 extended into 1978 with numerous shows in the United States. After concluding the domestic leg of the tour in Providence, Rhode Island in February 1978, the band flew to Japan, where it performed at Tokyo's famous Nippon Budokan arena in late March and early April. Kiss' five sold out shows broke the band's own record of four, which it had set in April 1977.

The band decided to top itself in a unique marketing manner. In September 1978, each member of the band released his own solo album. All of the LPs were moderate Top 40 chart successes except Criss' effort, which only reached #43 on *Billboard's* LP roster. But Criss' solo album wouldn't be his last. The band went back on the road and participated in a number of media interviews. One interview was particularly memorable.

On Halloween night 1979, the band appeared on NBC-TV's *To-*

morrow with Tom Snyder. Frehley was drunk and giggly, and Criss was having fun with his inebriated guitarist at his side. But Simmons was annoyed at both of them, especially Frehley. Snyder asked Criss about his interest in car racing. "I've wrecked quite a few cars in my time," confessed Criss to Snyder. "I'm very lucky to be here. So I stopped that."

Criss explained that he had other interests. He noted his appreciation for old gangster films and said that he was a gun collector who participated in target shooting.

"What is it about having a gun collection?" asked Snyder.

"I'm fascinated by them, maybe because I'm fascinated by gangster movies," remarked Criss. "If I could relive, I would love to be in the twenties and be like a [John] Dillinger or Baby Face Nelson." Simmons quickly added, "In the movies," as a way of spinning Criss' gun-flavored fantasy into an innocuous hobby that would not be interpreted negatively by anyone.

By the end of the decade, Kiss scored with *Dynasty*, another Top 10 LP. The album contained the dance-rocker "I Was Made for Lovin' You," which became the band's most successful *group* single to date. Despite the success, the group was disintegrating. Internal tensions, personality conflicts, accusations about musicianship – you name it – eventually led to a separation between Criss and the rest of the band. Even the breakup was the subject of interpretation: Criss said he quit; Simmons said he was fired. In any event, Criss was out of the band – and off came his Kiss makeup.

He also divorced his first wife in 1979, and married Debra Jensen, who had been *Playboy* magazine's Miss January 1978. A daughter, Jenilee, was born three years later.

Criss' departure from the band was accented by the release of his first non-Kiss solo album, *Out Of Control*, which was actually recorded in early 1980 while he was technically still a member of the group. He co-wrote ten of LP's tracks, except for "You Better Run," which was written by Felix Cavaliere and Eddie Brigati of The Young Rascals in 1966. An eleventh track, which lasted only seconds, had Criss delivering the first lines of "As Time Goes By," the memorable song from the motion picture *Casablanca*: "You must remember this, a kiss is still a kiss . . . ." Some fans were quick to point out that Casablanca was also the name of his record label – big time trivia for some in the ranks of the Kiss Army, the band's loyal followers.

Armed with his solo album, Criss set out on his first round of interviews – without wearing his familiar Catman makeup. Casablanca provided an official headshot of the artist, but it featured a slightly clouded profile image of Criss, thereby maintaining a sense of the old Kiss mystique. He was also provided with a label staffer who sat in with him on all interviews.

I was the first to interview him. Criss and his female assistant waited for me in one of Casablanca Records' offices, a room that was decorated with large, life-like dolls of his former bandmates. Although Criss was on his own as a performer, the other members of Kiss – at least in caricature form – were on hand to "witness" every word of our conversation. Criss was friendly but appeared a bit nervous.

"I've waited so long for this opportunity, said Criss. "It's not just because I'm finally doing what I want to do musically, but even offstage I'll be able to be myself."

He was quick to explain his departure from the band. "I was very frustrated in Kiss, especially during the last few years," he noted. "Many of my musical ideas were rejected by the other guys in the band. I admit that some of my songs didn't exactly fit the Kiss sound, but they were good songs. Take 'Beth,' for example. I was lucky to even get that on a B-side, but it turned out to be Kiss' first gold single."

Criss pointed out that his decision to leave the band was not done in haste. He contemplated departing the ranks during the band's previous concert tour. "I first thought of quitting back then, but I didn't go through with it," he said. "But it never left my mind. I really didn't have enough time to do what I wanted, and I was going through my divorce besides."

Criss also explained that life on the road was no longer enjoyable and he believed that the concert set lists were repetitive. As a result, he explained that he had not performed up to his own expectations.

"Back on tour I just wasn't giving the 110 percent that I always used to give," he declared. "The tours were not only extremely hectic but they got boring. I mean, every night we were expected to do three encores, and we did them."

Criss made the decision to leave Kiss shortly after his marriage to Debra Jensen. "The idea about leaving the band for good came during our honeymoon in Brazil," he said. "When we returned I told the other guys that I was quitting. It was kind of a surprise to them, but everything seems to have worked out. I'm still vice president of the Kiss business, so I've only really left the band as a performer, but the break is final."

Kiss replaced him with Eric Carr, a veteran of numerous New York-based bands. Carr's stage presence was characterized by a fox-like physiognomy. Criss held no animosity towards his replacement. "He's a good drummer, and it's definitely a good shot for him," stated Criss. "He's got a partner in Kiss; he draws a salary, just like the guys in my new band. But he's got a hard seat to fill in. Yet, I wish him and the band all the luck in the world. Kiss lasted for ten years and it will probably last for another ten."

Criss was optimistic about *Out Of Control* and his solo career. "If you listen to those songs, you'll understand – at least a little more – about how I view my new career," he said. "'By Myself' was written to show that I'm on my own now; it's like my version of Frank Sinatra's 'My Way.' As a matter of fact, Sinatra is one of my all-time favorites, but don't expect me to come onstage with a raincoat draped over my shoulder and a cigarette in my hand."

The accomplished hard rocking percussionist also confessed to liking other mainstream recording artists. "Besides Sinatra, I really enjoy The Eagles and The Commodores," said Criss. "And I really like what Bob Seger has been doing lately; he's also one of my favorites."

Criss viewed the upcoming decade with great expectations. "The eighties is a whole new era and I want to get into it," he pointed out. "I'm not in it for the money anymore; I just want to get off on the music."

Criss also explained that he wasn't going to be always shrouded by a wall of drums and cymbals; he was going to assume the role of a lead vocalist fronting a band, a rather challenging role.

"Yeah, I'll finally be upfront," he said with a smile. "But it's something I look forward to. Music is still a big part of my life. It's been that way ever since I was a kid."

Besides press interviews, Criss also appeared on a number of television talk shows, including a return to *Tomorrow with Tom Snyder*. The host recalled the band's first wild appearance on his show years ago and asked Criss if he and his former Kiss partners had ever used alcohol and drugs. "We were drinking moderately," replied Criss. "Kiss was never really into drugs."

Unfortunately, *Out of Control* was a commercial failure. In 1982, his next album, *Let Me Rock You*, also suffered poor sales. A year later, the remaining members of Kiss – minus Ace Frehley, who also had left the band – appeared without their makeup on MTV while promoting the new *Lick It Up* album.

Criss formed several bands during the subsequent years and even managed to temporarily join forces with Ace Frehley on the guitarist's 1989 album, *Trouble Walkin',* which failed to break *Billboard's* Top 100 album roster. It wasn't the best of times for Criss, who divorced his second wife in 1994.

In 1995, Criss learned about a Kiss convention that was being planned in Los Angeles and thought it would be a good idea to attend. He was warmly received by his former bandmates and was embraced by the fans when he sang "Hard Luck Woman" during an acoustic set. The success of the convention reunion led to something more organized, and it also involved Ace Frehley.

On August 9, 1995, Criss rejoined Kiss during a performance on *MTV Unplugged.* He was particularly effective as he sang "Beth" and shared the lead vocals on a rousing rendition of "Nothin' to Lose." Criss united with the band on its successful world tour which carried into 1997, but he was paid a salary instead of receiving a portion of the gross, which included ticket and merchandise sales. Although Frehley was also paid a salary, the guitarist was paid more than Criss. When Criss found out about the uneven financial arrangement, his friendship with Frehley fell apart.

Nevertheless, the following year Criss contributed drums to the group's studio album *Psycho Circus,* but his percussion work was only featured on one track, "Into the Void." The rest of the drum tracks were provided by Kevin Valentine. Ace Frehley's guitar work was also limited on the album; however, the LP reached #3 on the *Billboard* album chart. Criss, though, got married for the third time in 1998.

Psycho Circus also marked twenty-five years since Kiss debuted with its first album in 1974, which meant that the band was eligible for induction in the Rock and Roll Hall of Fame. But the select voters avoided the band like the plague. In 1999, Kiss was ignored; Billy Joel, Curtis Mayfield, Paul McCartney, Del Shannon, Dusty Springfield, Bruce Springsteen, and the Staple Singers were inducted instead. Every year that followed, Kiss was not even mentioned as an act that deserved to be recognized as one of Rock's greats, yet the Kiss Army protested. Eddie Trunk, host of VH1 Classic's *That Metal Show*, was the most vehement critic among those who condemned the Rock and Roll Hall of Fame's exclusion of Kiss. The hard Rock/Metal DJ became even more upset when such "rock and rollers" as Patti Smith, Leonard Cohen, and Abba were welcomed as inductees.

Criss split from the band again in 2000, but later rejoined the group once again a few years later and participated on *Kiss Symphony: Alive IV*, which featured the Melbourne Symphony Orchestra and Ensemble. In 2003, Kiss – Simmons, Stanley, Criss, and guitarist Tommy Thayer – joined Aerosmith on the Rocksimus Maximus Tour, one the year's most successful concert tours. Tensions reemerged among the band members and Criss was let go; Eric Singer became the new Kiss drummer but he adopted his predecessor's feline appearance.

Criss was highly critical of the new Kiss lineup, especially Thayer, who replicated Frehley's costuming, makeup, and playing style. He told Trunk on one of his shows that Thayer and Singer were "imposters."

In 2007, Criss released a solo album, *One For All*, on Megaforce Records, an independent label. The dozen-track collection only managed to reach the #36 position on the *Billboard* indie album roster.

In late 2007, Criss was diagnosed with breast cancer, a rare malady for males. After he had the lump surgically removed in 2008, he became actively involved in breast cancer awareness programs. Criss provided interviews about the disease to the national media in October 2009, which coincided with National Breast Cancer Awareness Month. But during a Reuters news service interview, he also suggested that he was finished with Kiss reunions. "Must I keep putting spandex and makeup on at [age] seventy?" he asked. "I don't think I really want to do that."

Over the next few years, Criss continued to speak out about breast cancer. In September of 2010, he participated in an American Cancer Society walk-a-thon in Point Pleasant, New Jersey. He returned to the Jersey Shore community the following year on October 16 and joined in the Making Strides 3K walk. On October 18, 2012, he was recognized for his cancer awareness activities by the Jersey Shore branch of the Cancer Support Community.

Criss was busy in 2012. He co-penned (with Larry Sloman) his autobiography, *Makeup to Breakup: My Life In and Out of Kiss*. The book was more than a sex-drugs-and-Rock-and-Roll diary; it carefully detailed Criss' street-guy philosophy; his explanation of Rock music as more than artistic expression; the Kiss reunion tour problems; his awkward relationships with his former band members; his battles with depression, tax problems, assorted debts, and much more. He was highly critical of many in his bio – especially his fellow band members – but he was more critical of himself, describing himself as a kid from Brooklyn who lived the Rock and Roll high life and became hooked on cocaine and other substances.

He did an extensive cross country book-signing tour in which *Makeup to Breakup* was described as a book that "traced the perils of stardom ... near suicides, two broken marriages and a hard-won battle with breast cancer." Since the book signings provided enthusiastic Kiss Army members with an opportunity to meet their beloved Catman, strict guidelines were established at some book stores in order for the fans to meet and greet their hero as quickly as possible. Fans that had purchased the book were not allowed to bring other items for Criss to sign, and flash photography and videoing were forbidden. The scene was reminiscent of the protection afforded him when he launched his solo career in 1980. Despite the rules, fans captured just about everything on their cameras and video recorders, and Criss didn't seem to mind. He seemed to genuinely appreciate his fans' loyalty.

He also made an appearance at a Kiss Expo in Edison, New Jersey on September 8, 2012, where he addressed the issue of breast cancer. Criss was determined to share his experiences with the disease to as many people who would listen to him.

Also in 2012, Gene Simmons and Paul Stanley (with Ken Sharp) published their co-autobiography, *Nothin' to Lose: The Making of Kiss, 1972-1975*. In interviews, Simmons made statements about "the madness that is Peter Criss and Ace Frehley." The bassist accused Criss of "false bravado," as someone who was "deeply insecure" and "unpredictable." The animosity among the members of Kiss continued.

In October of 2013, Criss participated in a number of breast cancer awareness programs: a luncheon at St. Johns University in New York; a Cancer Support Community "Celebration of Life" event at the Eagle Oaks Country Club in Farmingdale, New Jersey; and the Making Strides Against Cancer walk in Point Pleasant, New Jersey. And the Garden State is now home to Criss. He and his wife Gigi, also a breast cancer survivor, live in Wall Township, a suburban community in Monmouth County, New Jersey.

Criss was an invited guest to Eddie Trunk's 30th Anniversary shindig at the Hard Rock Café in New York City on October 24, 2013, where he joined Ace Frehley and a squad of galvanized musicians in a short energetic set of tunes that included the Kiss classic "Rock and Roll All Nite." "We're gonna do some stuff for Ed Trunk, who I love dearly," declared Criss as he sat down at a drum set. "I came here; I'm so excited!" Then Criss and the rest of the rockers launched into "Hooligan," a tune he co-wrote with Stan Penridge for the *Love Gun* album. It was a rare performance appearance for Criss, and he seemed to be having a ball.

The Rock and Roll Hall of Fame modified the way in which it inducted new members in 2013 by allowing fans to cast online votes for eligible performers. The Kiss Army, with Eddie Trunk in command, promptly went into action. Kiss was finally elected and an announcement was made on December 17.

"This is absolutely the best Christmas and birthday present I could get," said Criss in a statement to the Associated Press just a few days before his sixty-eighth birthday on December 20, 2013. "This is amazing, that something like this could happen to a kid from Brooklyn." Gene Simmons told *Rolling Stone* magazine that he was willing to perform with Criss and Frehley at the ceremony. It appeared that another Kiss reunion was in the works.

However, on February 21, 2014, Criss phoned Eddie Trunk's Q104.3 FM radio show in New York and informed the host that due to disputes among the Kiss band members, past and present, the group would not perform in its original lineup or its current lineup at the Rock and Roll Hall of Fame induction event. Criss put the blame on Gene Simmons and Paul Stanley. "They just shot down any type of reunion with us," explained Criss. "This is disgraceful, and I feel bad for the fans that were looking forward to the four of us being inducted together."

Criss made an appearance on *That Metal Show* a few weeks before the Rock and Roll Hall of Fame event, and admitted that it was "heartbreaking" that he would not be playing at the induction ceremony. He repeated that he was upset that Eric Singer, the current drummer, was still using the iconic Catman makeup. Although he didn't mention Singer by name, Criss reaffirmed his own status as the band's Catman.

Ten days before the ceremony, ten remastered Kiss albums were released, and it was announced that *Kiss 40*, a two-CD set of the band's landmark tunes, was scheduled for release after the Hall of Fame event.

Peter Gabriel, Hall and Oates, Nirvana, Linda Ronstadt and Cat Stevens, joined Kiss in the class of 2014, along with non-performers Brian Epstein, The Beatles' manager, and Andrew Loog Oldham, the manager of The Rolling Stones. The event took place at the Barclay's Center in Brooklyn, New York, Criss' home town, on April 10. For the first time, the induction ceremony was open to fans.

Tom Morello of Rage Against the Machine enthusiastically introduced the band. "And while there is often debate on who should and shouldn't be in the Rock and Roll Hall of Fame, I think the criteria are actually quite simple: impact, influence, and awesomeness, and Kiss have all three in spades," Morello pointed out. "Kiss has sold over 100 million albums worldwide, with twenty-eight gold albums in the United States alone. That's more than any other American Rock band in history."

Dressed in semi-formal and casual clothes, Criss and the rest of the original Kiss foursome delivered comments. Simmons spoke first;

Criss followed. "I want to say it's great to be home in Brooklyn," said Criss, who later thanked a roster of individuals who had helped him in his life. He also reminded the audience about the importance of early breast cancer detection. Before he concluded, Criss stated: "In or out of makeup, I'll always be the Catman."

Chapter 5

Danny and The Juniors

"Rock and Roll Is Here To Stay"

The Juvenaires were four Philadelphia teenagers – Danny Rapp, Joe Terranova, Frank Maffei, and Dave White – who were singing on a street corner one night in 1957 when singer-song writer John Madara, (then known as John Medora), a nearby resident, heard them.

"I lived on 54th Street, and one night, through the evening, I heard them singing," said Madara. "The next day, I asked a friend about who they were, and he said, 'Danny Rapp and *those* guys.' I eventually met them and connected with Dave White, who shared similar songwriting interests with me."

White had actually formed the group two years earlier. "I was initially inspired by the tenor in The Four Lads," explained White. The Four Lads were a Canadian quartet that included first tenor John Bernard "Bernie" Toorish. The group recorded a number of major hit songs including "Moments to Remember" and "No, Not Much" in 1955. "I really liked their sound, and the sound of the Four Coins. I later got into Rhythm and Blues by listening to such radio DJs as Jocko Henderson."

White started recruiting members of his singing group while he was a freshman at John Bartram High School in Philadelphia. "Out of the neighborhood, I recruited Artie Scotese, who was in the group for a while," said White, who served as the lineup's first tenor. "I was considering another guy, Joe Nazario, to be the baritone but selected Joe Terranova instead because Joe was so passionate about singing and being in a group."

Frank Maffei knew White from school but got to know him better thanks to a chance encounter. "A friend of mine took me to a corner one night where we were going to meet some girls," remarked Maffei. "It was about a mile away from where I lived but it was no big deal. When we got there, I noticed that Dave White was hanging out. We got to talking and he explained that he was putting a group together. I really didn't how to sing that well, but I did have an ear for music. Well, in any event, Dave brought me into the group. He taught me the vocal parts; he really knew his stuff. I learned a lot from him."

White also learned something from Maffei. "Frank Maffei was in the group as second tenor and he was the one who told me about Danny Rapp, who was attending nearby Shaw Junior High," said White. "Danny had more than an appropriate voice to be the lead singer; he was primarily influenced by R&B, and he sang with feeling."

White christened the group The Juvenairs, delegated the vocal parts, and secured the quintet's first gig – a non-paying performance at a nearby church hall. "We just kept singing in the neighborhood," said White, "and then John [Madara] heard us."

Madara, who had a regional hit with "Be My Girl" on Prep Records, and White collaborated on an uptempo tune called "Do The Bop," which celebrated the Bop, a popular dance at the time. "I approached Dave with the idea for the song and the melody," said Madara. "The kids on *American Bandstand*, which was still a local TV show, were dancing the Bop to Jerry Lee Lewis' 'Whole Lotta Shakin' Going On.' I wanted to make a song that had that 'Whole Lotta Shakin' Going On' influence, and so we started writing the song."

They brought the completed song to the attention of local producer Artie Singer. "He told me if I had some money he could make a recording of the song," said Madara. "Imagine, if *I* had the money! I was just a kid; what did I know. So I paid for the recording session. Well, actually it was my father-in-law who paid for it, about $180 to $200." Singer recorded the tune and released it on his Singular Records label, which stated that the "orchestra and chorus was conducted by Artie Singer."

"It wasn't supposed to come out," explained Terranova. "John was singing lead on it, not Danny."

"Yeah, that's right," said Madara. "I sang lead on the record."

The B-side was a wonderfully rich harmonic ballad that White wrote called "Sometimes (When I'm All Alone)," a song that would one day become a well respected doo-wop classic.

Singer and disc jockey Larry Brown changed the name of the group to Danny and the Juniors and brought the vinyl disc to the attention of Dick Clark, whose Philadelphia-based *American Bandstand* program went national in August 1957. Clark listened to the song and gave his assessment to Singer. "I liked the feel of the song and the beat but the lyrics are terrible," stated Clark in his 1976 autobiography, *Rock, Roll & Remember*. "The Bop is almost over as a fad dance; by the time you record and release it, it'll be out of date." The TV host suggested something else. "I've got an idea though," replied Clark. "Why don't you rebuild it to tell the story of what goes on at a record hop? You could call it 'At the Hop.'"

Everyone agreed with Clark's idea. Under Madara's guidance, the quartet went to Reco-Art Studio in Philadelphia and sang the rearranged composition with its revised lyrics; Rapp handled the lead vocals. "The whole production was my idea," said Madara. "I told the engineer what to do."

With only drums, piano, and bass, Danny and the Juniors recorded "At The Hop," which featured an earth-shaking piano solo by Walter

Gates. "We did thirteen takes," recalled Terranova. "I remember after the twelfth take, Walter said, 'I can only do this one more time!' Fortunately, we got it on the next take. That was the one that was released as the single."

The recording featured White's vocal arrangement in which each member of the quartet delivers a distinctive harmonic "bah" – first Terranova, followed by Rapp, then Maffei, and finally White. The infectious sing-a-long quality of the song was quickly embraced by teenage America.

Singer released "At The Hop" on Singular but the song's affiliation with the local label was brief. On December 2, 1957, "At The Hop" got a major boost when Dick Clark invited the quartet to appear on his show one afternoon when another scheduled guest couldn't appear.

"To this day, I still don't know who the act was that was scheduled to appear," admitted Maffei. "Supposedly, it was Little Anthony and the Imperials. Who knows? In any event, Artie Singer called us up and told us to get over to *American Bandstand*. Since Dave was the only one with a car, he drove us there. Fortunately, Dave was always looking for ways to make money, and he had sold enough magazine subscriptions to buy a used Pontiac."

The group lip-synched the song during the afternoon broadcast and soon everything changed for Danny and the Juniors. "The song had been played before on *American Bandstand*," said White. "In fact, I used to go to Danny's house where we watched the show on his TV. When we heard the song, we got excited. And when we first heard it on the radio, well, it was a thrill."

"But once it got played on *American Bandstand* after our appearance, the song took off," added Terranova. Singer later sold the recording to ABC-Paramount, which released it shortly after the group's debut performance on the program.

A week after the group's appearance on *American Bandstand*, "At The Hop" debuted at the #14 position on *Billboard's* "Best Sellers in

Stores" chart. It was the highest debuting single on the vinyl roster. Interesting enough, the second highest debuting single on December 9, 1957 was "Teardrops" by Lee Andrews and the Hearts, which entered the charts at #30. Andrews, like some of the other members of Danny and the Juniors, had also attended John Bartram High School.

Danny and the Juniors went on the road. The group performed several dates in the northeast during January 1958, including a stop in Rochester, New York on the 19th that starred the Everly Brothers and featured Jimmie Rodgers, The Rays, and Buddy Holly and the Crickets, among other acts.

Within two months after its release on the ABC-Paramount label, "At The Hop" knocked Pat Boone's "April Love" from the top of the charts. The group's song remained there from the beginning of January 1958 until February 10, when Elvis Presley's two-sided hit, "Don't" and "I Beg Of You," became the new #1 song.

During the early years of Rock and Roll, competing record labels would frequently produce versions of songs that were rising up the charts. On most occasions, the so-called cover versions featured White artists performing songs that had been originally recorded by Black singers and musicians. After it entered the charts, "At The Hop" was covered by Nick Todd, Pat Boone's younger brother. The Boone-to-Todd name change was created when the singer's record label, Dot, spelled its name backward (Dot became Tod) and added another D (Tod became Todd). The elder Boone boosted his career covering tunes by such performers as Fats Domino ("Ain't That a Shame") and Little Richard ("Tutti Frutti"). Boone's versions were bland and mechanical, and his younger brother's version of "At The Hop" followed in the same vein. Todd's interpretation entered the charts at the #92 position on December 30, 1957. It eventually peaked at #70.

"We thought, gee, Dot Records must think we're Black and are covering the song with a White artist," quipped Terranova. "Actually, we did *The Pat Boone Show* when his brother's record hit the chart. So much for brotherly love."

However, there was brotherly love within the ranks of Danny and the Juniors. "Frank had been down-to-earth as a teenager," said Bobby Maffei, Frank's younger brother, "and the guys were all that way, too. They would go on the road and all of them said that they all looked forward to coming home in order to hang out with the crowd. My family was amazed at Frankie's success. My family would gather around the TV to watch Danny and the Juniors on *American Bandstand* and the other national TV shows they appeared on, like *The Pat Boone Show* and *The Patti Page Show* in 1958."

Despite being bumped from the #1 position by Elvis, the song remained strong on the charts. During the first week of March in 1958, "At The Hop" was still in the Top 10 nationally when the group's follow up release, the hook-laden "Rock And Roll Is Here To Stay," debuted on *Billboard's* "Best Selling Pop Singles In Stores" Top 50 chart at the #47 position. Written by White, the song's lyrics boldy predicted that Rock and Roll was going to be a permanent part of the Pop music landscape – "Rock and Roll will always be/It'll go down in history" – despite criticism from authoritative adults across the country. Attacks on Rock and Roll came from every direction, especially from church and civic leaders. The same week that Danny and the Juniors first performed "At The Hop" on *American Bandstand*, John Charles Thomas, a well-known operatic baritone, appeared on Groucho Marx's TV show, *You Bet Your Life*, and critcicized Rock and Roll. "This present jitterbug music," stated Thomas, "from the odor of it, most of it comes from the Chicago stockyards." Groucho's adult audience applauded with gusto.

"Rock and Roll Is Here to Stay" became a counter-attack anthem for nearly everyone nineteen years of age or younger.

The demonstrative phrase that "Rock and Roll is here to stay" had first been used by Little Richard on the flip side of his 1956 recording of the Robert Blackwell-McKinley Millet composition, "All Around the World." The B-side, "The Girl Can't Help It," included the lyrical line "all around the world, Rock and Roll is here to stay."

"I only became aware of the Little Richard lyric *after* I wrote 'Rock And Roll Is Here To Stay,'" stated White. "And the original copyrighted version of his song didn't include the lyric. But it was added to the recording. It's kind of like a Rock and Roll mystery."

Another potential follow up to "At The Hop" was "Little Doll," which was written by Madara. "It was meant to be a piano-driven song like 'At The Hop,' but for some reason it wasn't released," explained Madara. "'Little Doll' was a cute little song," noted Terranova. "But ABC-Paramount didn't release it."

The group sang "Rock And Roll Is Here To Stay" on *The Dick Clark Show*, the host's Saturday night production, on February 22, 1958. During the concert-styled program, Clark presented the quartet with a gold record (which represented at least 1 million singles sold) from the Recording Industry Association of America for "At The Hop." Sitting next to Danny Rapp in the audience of the Little Theater in New York, Clark made the presentation. "In all its glory, there it is," said Clark, holding the framed golden disc. "Danny, you and the fellows deserve a great deal of praise because most recording artists – I presume you can tell this is a gold record; it's shiny enough – most record artists try somewhere along the line to get a gold record to put somewhere. I don't know how you're gonna cut this thing four ways – you did it first time out. First record; first gold record. It sold 1,500,000 copies."

"At The Hop" continued to sell; in fact, the song remained on *Billboard's* "Best Selling Pop Singles In Stores" until the publication's April 14, 1958 issue, a run of nineteen weeks in the Top 50.

"Rock and Roll Is Here To Stay" rose up the charts and reached #19 chart position on March 17; coincidentally, "At The Hop" was the #18 song at the time. "Rock and Roll Is Here To Stay" peaked at #19 and remained on the charts through April. The record's B-side, "School Boy Romance," a restrained composition, was also written by White.

The young singers made the most of their first performance royalty payment.

"We got $50,000, but half of it went to the accountants," quipped Frank Maffei. "We weren't rich but we did okay. We all bought new 1958 Chevy Impalas; Danny bought a black one and I bought a black hard top with red interior."

"Mine was a powder blue convertible," White pointed out. "And I bought my mom a house."

"I bought my mom a new dining room set, furniture, and a new bathroom," said Frank Maffei.

Terranova was only group member who didn't buy an Impala. "His father didn't want him to spend the money on an Impala, which was the top Chevy model," chuckled Frank Maffei. "So he ended up buying a Chevy Belair model. Joe eventually gave it to his father and he bought a used '56 Ford convertible."

"That's right," replied Terranova. "But it was a nice Belair model; it was turquoise with a white top. And I did give it to my dad when I bought the Ford."

Danny and the Juniors' popularity continued to soar and they soon received an invitation to appear in a motion picture. The group traveled to a sound stage in New York, where they lip-synched "At The Hop." The performance was included in a black and white low-budget Columbia Pictures' musical drama titled *Let's Rock*, which was based on the premise that "Rock and Roll is here to stay."

"We were filmed at a studio where the old Keystone Cops comedies from the 1920s were shot," explained Terranova. The film debuted in June of 1958 and starred singer Julius La Rosa as a mainstream balladeer who turns to Rock and Roll in order to save his struggling career. Paul Anka and Danny and the Juniors shared the next billing line on the film's theater poster although the performers were billed below Fats Domino, Jerry Lee Lewis, the Everly Brothers, and Buddy Holly and the Crickets at an actual Paramount concert in New York (the theater's marquee can be seen for only a few seconds on screen).

Just after the 52:00 mark of the film, Danny and the Juniors are introduced and promptly lip-synch their big hit to the enthusiastic teenage audience. After singing the song, the group briefly engaged La Rosa's character, Tommy Adane, in a scene backstage, which was shot with only one camera position:

Rapp:	Tommy boy!
La Rosa:	Hey, Danny. How are ya?
Rapp:	Where you been hiding? Long time, no see.
Maffei:	I heard your new side. You're singing great.
La Rosa:	Well, I just caught your act and you fractured 'em.
Rapp:	When you gonna come over and cut a few live ones?
La Rosa:	Look, I'll make a bargain: you don't record ballads, I won't record Rock and Roll.
White:	That's a deal. How about a cup of coffee?
La Rosa:	Ah, we'll do it later. Phone.
Rapp:	I dig. Alone time, ha?
La Rosa:	You got it. Goodnight, boys.
Rapp, et al:	Good night/See ya/We'll see ya.

Terranova was the only member of the group not to have specific lines in the brief scene. "But originally, I was supposed to have all of them," chuckled Terranova. "Julius La Rosa entered our dressing room earlier, looked at me and told me that I had all the lines. But when I delivered them, well, it didn't work out for the director."

British-born director Harry Foster, who had primarily supervised scores of documentaries and short subjects since the late 1930s – from

Table Tennis Topnotchers in 1944 to *Columbia World of Sports: Rodeo Daredevils* in 1956 – at first agreed with La Rosa that Terranova should handle the dialogue. The young singer certainly fit the bill for the big screen: he was tall, dark, and ruggedly handsome.

"But I couldn't act," confessed Terranova with a laugh. "The director told me, 'Listen, I don't have time to teach you how to act.' So he ended up giving the other guys in the group my lines. But I appreciated what he told me because later I realized that even in the music business you have to know how to act in order to be a more complete performer."

Frank Maffei was "pleasantly shocked" when he saw the film at the premier showing. "We weren't used to looking at ourselves," he said. "But it was a great experience. Still, it's the only line I ever spoke in a movie."

No one confused *Let's Rock* with such other 1958 motion pictures as *King Creole* or *South Pacific*, but the film proved to be innocuous fun that brought Danny and the Juniors to the big screen and an even bigger audience.

"I liked the movie," said Terranova. "And it could have been a bigger hit but a few weeks after it opened there was fallout from the Rock and Roll riot in Boston."

On May 5, 1958, a Rock and Roll concert at the Boston Arena produced by Alan Freed turned into a major brawl when the local police refused the legendary DJ's request to have the house lights dimmed for the show. Freed allegedly told the crowd, "I guess the police here in Boston don't want you kids to have a good time." The chaos resulted in at least fifteen people suffering serious wounds and injuries.

"As a result, the movie was distributed to smaller markets around the country instead of the big cities," said Terranova. "And there was more bad news associated with the riots and us. We supposed to appear on *The Ed Sullivan Show*, but he cancelled us. And for a while he didn't have many Rock and Roll performers on his show during the summer of '58."

Despite *The Ed Sullivan Show* cancellation, Danny and the Juniors continued to perform around the country as part of larger Rock and Roll tour shows. "We worked some of the Alan Freed shows and we also worked for General Artists Corporation," said Terranova. "All those tours have certain memories for me. Just meeting everybody, from the Everly Brothers to Buddy Holly and the Crickets, was a cool thing."

The popular quartet was invited by European promoters to perform in their respective countries. "But Danny didn't like to fly," explained Terranova. "So back then, we never performed in Europe or Australia where we were also in demand."

The group had a reliable substitute member: Frank's younger brother, Bobby. "If one of the guys couldn't perform, I was the fill-in," said Bobby Maffei. "I was singing in my own group, The Leisure Lads. All of us as teenagers sang on our corner, which was in southwest Philadelphia. And I filled in with Danny and the Juniors if someone couldn't perform on the date."

Terranova paid a personal price for being one of the most popular Rock and Roll acts in the nation. "Since I was performing regularly during my senior year in high school, I had to take my school work on the road with me," explained Terranova. "Fortunately, I found some girls to do my homework – no, seriously, I did the work. But I failed English. I think the teacher was jealous of me. In any event, it kept me from graduating."

White left Temple University. "I blew my entire gymnastics scholarship once I left school after Dick Clark started playing 'At The Hop,'" said White. "My mother was very upset, but I was excited. Music was something I wanted to do."

Dick Clark frequently had Danny and the Juniors on his two television shows, *American Bandstand* and *The Dick Clark Show*. In June 1958, the group appeared three times on the popular music host's programs. On June 4, the singers appeared on *American Bandstand*, and on June 7 and June 21 they performed on *The Dick Clark Show*. "Dick Clark certainly helped us out," said Frank Maffei. Over the years, the group appeared dozens of times on various Dick Clark-produced television programs.

On the quartet's June 21 appearance on *The Dick Clark Show*, the singers performed "At The Hop" as teenagers danced around them at the Shelburne Hotel on the Atlantic City boardwalk. The Jersey Shore became a second home of sorts to most of the Philadelphia-based artists during the summer, and Danny and the Juniors played nearly everywhere along the Garden State coast, including such popular locations as Wildwood and Atlantic City's Steel Pier.

The group's next release was "Dottie," which entered the national Top 50 on June 21. The Madara-Singer tune managed to break the Top 40 but stalled at #39. Several recordings followed but they failed to register on *Billboard's* newly created Hot 100 chart. Danny and the Juniors and ABC-Paramount went their separate ways after such unsuccessful 1959 releases as "Do You Love Me" and "Somehow I Can't Forget" and "Playing Hard to Get" and "Of Love."

"At about that time, I left the group," said White. "I had just got married and we weren't performing that much without a new hit."

"I filled in for Dave White often," said Bobby Maffei. "On one date in North Carolina, I think in 1959 with Dion and the Belmonts, I was asked by Dave to go on the date. When we returned, we all found out that Dave had eloped. Dave was probably nineteen years old, but he was happily married and had three beautiful children, all girls."

White looked for work that paid a steady wage. "I found a job at Link Belt, a business that made machinery in Philadelphia," explained White. "It paid $64 a week. I worked there for about a year and then rejoined the group when it got signed to Swan Records."

On Philadelphia's Swan Records, Danny and the Juniors scored with a Kal Mann-penned composition titled "Twistin' U. S. A." The tune, which capitalized on the national Twist craze, became the group's final

Top 40 chart hit; it reached #27 in the autumn of 1960. But the dance tune was even a bigger hit north of the border where it reached the Canadian Top 10.

Additional versions of the song, like "Twistin' Germany" and "Twistin' Italy, were recorded to cater to international audiences. "The record company thought it would be helpful promotion, and it probably was," said Terranova. "But we couldn't take advantage of it because Danny didn't want to fly."

The Madara-White writing relationship was revived at Swan Records. "It was during our association with Swan that I starting working again with John," said White. "We just started writing songs again."

Additional releases, like "Daydreamer," "Pony Express," and "Back To The Hop" managed to crack the *Billboard* Hot 100, and "Candy Cane, Sugary Plum," with its Chipmunk-like background harmonies, was a cute Christmas novelty tune, but the songs never sold well enough to reach the coveted Top 40 hit parade.

By 1962, Danny and the Juniors left Swan and signed with Philadelphia's Guyden Records. The group released "Oo-La-La-Limbo" but it barely broke the Hot 100. Another interesting Madara-White ballad was "Now And Then." Unfortunately, the Guyden single fared no better than "Oo-La-La Limbo." Still, the group continued to perform around the country with other contemporary acts. However, without hit records, the band experienced financial difficulties.

"There was even a brief time when Joe wasn't in the group," explained White. "He went to work for his family's catering business. For a while, it was just Danny, Frank, and me."

"Yeah, I was out of the group in 1962," said Terranova. "My son was born and I had to make ends meet." The group went through constant lineup changes. Eventually, Dave White left the group. Terranova returned, and Danny and the Juniors performed as a trio ever since. When Frank Maffei left, Bill Carlucci replaced him.

Then The Beatles arrived, and the oldies but goodies acts became the first casualties of the British Invasion. "We disbanded for a while in 1964, after The Beatles came to America," explained Terranova. "We didn't do much for most of the decade."

Although Danny and the Juniors were not as successful as they had been, White and Madara were accomplishing a great deal as writers and producers. They had written a number of pre-British Invasion hits, like Chubby Checker's Top 10 entry, "The Fly," in 1961 (Madara's electric razor gave the song its fly-like buzz sound).

Madara and White discovered and signed The Pixies Three, a talented young female vocal group, to Mercury Records and wrote the girls' first Top 40 hit, "Birthday Party," in 1963.

"John and Dave wrote almost all the songs we recorded, although I was delighted when they decided to use one of my songs, 'Our Love,' on the flip side of 'Birthday Party,' our first hit," explained Kaye (McCool) Krebs, an original member of the group. "That was really very generous because, in those days, the flip side got the same royalties as the A-side, and most producers put their own songs on the flip side to make more money. Both John and Dave were always fun to be with and highly professional. After every studio session, I would badger them to make a tape for us to take home for our parents and friends to hear. They always obliged."

Madara and White also wrote for such performers as The Secrets, Maureen Gray, and Billy and the Essentials, among other acts.

In late 1963, the pair wrote Leslie Gore's "You Don't Own Me," which went to #2 and remained there for three weeks on the *Billboard* Hot 100 in February 1964. Ironically, The Beatles' first American chart topper, "I Want to Hold Your Hand," prevented Gore's single from reaching the top spot. Another Madara-White creation (along with contributing writer Leonard Borisoff), Len Barry's "1-2-3," reached #2 on the *Billboard* Hot 100 in 1965.

The creative duo joined forces with radio personality Ray Gilmore in 1965 to form the Spokemen. The trio released an album that included the Top 40 single "Dawn of Correction," a patriotically optimistic ballad that countered Barry McGuire's powerful chart-topping single, "Eve of Destruction." On the LP cover, the three singers are standing, arms folded, with serious looks on their faces.

"That's the way we wanted to appear," said White. "We *were* serious."

So were the lyrics. The song began with a Cold War pledge: "The Western world has a common dedication/to keep free people from Red domination," which clearly reflected the writers' attitude toward the threat of international Communism. The rest of the tune addressed such other concerns as the war in Vietnam, voter registration, and integration. The lyrical innocence of "Rock And Roll Is Here To Stay" seemed to be a song from long ago.

For the rest of the decade, most of the acts that had scored big hits in the '50s were not performing – at least not performing regularly. The music charts were dominated by a new generation of artists who seemed to see the world differently. Even Elvis Presley, who had twelve #1 songs between 1956 and 1959, had only one chart-topping single between 1964 and 1969 – "Suspicious Minds" in 1969. The Madara-White partnership, though, was more successful. The pair penned dozens of chart hits for various artists that generated millions of record sales.

The music of 1950s, though, was about to make a comeback.

On Monday morning, August 18, 1969, Danny and the Juniors and every other oldies act received a positive jolt of career-resuscitation when Sha-Na-Na, the parody Rock and Roll act, performed a dozen blasts from the past – including "At The Hop" – at the historic Woodstock Music and Art Fair in Bethel, New York. The seeds of the Rock and Roll revival had been planted on Max Yasgur's farm.

That same year, Gus Gossert debuted his *Doo-Wop Shop* on WCBS-FM in New York. Gossert was particularly fond of classic ballads including

"Sometimes (When I'm All Alone)," the harmonic flip side of "At The Hop." The program became an instant listener favorite and groups from the 1950s regained some of their popularity during the age of progressive Rock. A few years later, WCBS-FM went to an all oldies format.

"After Gus Gossert's show became the #1 call-in radio show in New York, producer Richard Nader wanted to take advantage of it by putting on a concert show of his own," said Terranova.

"But I wasn't in the group at the time," said Frank Maffei. "I was married at the time and my wife wasn't too fond of me going back to perform. I was out of the group and was working in the optical business."

At about that same time, Dave White joined forces with Crystal Mansion, a vocal-instrumental group that performed an eclectic mix of progressive Pop and blue-eyed Soul. White wrote and co-wrote most of the band's songs, including the group's highest-ranking chart hit, "The Thought of Loving You," which reached #84 on the *Billboard* Hot 100 and was subsequently recorded by a number of diverse artists, including Spiral Starecase, Manhattan Transfer, and Wayne Newton, among others.

On October 18, 1969, Richard Nader showcased his "Rock and Roll Revival" concert at Madison Square Garden's Felt Forum. Danny and the Juniors – Rapp, Terranova, and Carlucci – were joined by the likes of Chuck Berry, Little Richard, Fats Domino, and other memorable artists. Excerpts from the concert, including an abridged version of "At The Hop," were featured in the 1973 film *Let The Good Times Roll*. The hit song, performed by Flash Cadillac and the Continental Kids, was also included in the 1973 film *American Graffiti* and appeared on the *41 Original Hits from the Soundtrack of American Graffiti* album.

A year earlier, *Grease* debuted on Broadway. The popular musical earned seven Tony Award nominations, including Best Musical, and won two Drama Desk Awards and a Theatre World Award. Old time Rock and Roll was on the Great White Way – and it was here to stay.

"And I was back in the group in 1974," added Frank Maffei.

On January 15, 1974, *Happy Days* debuted on TV, which helped underscore the re-interest in Rock's Golden Era. The Rock and Roll revival was also underway across the Atlantic. In 1976, "At The Hop" was reissued in Great Britain, where it reached the #39 position on the singles chart. "It was great," said Terranova. "And we were back."

Rolling Stone magazine, among others, saw the renaissance of early Rock and Roll as nothing more than a quirky fad, a musical expression based upon nostalgia rather than edgy socio-political substance.

"*Rolling Stone* has never given much due to the pioneers of Rock and Roll other than Chuck Berry or Little Richard," noted Terranova. "They have almost completely left out the groups. Once in the early '70s, they did cover a Richard Nader concert, where we and a couple of other acts rode the subway in from Long Island as a promotion. It was a chilly morning, and I offered to buy the *Rolling Stone* writer a cup of coffee – to which he bantered, 'You can't buy this interview.' I haven't been a fan of the magazine since."

Two decades after their initial chart success, Danny and the Juniors were still on the road. In the late 1970s, the singers were approaching their forties and they performed primarily on the club circuit.

"We do forty-two weeks on the road a year," said Terranova in an interview with me in 1978. "We've been paying our dues for a long time since we made it big without really trying too hard. So in a way, you could say that unlike other acts who worked years before they made it big, we did it just the other way around. We were fortunate and unfortunate."

They had developed a highly polished act that included a spectrum of tunes, satire and impressions, and comedy routines. Rapp's Frank Sinatra impression was a visual gem, and Frank Maffei's spoof of Paul Anka's "(You're) Having My Baby" generated side-splitting laughs from the audience.

"At the time, our manager told us: 'You guys gotta have an *act*,'" said Frank Maffei. "So the comedy part fell on me." But club patrons attended the group's performances primarily to hear the hits and the group delivered them all with energetic enthusiasm.

Sha-Na-Na provided another indirect musical assist to Danny and the Juniors when the parody group – as Johnny Casino and the Gamblers – performed "Rock And Roll Is Here To Stay" in the movie version of *Grease* in 1978. The song appeared on the film's soundtrack album, which was released on April 14, 1978, prior to the film's debut. Coincidentally, twenty years earlier on that same week, "Rock And Roll Is Here To Stay" was the 24th most popular song in the nation. Also, in 1978, "Rock And Roll Is Here To Stay" was performed by Prof. LaPlano (actually Kenny Vance, an original member of Jay and the Americans) and the Planotones in the Alan Freed bio-pic *American Hot Wax*.

However, the nostalgia renaissance didn't guarantee group unity. During the late 1970s and early 1980s, there were two groups performing under the name Danny and the Juniors. "Frank and I were heading one group," said Terranova. "And Danny was heading another one. But it was just him. He would hire a backing band with a couple of singers and he would go out on the road. But it never really bothered me."

Terranova's lineup was the headlining act at the Beacon Theater in New York on September 12, 1981. The concert included The Five Satins, The Shirelles, The Belmonts, The Drifters, and Little Anthony. It was a good time for Terranova and company, but Rapp was having a difficult time—and he frequently sought relief in alcohol.

On April 5, 1983, Danny Rapp was found dead in a Yacht Club Motel room in Quartzsite, Arizona, the victim of a self-inflicted gunshot wound to the head. The forty-one-year-old vocalist had just been performing at Phoenix's Point Tapatio Resort's Silver Lining Lounge.

"I think Joe called me and told me," said White. "It was definitely shocking. At that time, I was actually considering rejoining him. My royalties weren't doing that well, and Danny and I were talking about it. I had seen him perform in Arizona a few months earlier. He was in great shape at the time. He was sober and he was putting his son through college. He even brought me up on stage to see if I remembered the songs and the steps. How could I forget! It was fun, real fun, and we were up all night talking about everything."

"I was very saddened by the news of Danny's death," explained Madara. "It was shocking. I hadn't seen him in about fifteen years. He was a special guy, really special."

"Danny's death was more than shocking: it was disbelief," said Frank Maffei. "He didn't seem like the type of guy to do something like that. I found out about it when a member of his family called. And then they told us that they didn't have enough money to fly his body back to Philadelphia, so Joe and I paid for the expenses."

Frank Maffei still had concerns about Rapp's self-inflicted fatal wound. "I went out to Quartzsite, Arizona and spoke to the investigator who handled the case," he said. "I spent a couple of days there and went to Danny's motel, which was really nothing more than a bunch of connected trailers. I even spoke to the bartender, who told me that Danny was drinking rather heavy on the night he died. I was satisfied with what I learned and accepted that Danny took his own life."

Before the year was out, another macabre moment manifested itself. In December, 1983, "Rock And Roll Is Here To Stay" made its most unusual appearance when it was featured in the climax of the John Carpenter-directed thriller *Christine*, a film about a possessed killer car, a 1958 Plymouth Fury. In the scene, the evil vehicle played the song from its dashboard radio until it's crushed by a bulldozer. David White's lyrical line, "it will never die," has an added significance in the film's final scene.

Terranova took over the lead vocals for the trio which was subsequently billed as Danny and the Juniors featuring Joe Terry. A new "old" lineup change happened in the new century. "I had furthered my education after high school and became a large scale computer programmer, and I retired in the year 2000," said Bobby Maffei, who replaced

Johnny Petillo, a singer who had briefly joined the group. "My brother, Frankie, and Joe asked me if I wanted to go back on the road again. Of course, without hesitation I said 'yes!' My experience over the past fourteen years has been a fun-loving one. It still amazes me how the popularity has not changed for Danny and the Juniors and their hits."

The group was inducted in the Vocal Group Hall of Fame in 2003.

Danny and the Juniors continued to play outdoor concerts, festivals, special events, indoor venues, public functions, and theaters, sometimes teaming up with other oldies acts. Unlike most of their contemporaries, the trio occasionally recorded new music – both reworkings of other artists' songs and some originals.

The band members are grateful for their fans, especially those who were there from day one. Bobby Maffei particularly enjoys those who appreciated the group's doo-wop tunes. "I appreciate the fans who grew up in the northeast and how they liked and sang the song 'Sometimes' on the street corners of their own cities, such as the Bronx, Brooklyn, and Boston," he said. "'Sometimes' had a lot to do with the long-term success and sales of 'At The Hop.'"

They also kept busy by establishing a website [www.dannyandthejuniors.com] producing CDs of song compilations, hosting a radio program (*Rock and Roll is Here to Stay: The Radio Show*), and supporting Truth In Music legislation that would prevent bogus acts from performing as the original artists.

I saw them on August 11, 2006, when they performed with The Dovells at a Philly Doo-Wop show at the House of Blues in Atlantic City's Showboat hotel and casino. Competently backed by a basic combo, the trio performed with youthful-like exuberance. Four years later, my wife and I had front row seats when the group performed on Valentine's Day at the Ocean First Theater in Stafford, New Jersey. Once again, they delighted the crowd with a wonderfully nostalgic journey down memory lane. After the concert, the trio sat at tables in the venue's lobby and autographed copies of their CDs, including *Back to the Hop*, which features a dozen of the group's best-known recordings.

In May 2011, a South Carolina-based regional chart utilizing the old *Cashbox* magazine name on its internet-produced publication indicated that the group's new Terranova-penned single, "First Kiss to the Last," was number one on its Beach Music roster. The band issued a press release commemorating the event: "Danny and the Juniors Strike Gold Twice – 53 Years Apart."

There was no RIAA gold record award presented to the group for the new single since it didn't place on any of the *Billboard* charts, but it was accomplishment nonetheless for the group whose original members started singing on a Philadelphia street corner in 1955.

On April 18, 2012, Dick Clark, who had suffered from stroke eight years earlier, died.

"I can't say enough about Dick Clark," said Madara. "He was a beautiful human being; he was the best."

"He became a personal friend," added Terranova. "If he didn't suggest changing the name of 'Do The Bop' to 'At The Hop,' who knows what would have happened to us. We were fortunate that we lived in Philadelphia where Dick Clark's *American Bandstand* was broadcast from. It was the perfect fit for us. And it was very sad for me when I learned that Dick had died."

"I'm so grateful for Dick Clark," said White. "Without him there is no 'At The Hop.' He jump started my career, and he was always there for me. We always kept in touch. Even the year before he passed away, he always answered my phone calls. He was a true gentleman and a good friend."

Clark had been inducted in the Philadelphia Music Alliance's Walk of Fame in 1987, and five years later Danny and the Juniors joined him in the celebrated association that includes over a hundred Philadelphia artists, DJs, announcers, producers, music industry executives, and such contemporaries as Lee Andrews and the Hearts, Frankie Avalon, Chubby Checker, and Bobby Rydell, among many others.

On October 24, 2013, songwriters Madara and White, who penned hundreds of musical compositions during their careers, were also inducted. "I felt privileged and honored," said White. "It was a wonderful occasion to be honored by Philadelphia, my home town. And I'm thankful for John Madara."

"I was overwhelmed by it all," remarked Madara. "It was very special to see friends and performers who I had not seen in decades."

Members of The Secrets and The Pixies Three attended the ceremony. "It was wonderful to see three of The Secrets there," said White. "And Kaye from The Pixies Three was there, too. I hadn't seen some of those people in about fifty years."

The current Danny and the Juniors lineup was represented at the event. "I thought it was great that they were inducted," noted Terranova. "I was thrilled for them. They were a force out of Philadelphia as writers and producers, and they deserve the recognition."

On November 30 and December 1, Danny and the Juniors featuring Joe Terry performed at the Suncoast Hotel and Casino in Las Vegas. After the second show, Dave White and his wife, Sandra, paid the group a visit. It was a reunion of sorts for White, Terranova, and Frank Maffei. "We didn't have enough time to talk during the induction ceremony in October, so seeing them out here – we only live about ten minutes away from the Sun Coast Casino – gave us all an opportunity to relax and talk about old times," said White. "Sandra and I had a wonderful time with them."

Besides having generations of fans, the group members were fans themselves – sports fans, to be exact. The trio demonstrated its loyalty in early 2014. As the Philadelphia Eagles entered the National Football League playoffs, the group wrote and recorded a new song, "The Eagles Are (Unbelievable)," to show its support for the team. However, the Eagles lost to the New Orleans Saints, 26-24. "That was then and this is now," reasoned Terranova. "And the Eagles will be back! The team has a great quarterback in Nick Foles. Hey, he threw for seven touchdowns last year against the Raiders. And they've got a great coach in Chip Kelly."

Danny and the Juniors have been performing regularly on various winter and spring Caribbean cruises that showcase the talents of such Rock and Roll veterans as Leslie Gore, Freddie Cannon, and Johnny Tillotson, among others. The cruises allow Baby Boomers to spend lots of time with the artists they grew up with. "We enjoy doing them," explained Terranova. "They're a lot of fun and everybody has a good time. That's what Rock and Roll is all about."

Filmed performances of the group singing "At The Hop" and "Rock And Roll Is Here To Stay" in 1958 were featured on the PBS television special, *50s & 60s Party Songs (My Music)*, in the spring of 2014. Frank Maffei and Joe Terranova appeared with host TJ Lubisnky during a short fund-raising segment on the two-hour special that featured numerous other acts from Rock and Roll's first decade. When asked by Lubinsky about the long-term significance of "At The Hop," Maffei quipped, "It's gonna outlast us!"

I asked Terranova how many times he's sung "At The Hop." "Hmm, let me try and figure that out," he said. "Nobody's ever asked me that. You know what? I probably sang that song 100,000 times." But during all those years when Danny and the Juniors performed as a trio, how the group handled the four distinct "bahs" at the beginning and end of "At The Hop?"

"I did two of them myself," said Terranova with a laugh and a wink. "I carried the act for years."

Chapter 6

Judas Priest

"Breaking the Law"

On a perfect summer day on July 3, 1980, I drove to Asbury Park, New Jersey to interview Judas Priest. At the time, the British Heavy Metal band was touring the United States on the strength of its latest LP, *British Steel*.

The band – Rob Halford (vocals), Glen Tipton (guitar), K. K. Downing (guitar), Ian Hill (bass), and Dave Holland (drums) – was scheduled to perform later that evening at Convention Hall. The members of Judas Priest were staying at an inexpensive motel several miles away. By the time I arrived in the late afternoon, the band was preparing to travel to the venue for a pre-concert sound check.

Judas Priest's two guitarists, Glen Tipton and K. K. Downing, were the first to meet me as they stood outside their tour bus. After a few obligatory greeting exchanges, Downing said, "You've got to see this!" Tipton pointed the way to the band's unmarked vehicle in the motel's parking lot. "It's our new video for 'Breaking the Law,'" replied Downing.

Near the front of the bus, a portable video-tape player and monitor had been positioned for easy viewing. Downing, eager to show the video, hit the play button. He exchanged a quick smile with Tipton as the video began. The audio-visual production featured the band members as bank-robbing troubadours who manage to break into a vault filled with framed gold records. Although aware of the security camera – and with a guard watching – the band boldly performs the song and commits a grand theft.

Tipton and Downing were all smiles when the video concluded. Visually, the production was entertaining especially when the band made its daring getaway in a Cadillac convertible. Halford's lyrics about the desperation of unemployment and the need to "put some action in my life" underscored the band's rough and tumble beginnings in Birmingham, an English industrial city that had seen widespread unemployment and inflation in the late 1970s and early 1980s due to the recession that affected many countries in the world.

Judas Priest's origins can be traced back to 1969 when Downing, Hill, and another musician formed a local power trio called Freight that was inspired by the likes of such hard-rocking threesomes as The Jimi Hendrix Experience, The Who, and Cream. The band members also appreciated electric Blues. When singer Al Atkins joined the band, he persuaded his bandmates to change the group's name to Judas Priest. Influenced by its hard-edged, working-class surroundings, the band developed its own brand of Heavy Metal but failed to break out of the local and regional club scene. Lineup changes occurred over the next few years with Halford and Tipton joining the band. Powered by the Downing-Tipton guitar partnership and Halford's soaring vocal delivery, the band began fine tuning its pulsating style.

By 1974, Judas Priest had recorded its first album, *a Rolla*, on Gull, a British independent label. The album was produced by Rodger Bain, who had produced Black Sabbath's first three LPs. Comparisons to Black Sabbath were inevitable, but even from its first recording, Judas Priest was not merely following in the footsteps of the classic Heavy Metal band. Instead, Judas Priest was carefully crafting its own identify within the hard Rock spectrum. Two years later, the group released *Sad Wings of Destiny*. The Gull release featured the riveting "Victim of Changes."

Judas Priest not only had to overcome the normal challenges that every developing band faces but it had to contend with the tidal wave of Punk that dominated the British music scene at the time. Punk – and, later, its commercially acceptable step child, New Wave – established trendy barriers that only the most determined bands could hope to break.

Despite the lack of initial chart success, Judas Priest continued to build a following on the strength of its live shows. Columbia Records signed the band and released *Sin After Sin* in 1977. The LP reflected a harder approach – the band's "vicious sound," as *That Metal Show's* Eddie Trunk later described it – which spawned such staples of the group's concert set list as "Sinner" and "Diamonds and Rust." Leather-studded clothing and accessories also became Judas Priest's permanent fashion embellishments. Halford, in particular, developed a biker-like appearance that became the focal point of the band's distinct stage posture.

Stained Class, which included the classic-to-be, "Exciter," was released in 1978, and the band went on its first tour of the United States and Japan. Near the end of the year, *Killing Machine* (U.S. title: *Hell Bent For Leather*) was released, which secured the band's status as one of the world's better-known Heavy Metal acts. The LP's "Take on the World" became the group's first single to break the British Top 20.

A live LP, *Unleashed in the East*, recorded in Japan and released in September of 1979, became the band's biggest-selling album to date, earning platinum status by the Recording Industry Association of America. By late 1979, Dave Holland became the band's drummer (replacing Les Binks). For most of the next ten years, the bands' most well-known lineup of Halford, Downing, Tipton, Hill, and Holland remained in place.

British Steel's release in the spring of 1980 elevated the band's international profile and generated several hit tracks in Great Britain, including "Living After Midnight" and "Breaking the Law." Although the band failed to break the American singles charts, Judas Priest's modest album successes helped transform the band into an act capable of performing in larger halls and arenas.

"Our popularity is building slowly but steadily, unlike some other Heavy Metal outfits that started with platinum and double-platinum albums and then peaked," explained Downing on the tour bus. "We're playing to more people than ever before. There were times when we got apprehensive even headlining places with around 1,000 people, but now we're quite confident about what we're doing; I think we've come a long way from the old days."

Downing was also pleased that radio stations in both Great Britain and the United States were playing the band's tracks.

"I imagine that you can only ignore one of the most successful touring bands for only so long," he said. "But now, all the practicing and the traveling seem to have paid off. Every album has topped the sales of the previous one, and our concerts are packing in more and more people. It means that obviously something is happening. We used to be only considered as an underground or cult band, but it's completely different now."

Downing left the bus and returned to the motel; Tipton stayed on board to discuss Judas Priest's fan base.

"Our fans are a loyal lot," explained Tipton. "But sometimes they're too devoted in their loyalty. They're eager to meet us – and we're eager to meet them – but there are only a few spare moments in a day during a tour when you have time for yourself, I'm sorry to say."

Tipton excused himself and left the bus. He went to his room, retrieved his guitar, and returned to the parking lot where he awaited his ride to Convention Hall for the band's sound check. However, the rest of the band had gone and left him behind. "Now what do I do?" he exclaimed.

No problem. I offered to drive him in my wife's white Plymouth Horizon, not exactly a vehicle that was associated with chauffeuring Rock and Roll stars. He said, "Let's go!" He placed his guitar case in the back seat and we drove up to Convention Hall. During the ride, he asked about the Jersey Shore and the area's music scene. I told him about Bruce Springsteen, Southside Johnny and the Asbury Jukes, and the many bars and clubs which featured live music. As we approached Convention Hall, I noticed a small group of waiting outside the venue, but they never looked twice at the compact car that pulled up. Tipton exited, removed his guitar, and said, "Thanks." I parked the car and returned to the concert site.

Later that evening, Judas Priest took the stage; however, the quintet seemed to function more like a special operations military unit than a group of musicians. They acted as if they were fulfilling a clandestine mission rather than honoring a simple performance contract.

From the first ear-shattering power chords amidst a shower of lights, Halford, with a bullwhip in hand, rumbled onstage aboard a mammoth Harley Davidson motorcycle. With fog machines churning out billowy clouds of grey-white smoke and flash pots exploding controlled-flame blasts, the Hill-Holland rhythm section kicked in with a thunderous bottom followed by Halford's first stratospheric vocal blast. Downing and Tipton stood shoulder to shoulder and traded leads as they rocked back and forth in synchronization, their long locks swaying wildly. And the audience acted like a metal-church congregation that was eager to hear a passionate megawatt sermon.

Witnessing the organized mayhem, one understands the quasi-religious posture of the band and its name. As the concert progressed, Halford was no longer just a singer in a hard-Rocking band: he seemed more like a proselytizing metal clergyman who used dramatic theatrics to make his point. He also seemed to be winning converts with every anthem-like song.

"I think part of our success comes from our ability to play songs that have an anthem quality about them," said Downing after the concert. "They're the type of songs that get the audience singing along more often than not."

Halford joined the rest of the band in the relaxing, open-air backstage area of Convention Hall, which overlooked the Atlantic Ocean. "It's quite a nostalgic environment out here," he remarked. "It reminds me very much of England's coastline, actually. And considering those incredibly hot days we experienced in Texas, this is more than just welcome relief."

Halford explained the relationship between the band's songs and their fans. "Many of our songs have story lines that appeal even more to the audience," he pointed out. "If the audience gets involved with the lyrics as well as the music, a band definitely has some sort of advantage over other similar bands. You never really know what's going to happen next. You only have control over what you do, so you try and give your audience everything you can."

Our conversation was interrupted by shouts of "Judas Priest!" and "Rob, Rob, Rob!" from beneath the backstage area on the beach. Three male fans had climbed over the rock jetty to get as close to the band members as possible. Halford excused himself, walked over to the railing and acknowledged their collective clenched fists with one of his own. "Metal!" exclaimed Halford to his dedicated followers as they stood in awe of their hero. As he walked back to his seat, the fans left the area with contented smiles.

"New Jersey people are very similar in attitude to our British audiences back home in that both really set themselves out to enjoy a concert," said Halford. "I appreciate that."

As the evening wore on, the band members seemed to tire. To be sure, they were well aware that their demanding concert schedule would resume the following day. And there was a price to pay for that. "We got into this place at eight in the morning after playing in New York State, went right to sleep, and before we knew it, we were up, heading for the sound check," said Downing. "Then you return to your room, get dressed and head back to do the show. Then it begins again all over the next day. We're so busy we don't even have time to pick up a guitar to add a song to our concert play list."

Despite the grind of extensive touring, Downing was optimistic about the band's future. "I really feel by next year we'll be hitting our peak," he said confidently. "But I don't mean that will be the beginning of the end for the band. I think that we will be able to maintain that peak for most of the decade, as long as the fans keep turning out. The fans are what make us go."

Downing's words were prophetic: Judas Priest became an important Heavy Metal band in the 1980s.

In 1981, the band released *Point of Entry*, an engaging eclectic album that included undercurrent elements of scream-and-wail passion ("On The Run" and "All The Way"), galvanized sentimentality ("Don't Go"), captivating mainstream metal ("Heading Out to the Highway"), and punkish boot-stomping ("You Say Yes"). Armed with its new LP, the group sojourned on a two-continent World Wide Blitz Tour that numbered over seventy-five concerts. Iron Maiden joined Judas Priest on the U.S. leg of the tour.

Screaming For Vengeance followed in 1982. The band toured in support of the new album ("Electric Eye," "Devil's Child," and the driving "You've Got Another Thing Comin'" were particularly impressive tracks), and I spoke to Halford again following Judas Priest's October 2, 1982 concert at New York's Madison Square Garden. The small venue concert halls and assorted venues of the band's American tour of two years earlier had been replaced by large arenas. Halford was pleased that the band was selling out all of its concert locations including Manhattan's world-famous performance and sports facility.

"Playing before that sellout crowd gave us all a rather tremendous feeling, especially when they were chanting our name over and over again," he said. "But it wasn't the concert performance itself that provided that feeling: it was the realization that years of hard work had paid off. After all, we're not exactly an overnight success story. But we get our share of interviews by people who approach us with the just-another-heavy-metal-band kind of attitude. Actually, we really don't get bothered by those that think we just made it, because we know that there are those who *know* the Judas Priest story."

Another issue bothered the band: the reaction to its name. Like Black Sabbath before it, the band's name seemed to represent something more ominous than the moniker of another musical group. "The name Judas Priest, for some simple minded people, has additional meanings," said Halford. "But all we're doing is going out there and having a good time by playing our music. However, some don't see it that way. When we were in Milwaukee, there were some people who were burning our records and protesting our presence. But at least we were getting the royalties from those burned records. I believe in freedom of voice, but when it comes to making totally false – if not libelous statements – well, then that's quite another matter. Still, I feel the whole affair was nothing more than a small storm in a tea cup."

Halford remained confident that the band's dedicated work ethic was paying off. "Everything that we've set our sights on doing, we've done," he said. "Everything is the result of a drive and a commitment by the band. And that attitude is still as intense, if not more intense, than ever before because it breeds even more of an effort."

The singer was quick to point out that although the band's brand of Heavy Metal was unique, the Judas Priest sound would never be trendy. "We've always maintained an attitude of wanting to achieve and maintain a certain degree of professionalism," said Halford. "Essentially, we always wanted to *avoid* creating a sound that was fashionable. Yes, for us, it just happens that music seems to have come full circle again."

Halford was pleased that Judas Priest had an influence on other up and coming bands. "It's more like a compliment," he said. "We now hear that certain bands cite us as their inspiration. Actually, it's quite amusing, because at one time not too long ago we were in the same position. However, it's great that there's a new generation of Heavy Metal headbangers out there."

Despite Halford and his fellow band members' collective work ethic and dedication to their craft, one factor remained at the core of Judas Priest's success: the group's loyal fans. "We feed off our fans' enthusiasm," said Halford. "They help instill in us a rededication to go to greater heights. And there's nothing better when we see some of those old familiar faces out there, the ones that have been with us since the beginning. But we need them all – both the old and new fans; without them we simply don't exist."

The band continued its successful development as the decade evolved. *Defenders of the Faith* was released in 1984, *Turbo* in 1986, *Priest...Live!* in 1987, and *Ram It Down* in 1988. Each album reinforced the group's dedication to intensity, power, and passion. The band's live performances – from the World Vengeance Tour in 1982-83 and Live Aid in 1985 to the Mercenaries of Metal Tour in 1988 – elevated Judas Priest to a place among hard Rock's all-time greats. However, veteran drummer Dave Holland left the band in 1989.

Judas Priest's uninterrupted success streak hit a major non-musical roadblock in 1990.

The band was involved in a civil suit stemming from an allegation in which an alleged fan in Sparks, Nevada, committed suicide after listening to Judas Priest's music. Two days before Christmas in 1985, Raymond Belknap, an eighteen-year-old Heavy Metal fan, and James

Vance, his twenty-year-old friend, binged on beer and marijuana, and then shot themselves with a 12-gauge shotgun in a church yard. Belknap died instantly but Vance survived; however, his face was horribly disfigured. During his recovery, Vance wrote a letter to his late friend's mother in which he noted, "I believe that alcohol and Heavy Metal music, such as Judas Priest, led us or even mesmerized us in believing that the answer to life was death." He eventually died three years later. The parents of the deceased men pressed charges that resulted in a court case: *James Vance et al. v. Judas Priest*.

Heavy Metal has always suffered from the slings and arrows by those who condemned the genre for the overt and subliminal messages that were seemingly contained in everything from song titles and lyrics to band logos and album cover art. Judas Priest songs like "Genocide," "Evil Fantasies," and "Breaking the Law," and album titles, such as *Sin After Sin* and *Killing Machine*, certainly could not be confused with other more innocent-sounding, mainstream Pop creations. Although the band was not proselytizing anarchy, Satanism, or violence, its music could be broadly interpreted to suggest some form of anti-establishment behavior. Clearly, the essence of Rock and Roll is rebellion of one sort or another.

The trial began on July 16, 1990 in Reno, Nevada's District Court.

The prosecution focused on "Better By You, Better Than Me," an old Spooky Tooth song that the band included on its *Stained Class* album, which allegedly contained the self-destructive message, "Do it," amidst lyrical lines that included, "They'll find my blood upon her windowsill."

The band's defense attorney, Suellen Fulstone, asked Halford in court about the existence of subliminal "Do it" messages in the band's song. "Absolutely not," testified the singer, who actually sang a portion of the song in court.

Tipton, Downing, and Hill showed up in court to support Halford and his legal team. As the trial went on, testimony revealed that Vance had a number of personal problems that had nothing to do with Judas Priest's music. The charges were dismissed on August 24.

"We're about to start another tour in America," said Halford when he left the courtroom. "And we look forward to sharing our enjoyment and entertainment with millions of people around the world."

A month after the trial, the band released *Painkiller*, which had been completed earlier in the year. The ten-track collection, which featured Scott Travis on drums, included more rapid-delivered songs than the last few albums. The band's revived power was never more evident than on the title track on which each member of the band performed at an intense level of musicianship that rivaled anything that the group had previously done. *Painkiller* was eventually nominated for a Best Metal Performance Grammy. The album, though a moderate chart success, maintained the band's status as one of Heavy Metal's most well respected acts.

A year later after some in-band disagreements, Halford left the group with drummer Scott Travis and formed a new band called Fight, which released its debut album, *War of Words*, in 1993. A few additional Fight releases followed over the years that included some assorted collection packages. Halford, though, rejoined Judas Priest for a short time when the band was assembling *Metal Works '73-'93*, a compilation album. The remaining quartet eventually recruited Tim "Ripper" Owens, a performer in a Judas Priest tribute band, to replace Halford. The new lineup released a pair of studio albums: *Jugulator* in 1997 and *Demolition* in 2001, along with a live disc, *Live in London,* in 2001. Halford and Travis eventually returned to Judas Priest in 2003.

A new album, *Angel of Retribution,* was released in 2005, although Halford started his own record label and released his own material on it via the Internet's Popular Apple iTunes Store. Another album, *Nostradamus*, followed in 2008.

The band played a private show at the Hard Rock Café in New York

City on August 4, 2008, for Heavy Metal radio and TV veteran Eddie Trunk, who was celebrating twenty-five years behind the microphone. Trunk invited me and my wife, Debbie, to the event. We had a grand time, despite being the only folks who were not dressed in black.

In 2009, Judas Priest released *A Touch of Evil: Live*, a powerful assortment of concert tunes primarily recorded from the band's 2005 and 2008 tours. One track, "Dissident Aggressor," managed to win a Grammy Award for Best Metal Performance.

On December 7, 2010 Halford announced that the band's next tour – the Epitaph World Tour – would be the band's last concert venture. Downing retired from the band in 2011 and was replaced by Richie Faulkner. Only Halford and Hill remained from the band's original lineup. That same year, the band released *The Chosen Few*, a "best of" collection that was released via the Internet. Halford later remarked that the Epitaph World Tour might not be the band's last set of live engagements; as a matter of fact, the group announced that a new album would be forthcoming in 2014.

Judas Priest made its first public appearance in 2014 in a rather strange way. The group appeared as cartoon characters performing "Breaking the Law" on TV's *The Simpsons*. The appearance of the animated band in the episode, titled "Steal This Episode," coincided with an apology of sorts delivered by character Bart Simpson, who wrote "Judas Priest is not 'death metal'" on his school's blackboard. In an earlier episode, Judas Priest's metallic style had been incorrectly identified and Heavy Metal fans rose up in protest against the popular television program. D'oh!

On March 17, 2014, Halford was presented with the Man On The Silver Mountain award at the Ronnie James Dio "This is Your Life" tribute concert in Los Angeles. Halford was acknowledged for his efforts promoting the Ronnie James Dio Stand Up and Shout Cancer Fund. Dio, the celebrated metal vocalist who had played with Rainbow, Black

Sabbath, and other hard rocking lineups over a multi-decade career, died of stomach cancer on May 16, 2010. At the ceremony, Halford informed *Loudwire*, the online publication, that Judas Priest had completed a new album for release in 2014.

The new recording on Epic, *Redeemer of Souls*, generated excitement from the band's fans when a segment of one of the tracks, "March of the Damned," was released online in May. The album, which debuted two months later, coincided with the 40th Anniversary of the group's first album release.

For the band, it's been forty years of uncompromising musical mayhem, and once again, Judas Priest was "Heading Out to the Highway."

Chapter 7

Meat Loaf

"Bat Out of Hell"

Meat Loaf's performance of "Paradise by the Dashboard Light" remains one of rockdom's enduring moments, a tour de force of musical dramatics and emotional intensity. Many veteran fans can still vividly recall the rotund singer with the sweaty long hair and perspiration-soaked tuxedo shirt expressing his frustration about being unable to "go all the way" – at least initially – with a girl he swore love to until "the end of time."

The Jim Steinman-penned song was part opera and part Off-Broadway with a dash of Rock fury and monsters from the id thrown in for good measure. The composition was given its full measure of expression when Meat Loaf delivered its numerous nuances with verve, flair, and sense of vocal power that was unrivaled at the time. "Paradise by the Dashboard Light" remains a song that will probably be forever synonymous with the singer who gave it life.

Marvin Lee Aday was born in Texas on September 27, 1947. As an overweight youngster, he suffered from an alcoholic father who occasionally beat him; his mother, a school teacher who had sung in a Gospel group, once told him that he couldn't sing that well. Clearly, it was not the best of childhoods. Nevertheless, he managed to survive the pervasive negativity of his household by taking out his frustrations on the football field. In a way, hitting opponents on the gridiron was a way to strike back at his father.

After graduating from high school, where he had performed in a few stage productions, Meat Loaf attended college, but soon he was off to California, where he formed his first rocking Rhythm and Blues band, Meat Loaf Soul. His commanding vocal delivery was the distinctive feature of the band and the subsequent groups he belonged to, including Floating Circus. He and his bandmates recorded an indie single, "Once Upon A Time," and opened for such diverse acts as The Who and The Grateful Dead.

While in California, Meat Loaf successfully auditioned for the Los Angeles-based production of *Hair*, the popular counter-culture musical. Later, he teamed up with fellow cast member Cheryl Murphy (professional name: Shaun "Stoney" Murphy) on a 1971 Motown album titled *Stoney & Meat Loaf*. An advance single, "What You See is What You Get," managed only to reach #71 on the *Billboard* singles charts. Meat Loaf, Murphy, and Motown soon parted ways. Meat Loaf returned to New York and appeared in the Broadway production of *Hair*.

In New York, Meat Loaf auditioned for *More Than You Deserve*, a musical set during the war in Vietnam and written by Michael Weller and Jim Steinman. Meat Loaf got a part as one of the soldiers. He performed in a few more plays, including *The Rocky Horror Show*, in which he was cast as Eddie, the doomed biker, and the infirmed Dr. Everett Scott. Meat Loaf also worked in *The National Lampoon Show*, where he met fellow performer Ellen Foley. Meat Loaf later appeared in *The Rocky Horror Picture Show* 1975 film version, reprising his performance as Eddie (Jonathan Adams played Dr. Scott). While the film was in theaters, Meat Loaf and Steinman began their lengthy collaboration on what was to become one of Rock's all-time classic albums: *Bat Out Of Hell*.

Seemingly inspired by Bruce Springsteen's epic *Born to Run* album and the multi-layered production techniques of Phil Spector, Steinman forged ahead with his musical compositions. His adventurous and eclectic works reflected everything from symphonic orchestration to excessive expressionism, and he created unconventional arrangements that were filled with asymmetrical passages and lofty lyrical articulations. Steinman's creations were complex, at least by mainstream Pop music standards. As such, his musical portfolio required an artistic overseer to properly present it to a Rock audience.

Todd Rundgren, best known at the time for his hit singles "I Saw the Light" and "Hello It's Me," was invited to serve as the LP's producer, and he supervised the recording at several studios in New York and New Jersey. Rundgren, who had produced such diverse acts as Badfinger, Grand Funk Railroad, Hall and Oates, and The New York Dolls, embraced Steinman's epic goals but tempered them with enough Pop sensibility to make the album accessible to the public.

Released in October 1977, *Bat Out Of Hell* emerged as a grandiose vinyl tribute to the phenomenology of unrestrained teenage passion. Three singles from the album's seven tracks were released and all became Top 40 hits: "You Took The Words Right Out of My Mouth (Hot Summer Night)," "Two Out of Three Ain't Bad," and "Paradise by the Dashboard Light," which featured the demonstrative vocals of Ellen Foley and a memorable play-by-play broadcast by future Baseball Hall of Famer Phil Rizzuto of the New York Yankees.

"Steinman was writing the material for Meat Loaf's *Bat Out of Hell* at the time and my voice inspired him to write 'Paradise by the Dashboard Light' as a duet for me and the Meat," Foley told me in 1983.

"Paradise by the Dashboard Light" was more than another Pop single: the tune was a lengthy (it clocked in at at 8:28 on the album) and elaborate exhibition of vocal histrionics and musical overload.

Although Steinman wrote the memorable tune, Meat Loaf once

mentioned that the famous dashboard mentioned in the song was based on a feature in a 1963 Ford convertible that he once owned. Over the years, the singer wove tales – especially to members of the electronic media – that varied with each telling. The origin of his stage name, his football experiences, and his many adventures were embellished by the time and place, and he maintained a poker face smile during every explanation. In many instances, he seemed to want his interviewer to call his bluff so they both would end up laughing together. His innocuous tall tales were just that, and he meant no harm by them.

Onstage, though, everything was serious – at least it seemed so. His concert performances were theater-driven: Meat Loaf was an actor first, a Rock singer second. However, his concert delivery was not as exact as a script; as a matter of fact, he regularly altered the dynamics of songs and his onstage behavior as he fed off the collective pulse of an audience. To be sure, the best performers respond to audience reaction, but Meat Loaf's ability to internalize the collective sensibility of a crowd made him unique among his contemporaries.

FM radio embraced *Bat Out of Hell,* and *The Aquarian Weekly's* Theresa Allen called the LP the "outrage of '77!" Meat Loaf hit the road, with Karla DeVito replacing Foley as his on-stage love interest. The album took off, selling millions of copies. However, Meat Loaf's passionate stage show resulted in his near exhaustion on more than one occasion.

"I feel as well as anyone who has done fifty to sixty shows within a couple of months," remarked Meat Loaf in an April 1978 interview in *Entertainment Spectrum.* "I did have the flu, and it got to the point where I thought it would be easier to collapse than to perform. When I reached the hospital in the ambulance, my temperature was 103-degrees and my blood pressure was about 900 over 12,000,000! But I'm fine now."

He joked about his future on the road. "It depends on how long the album stays on the charts," he quipped. "If this album decides to sell

25,000,000 copies, I'll never do another one. I'll just sing 'Bat Out Of Hell' for the next ten years." To date, *Bat Out of Hell* has sold approximately 40,000,000 copies worldwide of which nearly 15,000,000 were sold in the United States.

At the end of the near year-long Bat Out Of Hell Tour in 1978, Meat Loaf experienced a near career-ending malady. "We came off the tour and prepared to start the next record," he said. "At the time, everything was fine. But then I took off for about three-and-a-half weeks. I went up to Woodstock and it got weird, real weird. I went back into rehearsal and I tried to sing, but I couldn't. I thought that I just might be rusty, or I had a cold, or maybe the allergies were acting up. It was cold out, it was snowing, anything could be wrong, or so I thought."

Meat Loaf sought a physician's opinion. "I went to a doctor and he told me that there was nothing wrong, except that my throat was a little red," he explained. "He told me not to talk for a while, so I didn't talk. This went on for months. But what was real weird during this time, some days I'd sound fine. It was like Jekyll and Hyde. Then I started to think it was psychological, since I believed that there was nothing really wrong with me physically."

His condition worsened.

"I started to develop mental blocks," he said. "I couldn't figure it out. I started to go to hypnotists, psychiatrists, psychologists. I had acupuncture, acupressure, and people started beating me up! Finally, I decided I needed another *medical* opinion. It was finally analyzed as a paralyzed vocal chord."

Meat Loaf sought the services of Warren Barigian, who had successfully aided such singers as Jackson Browne, Cher, and Bette Midler with his rehabilitative Vocal Bio Matrix technique. (In another interview, Steinman suggested that Meat Loaf was allergic to pollen and cat fur.)

"I found out that after the tour, everything was fine with my voice until I let it sit," he said. "Then it went into a state of shock. During that month when it realized that nothing was going on, it suddenly realized that it had been overworked. It swelled up at each base and stopped vibrating; it wouldn't move!"

But Meat Loaf kept on moving. He appeared in the comedy *Americathon* in 1979, portraying daredevil Roy Budnitz. A year later, he starred in *Roadie,* playing Travis W. Redfish, a commercial truck driver turned Rock and Roll road crew member. Then, Meat Loaf led his softball team to a championship in the New York Pro Sports and Entertainment League. "Our first championship in nine years of play!" he exclaimed.

Near the end of 1980, Meat Loaf regained his vocal strength and returned to the studio to record a new album, *Dead Ringer*. He teamed up with Steinman, who once again wrote all of the album's lyrics, and producer Stephan Galfas of West Orange, New Jersey's House of Music recording studio.

Dead Ringer featured Meat Loaf's characteristic brand of soaring, operatic-like vocal acrobatics and an all-star lineup of musicians who contributed to the eight-song collection: keyboardist Roy Bittan and drummer Max Weinberg from Bruce Springsteen's E Street Band; horn players Alan Rubin, Lou Marini, and Tom Malone of the Blues Brothers Band; Nicky Hopkins; Mick Ronson; Davey Johnstone; and Cher, among others.

"*Dead Ringer* is the reaction to *Bat Out of Hell*," he told me when we sat down at his rehearsal facility in August 1981. "It's a little more straightforward in its style. It's gut level emotion." The album still featured lush arrangements, epic lyricism, and Meat Loaf's roller-coaster vocals.

Meat Loaf expected to exceed the recording's power when he and the band went on the road. The singer's requirements were fulfilled; in fact, during the rehearsal, the songs were performed much heavier than they were on record. Of course, all live concert experiences featured high levels of volume that exceeded those on vinyl recordings, but there was a commanding emphasis and a spirited instensity that

Meat Loaf and his fellow musicians displayed that was quite different than *Dead Ringer's* studio mix.

Bat Out of Hell was released at the beginning of the Punk-New Wave movement, but by 1981, stripped down minimalist tunes were in vogue, and MTV was on hand to showcase the new bands with the new sounds. In a way, *Dead Ringer* seemed anachronistic compared to the latest talent wave, but Meat Loaf didn't seem too concerned, at least during our interview. He reached into a box of frozen yogurt pops on sticks and started to devour them one at a time – each one with a single gulp.

"I don't know what the current Rock scene is all about," he admitted after finishing one of the yogurt pops. "But I'm probably going to find out in the next ten weeks during the tour. I don't really pay attention to everything that's going on; I go in and do what I do. I do it because I like the way it sounds."

His "sounds" had little in common with the Pop music scene at the time. New Wave artists specialized in quick-hitting tunes that lasted only a few minutes, like early Rock and Roll recordings. Furthermore, Spectoresque production techniques of the past were frowned upon by most of the new acts. It was a new age where less was more.

"But there's not much stuff on this record!" countered Meat Loaf. "They talk about overproducing, but it's just how you put it together. The album sounds great because the songs lend themselves to that style, and if you didn't do it that way it would sound *stupid*! If anything's good musically, there's a market for it."

Meat Loaf paid special attention to those he assembled his touring band. Like the musicians that played on *Dead Ringer*, the road lineup was impressive: keyboardist George Myer (who had performed with Ian Hunter); Rockpile drummer Terry Williams; guitarist Mark Doyle (who had recorded with Hall and Oates); pianist and musical director Paul Jacobs (who had worked with Edgar Winter); vocalists Eric Troyer (who had provided vocals on John Lennon's *Double Fantasy*) and Ted Neeley (the star of *Jesus Christ Superstar*); bassist Steve Buslowe (who had recorded with Paul Stanley and Ian Lloyd); and Davey Johnstone, Elton John's guitarist.

Although most of the accomplished musicians were relatively low-key types offstage, Meat Loaf cited one exception: Davey Johnstone. "He's the classic Rock and Roller," said Meat Loaf. "He lives a very dramatic life, you know, the women and all that. The guy's phenomenal."

Meat Loaf reserved most of his praise during our conversation for Steve Buslowe. "The guy deserves the Congressional Medal of Honor," quipped Meat Loaf. "He went through four years with me since the first album. He believed in this project – the album and the tour – so much that he has turned down some great offers. He held the last band together, and as good as are the players that I have now – and they're *great* – he's holding this one together."

Besides the boys in the band, Meat Loaf added vocalist Pam Moore, who contributed to Bob Seger's *Nine Tonight* LP. Moore was also the newest member of the touring band, having been contracted on September 4, 1981, after a lengthy audition process. "It's very difficult to find a girl who sings well, looks good, and is able to wear white spandex!" declared Meat Loaf with a grin.

Moore auditioned at the Westchester Premier Theatre in Tarrytown, New York, where Meat Loaf was holding rehearsals. After going through a few songs with Jacobs and Neeley, Moore prepared to begin her part on "Paradise by the Dashboard Light." As the song got underway, Meat Loaf entered the auditorium and walked towards the lower seating section near the front of the stage. He carefully looked at Moore and listened to her closely. Following the classic Phil Rizzuto portion of the song, Meat Loaf jumped up on stage and told Moore to sing the "do you love me forever?" lines directly at him. Meat Loaf followed with his deliberate lyrical procrastination, and then Moore shouted out the "I wanna know right now!" line with gusto. In a way, Moore was not only performing but asking about her fate. Meat Loaf answered enthusiastically in the affirmative. It was a memorable moment.

He pointed out that he had just completed filming *Dead Ringer*, a promotional movie that was part live-concert footage and part drama. He described his character, but in a way, he was also talking about himself.

"When I play Meat Loaf, I understand who Meat Loaf is, but Meat Loaf is not me," he explained. "I also play another character: Marvin. Marvin happens to be my real name; Meat Loaf happens to be my stage name."

Then he made a perplexing comment: "I don't have a name. I'm a nameless person. I don't want anybody to know who I am. Nobody ever has and *nobody* ever will – and that's just how it is."

Dead Ringer was a moderate LP hit that reached #45 on the American album charts, but it topped the vinyl roster in Great Britain. The film, however, was generally panned by critics.

The 1980s was a mixed bag of personal and career ups and downs for the performer. A disagreement with Steinman resulted in Meat Loaf releasing *Midnight at the Lost and Found* on his own. The 1983 album contained songs written by a diverse lineup of musicians including such loyal sidemen as Steve Buslowe and Ted Neeley. Guitarist Rick Derringer, E-Street drummer Max Weinberg, and former Lynyrd Skynyrd guitarist Gary Rossington were among a number of veteran musicians who also played on the recording. The Epic Records disc was a commercial disappointment and failed to chart. Meat Loaf left Epic and began label jumping.

Meat Loaf joined forces with Arista Records and released *Bad Attitude* in 1984, but the album only reached #74 on the *Billboard* charts. The singer's *Blind Before I Stop* on Atlantic Records failed to chart.

Several years later, his reconciliation with Steinman resulted in *Bat out of Hell II: Back into Hell* in 1993. The MCA release was a major comeback success, topping the album charts in several countries and spawning the #1 single "I'd Do Anything for Love (But I Won't Do That)." Arguably, the most interesting and arresting track was "Objects in the Rear View Mirror May Appear Closer than They Are," which included lyrical passages that reflected the singer's problematic childhood relationship that he had with his father.

The album's popularity coincided with the singer's increasing appearances in films and on television. Meat Loaf was especially active in the late 1990s, working on a number of offbeat motion pictures, such as *Black Dog* (1998), *Crazy in Alabama* (1999), and *Fight Club* (1999).

Meat Loaf kicked off the twenty-first century with over a half dozen film appearances in 2001, including the profanity-laced *Formula 51* (aka *The Fifty First State*), in which his character, Lizard, experiences a memorable gross-out death. He continued to act throughout the next decade, although most of the films were minor productions like *Extreme Dating* (2005), *Urban Decay* (2007), and *Beautiful Boy* (2010). However, he managed to land a few small roles in a few quality TV programs like *Monk* and *Glee*.

In between the release of two relatively unsuccessful albums, *Welcome to the Neighbourhood* and *Couldn't Have Said it Better*, the singer published his autobiography, *Meat Loaf: To Hell and Back* in 2000. Co-written by David Dalton, the book emphasized the traumatic experiences of Meat Loaf's early years in Texas, the singer's zany school tales, and his struggles involving the creation of the *Bat Out of Hell* album. The book was also made into a TV movie: *To Hell and Back: The Meat Loaf Story*, which starred W. Earl Brown as the singer in the Jim McBride-directed production. Interestingly, the title *To Hell and Back* wasn't the first time a Texan used it for an autobiography and a movie. Medal of Honor recipient Audie Murphy, the most decorated combat veteran in United States history, used the phrase in his 1949 autobiography and his 1955 Universal-International bio-pic.

In February 2004, Meat Loaf sojourned to Australia for a tour that involved working with the Melbourne Symphony Orchestra and the Australian Boys Choir. The collaboration resulted in *Bat Out of Hell: Live with the Melbourne Symphony Orchestra*, an impressive nine-track collection that featured *Bat Out of Hell's* seven original songs. Unfortunately, the album wasn't extensively distributed and it only generated semi-respectable sales in the United Kingdom.

Meat Loaf rebounded in 2006 with *Bat Out of Hell III: The Monster is Loose*, which went to #8 on the charts. The best song on the album – arguably the most moving and romantic song Steinman ever wrote – was "It's All Coming Back to me Now." The song emerged as one of Meat Loaf's most impressive vocal performances of his career. An earlier dispute between Steinman and Meat Loaf about who should sing the song first resulted in the composer giving the song to Pandora's Box, a female group, in 1989.

Canadian thrush Céline Dion's version in 1996 reached #1 in her country and #2 in the United States. Meat Loaf's memorable version, which included a shared vocal by the gifted Marion Raven, was accompanied by a hauntingly arresting video that displayed the sorrowful and passionate pain of an endless love. Coincidentally, the video, directed by P. R. Brown, shared some of the same visual features used in Céline Dion's video, which was directed by Nigel Dick. Meat Loaf also sang an abridged version of the song with *American Idol* runner-up Katherine McPhee on the Grand Final episode of the TV program's 2006 season.

Meat Loaf helped promote *Bat Out of Hell III: The Monster is Loose* with an aggressive lineup of over a hundred concerts in 2007. The Seize the Night Tour began in California early in the year and then moved to Canada before shifting to the east coast of the United States. In May, Meat Loaf took the tour to Western Europe, and in the summer he returned to the United States and began a series of dates in July. From there, the tour bounced back to Canada, the United States, and Europe.

On October 31, 2007, during a concert in Newcastle upon Tyne,

Meat Loaf stopped the show because he claimed he was unable to sing any further. He wished the audience well and proclaimed "goodbye forever" to the throng. The cause of his condition was later diagnosed as a cyst on his vocal chords. The rest of the concert dates were cancelled.

Bat Out of Hell III: The Monster is Loose was Meat Loaf's last commercial and critical success. Over the years several "best of" and live albums were released by various labels, although none were big sellers in the United States.

In 2010, Meat Loaf released *Hang Cool Teddy Bear*, which featured a non-stop lineup of hard-edged rocking tunes. The album made a respectable showing on the *Billboard* charts, peaking at #27. His Hang Cool Tour followed and continued into 2011.

Another project in 2011 elevated Meat Loaf's Pop profile when he appeared on TV's *Celebrity Apprentice*. The performer participated in the reality game show and was successful in his apprentice endeavors until he was "fired" by host Donald Trump in the twelfth week. Of course, Meat Loaf's most unforgettable moment on the program was when he went into a profanity-laced rage against actor Gary Busey. However, Meat Loaf raised over $200,000 for his selected charity, the Painted Turtle, a camp in California for seriously ill children.

Hell in a Handbasket in 2011 failed to recapture the popularity of the *Bat Out of Hell* releases, but Meat Loaf was seemingly content to make new music, tour, and perform in new films, and there was talk of a new collaboration with Jim Steinman in 2014.

Although interviewed numerous times, Meat Loaf noted one thing as we ended our discussion: "Nobody ever asks me my real name and nobody ever asks me how I got the name Meat Loaf."

However, his response wasn't true. He had told various stories over the years about the origin of his unique professional name, most of them different from each other, although some were repeated. There was no reason for me to press the question because I wasn't going to get the correct answer anyway; as a matter of fact, it really didn't matter.

Meat Loaf smiled, shook my hand, and walked back to the stage and completed his rehearsal. In a few days, musical mayhem would erupt in concert halls across the country. He wouldn't have it any other way.

Chapter 8

Motörhead

"Everything Louder than Everyone Else"

Morning interviews with Rock and Roll performers are extremely rare; as a matter of fact, I only conducted one professional conversation when the sun was still rising in the sky. It was in July 1983, and it was with a memorable performer: Lemmy Kilmister, the bassist and vocalist of Motörhead, the aggressive, full-speed-ahead Heavy Metal band.

I arrived at the offices of PolyGram Records in Manhattan and took the elevator to the thirty-third floor. A member of the the label's public relations staff escorted me to an empty room where the interview was scheduled to take place. It wasn't quite noon.

A few minutes later, Lemmy walked in. He looked like a cross between a tough grizzled biker and a pirate from the Golden Age of sail, although the empty ammo cartridge belt he wore around his waist suggested a modern-day bounty hunter's persona. He also carried a bottle of Heineken beer in each hand. There was something earthy and genuine about Lemmy, and he seemed to possess a personal quality that was free of anything artificial or pre-programmed. However, he didn't smile.

After being introduced to each other by a PolyGram staffer, Lemmy (full name Ian Fraser Kilmister) and I sat down for the interview. He adjusted his cartridge belt after it temporarily caught the edge of the large desk next to his chair. He placed one beer bottle on the table and began drinking the other.

Lemmy looked around the room and gazed at the file cabinets, book cases, and wall hangings. "I don't particularly like places like this," he stated in his rough textured voice. "There's a lot of shit that goes on in places like this – corporate business shit. But at least PolyGram supports Motörhead."

Still, no smile.

He explained that he tried to keep his distance from the business side of the music industry. "I'm involved as much as I have to be," he said with a shrug. "I just don't like talking to all the business types. In fact, if I had to, I wouldn't even cross the street to kick them! But I'll talk to the kids anytime. We play for them, not the critics or anybody else."

Lemmy finally smiled as he took another swig of beer. Instantaneously, the atmosphere of room changed. Despite his earlier posture and opening remarks, he became as friendly and polite as anyone I ever encountered in the music business. He was generous, too. He offered me one of his imported beers and some unidentified white powder that he placed on the table in front of him. I respectfully declined his offerings.

Lemmy was quickly joined by guitarist Brian Robertson and drummer Phil "Philthy Animal" Taylor. The pair looked like Attila the Hun's personal body guards, and they looked like they were ready for a rumble; as a matter of fact, they appeared as if they had just come from a no-holds-barred punch up. They stood there and didn't say a word; Lemmy was the exclusive voice of Motörhead on that day. He beckoned to his Metal mates to be seated, and then he continued with the interview. Lemmy consumed the white powder that he placed on the desk and smiled once again. Then he recalled his early days of Rock and Roll.

Lemmy explained that he was weaned on the early recordings of Elvis Presley, Little Richard, Jerry Lee Lewis, and Chuck Berry. As a teenager, he attended Liverpool's Cavern Club where he saw The Beatles – with Pete Best on drums. Inspired by both American and British artists, Lemmy taught himself how to play guitar and eventually joined a local band. In the 1960s, he bounced around from group to group before joining The Rockin' Vickers in 1965. Lemmy stayed with the band for a couple of years; however, the group broke up in 1967.

His later became a member of Sam Gopal, an acid-Blues quartet that recorded an album, *Escalator*, in 1969. Lemmy, listed on the LP as Ian Willis (a temporary name based on his stepfather's last name), provided guitar and vocals and wrote five original songs on the Stable Records release.

Lemmy joined Opal Butterfly for a short time and served as a roadie for Jimi Hendrix before linking up with Hawkwind, an edgy progressive outfit that specialized in what some called "Space Rock," in September 1971. Lemmy characterized the band and its music as "*Star Trek* with long hair."

Hawkwind had been active since 1969, and had released a self-titled LP in 1970 and a follow-up album, *In Search of Space*, in 1971. Lemmy was surprised to be named the band's electric bassist at his first Hawkwind gig. Although he had never played the instrument, his on-the-job training commenced immediately. He later contributed to *Doremi Fasol Latido*, the band's third album and a Top 20 chart success. Lemmy and Hawkwind followed with two more Top 20 albums: *Hall of the Mountain Grill* in 1974 and *Warrior on the Edge of Time* in 1975.

Before the year was over, Lemmy began a new and significant chapter in his personal and musical life.

He was arrested for a controlled substance at the Canadian border, which resulted in a two-day incarceration and the cancellation of a number of Hawkwind bookings. Hawkwind ejected him from its ranks, but Lemmy departed with the last song he wrote for the band: "Motorhead," a power-packed ode to mind-and-body-altering properties ("motor head" is a term that also means "speed freak"). The tune, which had been released as the flip side of Hawkwind's single "Kings of Speed," had a guitar riff intro that sounded like Bo Diddley-gone-Metal. "Some of our riffs come from way back, but our music is strictly our own," said Lemmy. "Above all, it's the myth of Rock and Roll – and I'm in *love* with it!" Throughout the interview, he continued to talk about the band's hard-hitting "Rock and Roll" style and never used the term "Heavy Metal."

Lemmy formed Motörhead in 1975 when he recruited guitarist Larry Wallis and drummer Lucas Fox. The trio played in and around London and managed to secure a supporting act gig for Blue Öyster Cult in October 1975. Signed to United Artists, the trio recorded an album but the label didn't release it until the band became more popular years later. Fox was replaced by Phil Taylor, and "Fast" Eddie Clarke was hired as another guitarist. Wallis, however, quickly departed from the band.

Motörhead struggled until 1977 when Chiswick Records, a British indie label, signed the band and released the "Motorhead" single in June and the *Motörhead* album two months later. The recording's rough and tumble raw power recalled the aggressive underpinnings of embryonic Punk, ZZ Top-like swagger, and psychedelic Blues. The group demonstrated its interpretation of audio shock and awe by performing as frequently as possible to willing audiences. Ironically, the trio even opened up for Hawkwind.

The debut album's cover featured a unique creature created by artist Joe Petagano. The so-called war-pig (the artist named it "The Bastard") or Snaggletooth would grace nearly all Motörhead album covers in the years to come. The ferocious image was also as closely associated with Motörhead as "Eddie," the zombie-like mascot, was to Iron Maiden.

The next year, Lemmy and company were signed to Bronze Records, a subsidiary of PolyGram. The group released a straight-forward version of "Louie, Louie," The Kingsmen's 1963 classic, which resulted in modest British chart success.

The band's *Overkill* album followed in 1979. The ten-track collection, which was punctuated by Taylor's thrashy, double bass drum kicks, reached the Top 40 roster of the British album charts, and two tracks, the memorable love anthem "I'll Be Your Sister" and the LP's self-titled tune, became hit singles. Motörhead, in its uncompromising posture to maintain its instrumental and lyrical integrity, emerged from the Heavy Metal pack as a group to be reckoned with. "People were starting to get the message back then about us," said Lemmy.

So did United Artists. The label finally released 1975's *On Parole* in 1979. The group followed *Overkill* with *Bomber*, a Top 12 UK chart hit, and an extensive tour of Great Britain. Lemmy paid the price for the hectic schedule (the band played a show a night for nearly two months straight): he lost his voice. However, he regained his vocal strength thanks to a successful electroacupuncture treatment program.

The all-female Metal band, Girlschool, opened for a number of Motörhead concerts in 1979. "Playing on their tour helped us tremendously," explained Girlschool guitarist-vocalist Kim McAuliffe. "Our sound got somewhat more aggressive, although it's hardly the bash-bash kind of stuff that you might expect; as a matter of fact, we're not quite the Heavy Metal kind of band that you might think we are." Girlschool and Motörhead would join forces again.

In 1980, Motörhead released a successful EP, *The Golden Years*, and the memorable album *Ace of Spades* which featured its powerful title track about gambling, "dancing with the devil," and fatalism. The album was a Top 5 smash in Great Britain and the single, which was a Top 15 hit, became *the* essential concert song for the band. *Ace of Spades* also contained such solid no-nonsense rockers as "The Chase is Better Than the Catch" and "Love Me Like a Reptile."

Motörhead briefly teamed up with Girlschool as the hybrid band

Headgirl on "Please Don't Touch." The track, which was powered by Girlschool guitarist Kelly Johnson, was featured on the *St. Valentine's Massacre* EP in 1981. The record's cover featured Lemmy and the other musicians dressed as armed gangsters and gun molls from 1929, the year of the infamous St. Valentine's Day Massacre in Chicago. Everyone on the cover looked like they had dressed for a fun-filled Halloween party; Lemmy looked as if he was about to rob a bank.

The group followed up with impressive chart successes courtesy of 1981's *No Sleep 'til Hammersmith*, a live album that eventually topped the British charts.

Iron Fist followed in 1982. In the Waxing Hot section of *The Aquarian Weekly*, I noted that the album's "galvanized assortment really slam bangs from the opening speed chords of the title track to the powerful closing of 'Bang to Rights.'" But the speed metal vinyl offerings were a bit too aggressive and uneven (Motörhead split from its producer during the album's development) for many hard Rock fans in the United States. The "Iron Fist" single was a minor hit in Great Britain but it failed to chart in America. The album was a Top 10 smash on the band's home turf but American sales were sluggish, to say the least. *Iron Fist* maxed out at #174 on the album charts. However, Motörhead's popularity on the European continent continued to grow, especially in Germany and the Scandinavian countries.

The band went on tour to promote *Iron Fist* and display its powerful chops and rugged image. For Lemmy, playing live was the important thing, whether the band had a new recording in circulation or not. But the lineup underwent another change in May 1982: Clarke left the trio following a dispute about Motörhead's involvement with Wendy O. Williams of the Plasmatics during the recording of the *Stand by Your Man* EP. Lemmy moved quickly and secured the services of Brian Roberston, who had been a member of Thin Lizzy of "The Boys are Back in

Town" fame." After a short series of rehearsals, Motörhead's new lineup hit the road.

On stage, Lemmy is the focus of fans' attention. He remains steadfast at his microphone, which is arched on its stand and positioned above his head. In turn, it causes him to look upward as his sings. It's an ungainly position, but it results in one of metaldom's iconic stances. His gravelly voice sounds anger-filled, although his delivery is based more on power and intensity than animosity. The Rock and Roll spirit of anti-authortarianism and counterculturalism is evident in nearly every lyrical line. As a musician, Lemmy produces solid and chunky bass lines on his sturdy Rickenbacker bass thanks to his heavy-handed use of a pick and an emphasis on mid range tones. He occasionally uses two-note chords, an expression of his rhythm guitar background, to accent the power of a song. Lemmy demonstrates this stylistic attack, for example, on his most identifiable song, "Ace of Spades."

Despite the band's steady success at home, Motörhead was still unable to make significant inroads in the United States.

Lemmy had an answer to that dilemma. "The main thing is that we were too vicious for American radio," said Lemmy. "We're still too vicious for 'em."

Nevertheless, armed with their catalogue of crunch rockers, Motörhead toured America with great expectations, but the American chart failure of *Iron Fist* – to say nothing of the band's previously unsuccessful stateside releases – seemed to be problematic. However, Motörhead didn't hit the panic button.

"Well, we had no reason to sit around with our thumbs up our asses and our brains in neutral," said Lemmy. "As a matter of fact, we don't look at our music as a kind of progression. We just go out and do it."

What the band did was create *Another Perfect Day* in 1983. The Mercury album's eight tracks escalated from hard and fast to hardest and fastest. Aggressive songs like "Marching Off to War," "Die You Bastard," and "Dancing on Your Grave" reflected the group's ability to maintain an uncompromising stance of musical deviance based upon a frantically delivered rhythmic assault.

"We came up about the same time the Punk bands were coming up," he said. "Look, even though we had long hair and the like, we avoided the extended guitar solo just like the punks. When it comes to music, the Motörhead approach is 'smack it in on the mouth and move on!' We've always written songs with a kick to them."

Along the way, Motörhead's direct no-frills "kick" approach influenced a number of important Metal bands, such as Anthrax, Metallica, and Slayer, whose members have acknowledged Lemmy's contributions to their respective styles.

As my interview with Lemmy neared its conclusion, his supply of beer ran out, but like watching a magician at work, a bottle of vodka and a container soon emerged from under the table. Another smile grew on his face. Lemmy offered his "favorite drink" to me, but again I respectfully refused.

Lemmy told me that the band would be hitting the road once again. I asked him about how he and his fellow musicians viewed themselves on the road. "Acting like the lone horsemen, riding into town and looking for action," said Lemmy with a confident smile. Then he finished his drink in one large gulp, lit a cigarette, and left the room.

Before the year was out, though, Roberston was dismissed from the band (the guitarist was seemingly reluctant to play earlier Motörhead songs) and replaced by two guitarists: Phil "Wizzö" Campbell and Michael "Würzel" Burston.

In the mid-80s, Motörhead continued to tour and record, although the lineup and its label changed from time to time. The band released a live LP, *What's Words Worth*, in 1984, and followed with a studio LP, *Orgasmatron* (on GWR Records with Pete Gill on drums), in 1986. *Rock 'n'*

Roll, with Phil Taylor back on drums, was released a year later. Another live album, *Nö Sleep at All,* which reflected the band's uncompromising approach to its craft, followed in 1988.

During the 1990s, Motörhead released a new studio album nearly every year but under three different labels. In 1991, the band cranked out *1916*, which featured "Going to Brazil," a back-to-basics, one-four-five structured Rock and Roll tune that recalled Lemmy's affection for uptempo Rhythm and Blues rockers from the late 1950s. The album, which was nominated for a Grammy, also included "R.A.M.O.N.E.S.," a tribute to the seminal New York punksters, and the powerfully aggressive "I'm So Bad (Baby I Don't Care)."

In 1992, Lemmy and his fellow musicians were characterized in *Motörhead*, a "brawler" video game. Years later, Lemmy did the voice of Kill Master in the video game *Brütal Legend* and appeared as himself in the video game *Guitar Hero: Metallica.*

Motörhead albums following *1916* included *March or Die* in 1992, *Bastards* in 1993, and *Live at Brixton '87* in 1994.

The following year was another important one for Lemmy: Motörhead released *Sacrifice*, the last album to feature a four-man lineup (Würzel soon departed), and the front man celebrated his fiftieth birthday in grand style at the Whiskey A Go Go in Los Angeles. Metallica and a jam-packed crowd maintained a high level of excitement at the club until Lemmy and his musical partners elevated the intensity when they came on stage. "We are Motörhead and we are gonna kick your ass!" declared Lemmy, who promptly kicked off a rousing version of "Ace of Spades."

Overnight Sensation followed in 1996, *Snake Bite Love* debuted in 1998, and *Everything Louder than Everyone Else*, a double live album recorded in Germany, was released in 1999. The band's lineup continued to change; Mikkey Dee (formerly with King Diamond and Don Dokken) replaced Phil Taylor on drums.

The band celebrated the new millennium with *We Are Motörhead* and another extensive tour. Without skipping a beat, the band continued to record and tour.

Every other year, the group released an album. *Hammered* in 2002 was followed by four Cameron Webb-produced CDs: *Inferno* in 2004, *Kiss of Death* in 2006, *Motörizer* in 2008, and *The Wörld is Yours* in 2010.

In the middle of the decade, the band earned a Grammy Award for its version of Metallica's "Whiplash." On November 19, 2005, Lemmy teamed up with Girlschool at the Apollo Hammersmith in London for a nostalgic 25th Anniversary musical salute to "Please Don't Touch," which was the centerpiece of the *St. Valentine's Day* EP.

In March 2010, *Lemmy*, an entertaining documentary made by Greg Oliver and Wes Orshoski, debuted. The musical portions of the production were fundamentally interesting but the sequences away from the Motörhead performances were particularly intriguing. The Metal master chain smoker was shown spending most of his offstage hours in Hollywood where he maintained a Spartan apartment filled with memorabilia – everything from framed gold albums and assorted photos to unique figurines and Nazi collectibles from World War II. Lemmy also enjoyed spending time at the Rainbow Bar & Grill on West Sunset Boulevard in Los Angeles playing electronic trivia games. The popular watering hole also served as a place where metaldom's fans showed up to pay their respects to the hard Rock icon.

The *Lemmy* DVD was favorably reviewed by both Rock music and general entertainment publications. "You don't have to be a metalhead to love 'Lemmy,' an awestruck depiction of a rock god," wrote John DeFore in *The Hollywood Reporter*.

The DVD sold over 50,000 copies in the United States, which qualified it for a gold award from the RIAA, and it generated sales of over 25,000 units in the United Kingdom, which netted a gold award from the British Phonographic Industry. German fans also elevated the DVD to precious metal status.

On May 8, 2010, Lemmy made his first appearance on *That Metal Show*, VH1 Classic's popular cable television show that was beginning its fifth season. "I was honored to have had Lemmy on my radio and TV shows several times over the years," explained host Eddie Trunk. "He is the genuine real deal. In a business that can often be filled with people projecting an image and not really being in real life what they portray, Lemmy is one hundred percent genuine. But he doesn't think his band was ever a Metal band, just a very loud Rock band. Lemmy is also a very underrated musician and songwriter. The guy is simply an icon."

On December 24, 2010, Lemmy turned sixty-five years old, and he took to the road with his band the next year. He also showed up at various hard Rock and Metal concerts in the Los Angeles area when he was in the area. Of course, he never came empty handed.

"In 2011, I was in Los Angeles seeing Slash play at the House of Blues, and Lemmy was there," said Trunk, who had just completed another season of *That Metal Show*. "After the show, I went backstage and in the middle of the room was Lemmy, holding court with a Jack Daniels and coke in his hand and a stripper under each arm."

In 2012, the Motörhead juggernaut continued with concert dates in the United States and Canada.

Motörhead expanded its enterprises beyond recordings and the usual Rock group merchandise offerings when the band listed assorted alcoholic beverages for sale on its website. The first product was an Australian-produced Shiraz made by Brokenback Winery in New South Wales that featured the band's classic war-pig logo on the bottle's label. Lemmy promoted the wine in print ads that noted: "My advice is – approach it with caution. I mean, wine is deceptive, anything can happen."

Additional alcoholic offerings included a Rosé, a Swedish crafted vodka, and beer. All carried the Petegano-created band image on their bottles. Bastards lager, an inviting brew, catered to metal heads everywhere with the printed phrase "beer drinkers and hell raisers." The band also sold custom high quality wine and beer glasses, a whiskey carafe, shot glasses, and coasters. The entire enterprise may have seemed a bit too corporate for the denim and leather crowd, but the prices of the beverages were fair, although some of the glassware sets were rather expensive.

Lemmy returned to *That Metal Show* on April 28, 2012, and was welcomed with fanfare usually reserved for Rock royalty. "There's only one Lemmy," noted Trunk. "He's one of a kind."

In December 2012, Universal Music Group (UMG), which owned the rights to most of the band's early recordings catalog, released *Motörhead: The Complete Early Years* multi-CD box set that carried an initial price tag of over $600. Although the music was readily available on previously released records and CDs, the limited edition set on UMG's Sanctuary label was augmented with a 300-page collector's guide, an 84-page concert photo book, and other items.

Lemmy was furious.

"These are fine examples of corporate greed: reissuing the same stuff over and over again, overcharging the customers with outrageous pricing, basically trying to rape our fan base," he noted in a public statement.

The band returned to the recording studio in early 2013 for its twenty-first studio album, *Aftershock*. After completing the album, Motörhead went out on tour, but in June the band had to cancel some dates when Lemmy was diagnosed with a hematoma, a clotted blood condition. He received an implanted cardioverter defibrillator, which was designed to help treat his irregular heartbeat. After a short recovery, he promptly resumed his band activities.

Despite the health concern, Lemmy was pleased to learn that he was named "Best Bassist" at *Revolver* magazine's Golden Gods Awards ceremony in May. The award, named in honor of the late Paul Gray, a founding member of Slipknot, was presented to Lemmy by the deceased bassist's band members. "Thank you from the bottom of my heart," remarked Lemmy to the audience. No doubt some understood his unintentional ironic reference to his cardiovascular system.

Aftershock, produced by Cameron Webb, was finally released in October 2013. Most of its fourteen tracks were delivered in typical uncompromising Motörhead fashion: direct, powerful, and heavy. The first track, "Heartbreaker," was the ideal song to kick off the album since it featured every aspect of the band's characteristic style, and it was released as a single. One of the most interesting tracks was "Lost Woman Blues," a restrained Blues rocker that featured superb guitar work by Campbell and a heart-felt vocal delivery by Lemmy.

Aftershock, though, was not well received in the United Kingdom; it failed to break the Top 100 albums roster. However, the album became the band's highest charted long-play recording in the United States: it reached #22. The album also did well on various European charts, breaking into the Top 10 in Austria, Finland, Germany, Norway, Sweden, and Switzerland.

Motörhead scheduled a busy concert lineup for 2014. The tour kicked off in Scotland on February 13, and continued in the United Kingdom before heading to other western European nations. Some of Lemmy's fans, though, were still worried about the aging performer's health.

In 2015, Lemmy will turn seventy. He continues to rock.

Chapter 9

Peter Noone

"I'm Into Something Good"

At one time during the 1960s, Herman's Hermits were cranking out hit records almost as fast as The Beatles. In 1965 and 1966, The Beatles placed fourteen singles on the *Billboard* Top 40; Herman's Hermits scored thirteen hits, including two chart toppers: "Mrs. Brown You've Got a Lovely Daughter" and "I'm Henry VIII, I Am." Clearly, the band from Manchester, England must have been doing something right.

The band – Peter Noone (lead vocals), Keith Hopwood (guitar and vocals), Karl Green (bass and vocals), Derek "Lek" Leckenby (guitar and vocals), and Barry Whitwam (drums) – was actually more popular in the United States than in Great Britain. The group's first single hit, "I'm Into Something Good," co-written by Gerry Goffin and Carole King, reached the top of the British charts, but the quintet never had another #1 single at home.

Catchy Pop tunes produced by Mickie Most, a wholesome-looking teeny bopper lead singer (Noone was sixteen years old when the record was released), and America's love for all things British helped elevate Herman's Hermits' popularity. For several weeks during the spring of 1965, Manchester – not Liverpool – became the epicenter of British

Rock, as three Manchester-based bands had a lock on the #1 single position for several weeks in America: Freddie and the Dreamers ("I'm Telling You Now"), Wayne Fontana and the Mindbenders ("Game of Love"), and Herman's Hermits ("Mrs. Brown You've Got a Lovely Daughter").

On May 21, 1965, Noone's photo was part of a *Time* magazine front cover collage dedicated to Rock and Roll. At the time, Noone and his fellow musicians were riding high on the charts with "Mrs. Brown You've Got a Lovely Daughter," which had spent the three previous weeks at #1. The song, which was written two years earlier by English actor Trevor Peacock and performed by fellow thespian Tom Courtenay in *The Lads* on British TV, was eventually nominated for a Grammy. At the time, "Mrs. Brown You've Got a Lovely Daughter" held the distinction of being the highest debuting single in *Billboard* Hot 100 chart history; it entered at #12. Unknown to fans, though, were the musical contributions of studio musicians Jimmy Page and John Paul Jones on various Herman's Hermits recordings. Page and Jones would, of course, later emerge in their own right as members of Led Zeppelin.

Before 1965 was over, the group had scored enough hits to release *The Best of Herman's Hermits*. The album, which reached #5 on the American charts, was followed the next year by *The Best of Herman's Hermits, Vol. 2*.

Armed with over a dozen Top 40 chart hits in the United States, Herman's Hermits launched a headlining tour in 1967. During the American sojourn, The Who appeared a number of times on the same bill with Noone and company. Audience members got a chance to experience both the Hermits' nursery rhyme-like sing-a-long tune "I'm Henry VIII, I Am" and The Who's powerfully destructive "My Generation." It was an historic juxtaposition of musical styles, but it happened frequently on concert bills in the 1960s.

I first crossed paths with Peter Noone backstage at a Herman's Hermits-Who-Blues Magoos concert in Asbury Park, New Jersey's Convention Hall in 1967. After The Who had performed "My Generation," the quartet's final song, Noone stood with his band members outside the dressing room area and waited for Keith Moon's strewn and battered drum kit, scattered microphones, and pieces of Pete Townshend's broken guitar to be cleared from the stage. It was a tough act to follow, and The Who's dynamic performance had left most in the crowd in a state of shock. Noone had seen The Who's antics before; however, the young singer looked as if he might have a hard time winning over everyone in the crowd.

"Imagine The Who opening for Herman's Hermits," laughed Noone during an interview with me during the summer of 1980. "But let me tell you something: Keith Moon and I were a crazy pair back then. Most people thought I was such a good lad, but in fact, I kind of got Keith into some of his stunts. On the tour, we were always jumping from motel room windows into the pool and we were always challenging each other to go one floor higher. Well, one evening in Asbury Park, Keith challenged me to jump off the Convention Hall pier into the ocean below. But I said I would only if he would. So we both jumped off. I thought he was going to drown under those waves. It was something."

Herman's Hermits made several hit records in 1967 – "There's a Kind of Hush" and "No Milk Today" was an impressive two-sided hit – but the next year, the band managed only one, "I Can Take or Leave Your Loving." The group continued on but its bubble-gum image could not stand up to the sophisticated, psychedelic social consciousness that was pervading Rock music in the late 1960s. Yet, the band delivered a number of non-teeny bopper recordings, like a re-working of The Kinks' "Dandy" and Donovan's "Museum."

"We were a good band until 'Mrs. Brown You've Got a Lovely Daughter,'" said Noone. "But after that release we were always thought of as a kind of novelty act. Even today, if I try and bring up some of our better songs like 'Kind of Hush' or 'No Milk Today,' all people really want to talk about is 'Mrs. Brown You've Got a Lovely Daughter' and 'Henry VIII,' the only two songs that were actually novelty tunes of a sort."

Following in The Beatles' multi-media footsteps, Noone and his fellow band members made several film appearances. Herman's Hermits performed "I'm Into Something Good" in *Go Go Mania* (1965) (UK title: *Pop Gear*), a collection of filmed musical performances featuring a number of British artists. Later that year, the band appeared in the MGM musical *When the Boys Meet the Girls*, which included such diverse acts as Liberace and Sam the Sham and the Pharoahs.

In 1966, the band starred in its own film, *Hold On!*, a harmless cinematic exercise of romance, Rock and Roll, and space flights. *Mrs. Brown, You've Got a Lovely Daughter*, a big-screen comedy feature, followed in 1968. Of course, acting wasn't new for Noone; as a youngster, he portrayed Stanley Fairclough on the long-playing British soap opera *Coronation Street*.

On November 5, 1968, Noone celebrated his twenty-first birthday and married Mireille Strasser, twenty-two, whom he had known for about a year. "The main reason you get married is to let everyone know you love each other," he said in another interview. Their marriage would last longer than any other of his music business contemporaries.

Although the quintet still managed to place hits on the British charts in 1968, the band's musical fortunes in the United States continued to decline. *The Best of Herman's Hermits, Vol. 3* failed to break into the Top 100 *Billboard's* LP chart, and the soundtrack album, *Mrs. Brown, You've Got a Lovely Daughter*, was a commercial flop, stalling at #182. Each successive single release did worse than its vinyl predecessor. "I Can Take or Leave Your Loving," released early in the year, made it to #22, but "Sleepy Joe" failed to chart among the Top 40, and the next three singles never entered the Top 100.

In 1969 and 1970, five additional single releases failed to chart in the United States; however, "My Sentimental Friend," a touching song about a failed relationship, reached #2 in Great Britain. The hit single was just an aberration; the best days of Herman's Hermits had passed. In 1969, Noone performed in *Aladdin*, a pantomime that was staged at the Streatham Odeon in London and the Oxford New Theatre in Oxford.

In 1971, Noone left the band, which carried as The Hermits; Peter Cowap assumed the lead vocal responsibilities. Noone, however, didn't leave the music business. "I had done some work on English television and some studio work with David Bowie after I left the Hermits in 1971," he said. Bowie wrote and played piano on Noone's "Oh! You Pretty Things," which was a Top 20 hit in Great Britain in 1971. "So I really wasn't out of the musical scene entirely. But I clearly wasn't keeping up the same pace as the old days."

He also returned to the stage. In 1972, Noone appeared in *Dick Whittington*, a pantomime production based on the fanciful English folklore tale about the title character and his amazing cat, at the Bristol Hippodrome in Bristol, England. His dramatic efforts were well received by both critcics and audiences.

Noone reunited with the band in 1973 during the nostalgic revival that was sweeping both Great Britain and the United States. Herman's Hermits joined forces on stage with the likes of such fellow British rockers as Gerry and the Pacemakers, Billy J. Kramer and the Dakotas, The Searchers, and Wayne Fontana and the Mindbenders.

The 1960's stars' reunion was brief. It had been nearly a decade since Noone first broke out on the Pop scene and much had changed in the world of music. In Great Britain in 1973, Gary Glitter, David Bowie, Slade, and T-Rex were at the forefront of the glam Rock movement; Roxy Music and Pink Floyd were expanding the boundaries of progressive Rock; Led Zeppelin, Black Sabbath, and Deep Purple were at the vanguard of hard Rock and Heavy Metal; and the bubble-gum Rock crowd's new idols were young American artists Donny Osmond and David Cassidy.

Noone carried on the middle of the 1970s on a new label, Casablanca (home to Kiss, The Village People, and Donna Summer), and recorded a handful of singles, including "Meet Me Down on the Corner at Joe's Café" and "Something Old, Something New." However, his efforts were not successful, and he moved to Bus Stop Records, where he released "One of the Boys" in 1976. The innocuous Pop tune got lost in a sea of Disco, smooth Soul, Southern Rock, and "Silly Love Songs." Noone moved to France and then New York.

Rock music continued to evolve in the late 1970s with the birth of the Punk movement and its accessible Pop spin off: New Wave. Noone saw an opportunity and he took advantage of it. He returned to the music world as a New Wave artist – and armed with a guitar – in The Tremblers, a quintet that released a debut LP, *Twice Nightly*, in 1980. The album was released on Beach Boy Bruce Johnston's CBS-distributed label, Johnston Records.

The Tremblers included Greg Inhofer (keyboards, guitar, and vocals), George Conner (guitar and vocals), Mark Browne (bass), and Robert Williams (drums and vocals). The band's naughty name was short for "knee trembler" – British slang for stand-up sex. Clearly, the freshly-scrubbed adolescent innocence of Noone's Hermits days was over, and, after all, he was thirty-three years old. Furthermore, unlike Herman's Hermits, Noone did not want to be the focal point of the group.

"I want to be reborn as a Trembler, not The Tremblers featuring Peter Noone, formerly of Herman's Hermits, who used to know Paul Revere and the Raiders," he said with a chuckle. "I'm just one of The Tremblers." Despite his efforts to remain as just another member of the band, Noone was the group's centerpiece, the performer who received most of the media attention and interview requests.

When asked if it was difficult to start a new band a decade removed from his very successful tenure with Herman's Hermits, he stated: "No, not at all, actually. I enjoy driving across the country with the band, sometimes practicing in garages and using borrowed equipment. I'm not a star any more; I'm just a musician."

He also enjoyed playing live again. Noone admitted that his six-string skills weren't designed to challenge the likes of Eddie Van Halen or Eric Clapton. "I just throw in one of those Chuck Berry riffs now and then," he said with his familiar grin.

On *Twice Nightly*, Noone displayed an energetic vocal urgency on such tracks as "I'll be Taking Her Out Tonight" and "You Can't Do That," but the tunes, written primarily by the singer and Iren Koster, didn't make any headway with the power Pop audience. Still, The Tremblers continued to tour, primarily in clubs and small theaters. On occasion, though, the band opened a number of large arena concerts for The Beach Boys.

Noone viewed the 1980s as a decade with new musical challenges, but he still maintained connections with his musical past. One of his closest friends was Dave Clark, the leader of the popular British band, The Dave Clark Five, which scored seventeen Top 40 hits on the *Billboard* Hot 100 during 1964-1967.

"Dave is such a super-intelligent person," said Noone. "He's given me good advice over the years, and he played drums on 'Little Lover' and 'I Screamed Anne' on *Twice Nightly*. You might even call Dave Clark my unofficial manager."

With the exception of Noone, all of the other Tremblers were citizens of the United States. I asked him if he ever thought of giving up his British citizenship. "Oh no!" he exclaimed. "I'm never going to give that up – that would be embarrassing to say the least. Anyway, that's not a major concern for me right now. If anything, the road will be my home for the next two years. I'm back into Rock and Roll."

After his brief run with The Tremblers, Noone recorded a solo album, *One of the Glory Boys*, in 1982. The LP was filled with edgy rockers, like the title track, and spirited re-workings of the Alan Parsons Projects's "Nothing Left to Lose" and the Chairmen of the Board's "Give Me

Just a Little More Time." The album never found its audience, so other ventures followed. "I did a couple of projects that were out of the box – one with Ginger Baker for a Who tribute," he explained.

A few years later, I crossed his path one evening at Newark International Airport when a mutual friend invited me and my wife, Debbie, to join Noone for a few hours while the singer awaited his flight to California. Noone, who had purchased a house in Santa Barbara in 1985, was relaxed, friendly, and charming as ever.

During the 1980s, he appeared in a diverse roster of TV productions and motion pictures, including *Laverne & Shirley* and *My Two Dads*. Noone also appeared onstage in *The Pirates of Penzance*, in which he portrayed Frederic, the "pirate apprentice."

Noone and his wife became parents with the birth of a daughter, Natalie, on July 3, 1986. Herman's Hermits producer Micky Most, who also supervised many of the recordings of such artists as the Animals and Donovan, among others, was named Natalie's Godfather. Natalie grew up listening to her father's record collection of oldies but goodies, British Invasion classics, and other Pop hits. By the time she was a teenager, she began writing songs and playing guitar.

Two years later, Noone returned to the big screen. He sang a revived version of "I'm Into Something Good" which played during a fun-filled scene in the comedy flick *Naked Gun: From the Files of Police Squad* in 1988.

"We had Peter sing the song over for the movie," said David Zucker, the film's director. "We used the same arrangement as the original song but added a different guitar bridge. I was in the studio when he recorded it, and I got a chance to sing back up and do some of the hand claps during the session. It was fun to do, and Peter was just great to work with."

In 1989, Noone began hosting VH1's *My Generation*, and in the 1990s he made appearances on several TV shows. He also revived his famous band from decades earlier with a modified name: Herman's

Hermits Starring Peter Noone. Original Hermits Barry Whitwam, Lek Leckenby, and Karl Green had toured as Herman's Hermits since the 1970s, but Noone did not have legals rights to the name so he added the tag "starring Peter Noone" to his incarnation of the group. Surprisingly, that title had been initially used in an introduction for him and the band on a 1965 broadcast of *Hullabaloo*, an American Pop music and dance TV show. Noone's current line up features lead guitarist Vance Brescia, who also serves as the band's musical director.

Noone continued to act. One of his most amusing TV gigs was an appearance on November 15, 1992, when he played himself on the popular sitcom *Married With Children*. He was joined by fellow rockers Richie Havens, The Doors' Robby Krieger, Spencer Davis, John Sebastian, and Mark Lindsay of Paul Revere and the Raiders in a episode titled "Rock of Ages" in which cast member Ed O'Neill's character, Al Bundy, assumed the fake identity of "Axel Bundy," a so-called Rock star from 1969, in order to enter an airport's VIP lounge. "I'm a big fan," said Noone to Bundy. "I've got one of your records. You remember: the one that sold?" Noone continued with a fun-filled exchange with Bundy's wife and kids. "Why don't you jam with us?' asked Noone. A surprised Bundy immediately complied. Later, Noone and the other musicians participated in a mock benefit performance, "Old Aid." It was a funny bit, and Noone looked the most comfortable among his fellow artists.

After working on the popular television show, Noone was back on the road with his band. Original Hermit Lek Leckenby died in 1994. "Sadness," remarked Noone when asked about his initial reaction to his former bandmate's passing.

Noone still keeps in touch with some of the other original Hermits. "I have a weekly and friendly contact with Keith Hopwood, but no contact with Karl Green other than an odd sorry-to-hear-about conversation when someone we mutually love passes or gets out of jail," he said. "Barry has decided he is Herman's Hermits, much to the collective anger of all the living Hermits and the spouses who remember that he was the drummer."

On December 8, 1995, Noone performed "In My Life," a classic Beatles song, at the Hard Rock Café in New York. He explained his friendship with John Lennon and dedicated the song to his late friend.

A year later, Noone appeared with his daughter on the televised Unity Telethon 25th Anniversary Celebration, a fund-raising event for the Unity Shoppe, a Santa Barbara, California-based enterprise which distributes food and clothing to the needy. "Natalie was the person who wanted to support Unity," explained Noone. The pair sang "The Angels are Crying in Heaven," a poignant tune about the plight and sorrows of a young girl. "I like her singing," he noted. Over the years, Noone and his daughter appeared at the Unity Telethon, singing the same song.

Noone joined forces with 1960s British thrush Lulu of "To Sir With Love" fame to advise a group of finalists on the popular TV show *American Idol* in March of 2007. Noone also sang "There's a Kind of Hush" to a national audience on the program.

The following year, his daughter left the Noone household and traveled to Nashville, where she fell in love with the music scene. She established her own musical identity as the guitar-playing lead singer of Natalie Noone and the Maybes.

Noone, who also resides in London, was particularly impressed with one of his daughter's original songs, "I'd Rather Be Lonely," an accessible ballad. "I liked the song and was there as it was being written," explained Noone. "As a youngster in the business, I was sometimes able to make something different and appealing about someone else's song, for example, 'Silhouettes' and 'Wonderful World.' Vance Brescia suggested we try it ala 'No Milk Today,' and we did it on a British TV show to test it out. We got a great reaction, so I think it's a hit song for someone if they use the right approach." The song was eventually included on Natalie Noone and her band's *So Far*, a 2012 EP, and is currently featured in her concert song list.

Over the last few years, Herman's Hermits Starring Peter Noone has continued to tour extensively, performing at such places and events as Denver's "A Taste of Colorado" fest, the Las Vegas Hilton, the Resorts Hotel and Casino in Atlantic City, and the Flower Power concert series at Walt Disney World.

Noone has also participated in a number of Pop music television documentaries, including *British Blues Explosion* in 2010, *Beatles Stories* in 2011, and *My Music: '60s Pop, Rock & Soul* in 2011.

In 2012, Noone appeared at the 60th Annual BMI (Broadcast Music, Inc.) Pop Awards ceremony in Beverly Hills, California, where singer-songwriter Carole King received the prestigious BMI Icon Award. "I'm happy for Carole," he said during a pre-event interview. "My first record was one of her songs, 'I'm Into Something Good,' so they asked me to sing it to her. It was pretty great for me to sing the song to her."

The talented performer added an additional performance gig to his work load of late: hosting Sirius-XM Radio's *Something Good with Peter Noone*, a three-hour program featuring 1960s songs and interesting fun-filled commentary. Noone's smooth on-air delivery sounds as if he's sharing his stories from the British Invasion years with just one listener at a time. In fact, Noone sounds particularly comfortable operating in any kind of media outlet. "I'm not afraid of the media because I started in 1961, and learned if you always tell the truth or stay close to it, you are in a safe zone," he said.

Besides his tour dates with Herman's Hermits Starring Peter Noone in 2013, the veteran performer sang "Something Old, Something New (Something Borrowed & Blue)" on Plowboy Records' *You Don't Know Me: Rediscovering Eddie Arnold*, a tribute album. That same year, he teamed up with Restless Heart, the popular Country band, to record a new version of "There's a Kind of Hush." Noone also appeared at Beatlefest in New Jersey and sang "Mrs. Brown You've Got a Lovely Daughter," "I'm Henry VIII, I Am," and "There's a Kind of Hush" to an enthusiastic audience. In November 2013, Noone and his wife celebrated their 46th wedding anniversary.

Noone and his band kicked off 2014 with a performance at the Palace Theater in Stamford, Connecticut, where he was joined by Micky Dolenz of The Monkees and Mark Lindsay of Paul Revere and the Raiders in a benefit for the Greenwich United Way's 80th Anniversary.

We communicated in early 2014, and I asked him about how he assessed his life and family, fifty years after The Beatles-led British Invasion.

"We are a working class family," said Noone, "living beyond our means and loving every minute of it!"

Chapter 10

Platinum Hook

"Standing on the Verge"

Expectations were high for Motown's newest act, Platinum Hook, in 1978.

The band had a talent-rich lineup of experienced musicians. They were certainly capable of reaching "platinum" status on the record charts, and they were managed by Benny Ashburn, who also managed The Commodores. Drummer-vocalist Stephen Daniels was the band's leader, and he had worked diligently for over a decade to make it big in the music industry before being signed to Berry Gordy's label.

"We had worked hard and tried our best," said Daniels. "And we were hopeful that we would make it."

Daniels formed his first band, The Soul Dukes, in 1966. Primarily made up of fellow teenagers – Glynn Nesbitt (guitar), Richard Nesbitt (trumpet), William "Stag" Ford (saxophone), John Alston (saxophone), and Mel Caulton (bass) – from Essex County, New Jersey, the band quickly made a name by playing at up to four different venues on a weekend. "We sometimes played at one place in the afternoon and another at night," explained Daniels. "We were working hard."

The Soul Dukes were all compentent musicians, but two band members were particularly impressive. Glynn Nesbitt was a gifted guitarist, who was comfortable playing everything from edgy Funk licks to cool Jazz riffs, and Daniels possessed the rare ability of being able to sing diversified Rhythm and Blues tunes (his vocal style also recalled the expressive delivery of Levi Stubbs of The Four Tops) while executing complex percussion tasks on his drum kit.

A year later, The Soul Dukes were offered a job to open for and back up Motown's Four Tops at a scheduled concert in Newark, New Jersey in July. The vocal group had ten Top 40 hits to its credit, including a pair of chart toppers: "I Can't Help Myself (Sugar Pie Honey Bunch)" and "Reach Out I'll Be There." The Soul Dukes rehearsed all of the group's hits and other songs in the quartet's catalog. "We were prepared and ready to play," said Glynn Nesbitt. "I had really looked forward to backing up The Four Tops. We had previously backed up The Intruders earlier that year and a few other local recording artists. We had earned a reputation as being a pretty good band in the Newark area at that time and thought that this performance behind The Four Tops may get us noticed by Motown."

However, the concert was cancelled when urban rioting erupted in the city. "My father worked in Newark and he knew how bad it was down there," said Nesbitt, who resided in nearby Orange at the time. "I told my father that perhaps the musicians union would be able to provide security for us, and that the concert would go on. My father knew otherwise. He was not able to go to work in downtown Newark due to the riots. I called Steve Daniels and asked if we could get the music union to provide protection for us. My father heard me and he said, 'Are you crazy? People are being shot in Newark. You can't go there!' And so, that ended our chances of being discovered by Motown in the summer of 1967. I can remember seeing the poster of the show in the background of a photo of the riots in a *Life* or *Ebony* magazine."

"I though that there was a chance that we could have hit it big in the business at that time, since we were playing with an established

Motown act," said Alston, an accomplished musician who also played drums and all of the woodwind instruments. "But the riots happened."

Daniels placed the cancelled concert in perspective. "It would have been a great opportunity for us," he said. "But we were a young group and we realized that other chances would one day come our way."

In early 1968, the band reorganized its lineup: this writer replaced Caulton on bass [see Author's Introduction], and Daniels' younger brother, Charles, was brought in as a percussionist-vocalist. The Soul Dukes primarily performed at African-American venues but also played at such well known outdoor concert facilities as Palisades Amusement Park in New Jersey, where the band shared the stage with such performers as Johnny Nash, Melanie, and Billy Joel's first band, The Hassles. One of the park's masters of ceremonies was DJ Hal Jackson, who interviewed the band on his radio show after the concerts.

"It was exciting to be performing at Palisades Park," said Nesbitt. "But then to be invited to Hal Jackson's show and be interviewed on the air was something special." The band members appreciated talking about their live show to Jackson, but they were determined to have him play their first record. Glynn Nesbitt and Stephen Daniels started composing the group's first original composition, "Don't Leave Me Girl," a song which avoided formula Pop and Soul by utilizing a Jazz-like undertone within a powerful Motown-flavored structure.

On Tuesday, May 21, 1968, The Soul Dukes independentally recorded the two-sided "Don't Leave Me Girl" and "Jellyfish," but it failed to generate attention from any of the New York-based labels. "'Don't Leave Me Girl' was too sophisticated for the average Soul-record buyer back then," said Daniels, who pledged the make the band's next vinyl effort more commercially accessible.

The band continued to play larger venues and generate attention. During a gig at the Terrace Ballroom in Newark, Sam and Dave of "Hold On I'm Comin'" and "Soul Man" fame were playing nearby at Symphony

Hall. After the duo's performance, they stopped by briefly to view The Soul Dukes' show. "That was something," said Daniels. "But we never got a chance to meet them."

The Soul Dukes returned to Palisades Park for a pair of afternoon concerts on June 15 and 16. "They were all great shows," said Alston. On the first night, the band performed at Newark's Symphony Hall and played a club date the following evening. "It was a very busy time for the band," recalled Daniels. At the time, the only other New Jersey Soul band that was increasing its fan base was Kool and the Flames, a Jersey City-based unit that later changed its name to Kool and the Gang.

After a successful audition, The Soul Dukes were hired to play for several consecutive weeks at the Cheetah, New York City's major dance club, in the summer of 1968. "We had a guitarist and a bass player, who played certain instrumental passages with their teeth!" stated Daniels with a laugh. "We definitely put on a show."

"The Cheetah dates gave us another opportunity to hit it big," said Alston. "It was a great time for us." One night, Academy Award winner Sidney Poitier came by to check out the band, and later NBC-TV filmed the group for a future broadcast special titled "Noise Boom" on *New York Illustrated*. Near the end of the first week at the Cheetah, The Soul Dukes were headliners at a Palisades Amusement Park concert on August 17. Although the band had no record out, The Soul Dukes were still billed over Johnny Nash, who had a top five hit the year before with "Hold Me Tight."

During the first week at the Cheetah, The Soul Dukes were joined by a new band from Tennessee called The Commodores.

"I remember seeing the guitar player's small Fender amp and hearing them talking with their country accents and thinking that these guys won't be that good," recalled Nesbitt. "Well, when show time came around, the air conditioning temperature setting had been turned down to what felt like forty or fifty degrees. We performed first, and what a disaster that was. We sounded terrible, but when The Commodores came on, they were perfect. They sounded great and their routines were polished. I think the guy who loved us at the audition and hired us wanted to fire us that night. Fortunately, we did finally redeem ourselves with a very polished and flawless performance that first weekend when a lot of our New Jersey friends came to see us perform."

The two bands played alternate forty-five minute sets, from nine p.m. to three a.m. every night (the club was closed on Mondays). At the time, Commodore Lionel Richie, who would later go on to superstardom as a solo artist, was primarily a saxophonist. Bassist Michael Gilbert, who handled most of the band's lead vocals, and charismatic saxophonist Jimmy Johnson were the focal points of the group. The band also featured the talented keyboardist Milan Williams.

Benny Ashburn, The Commodores' manager, had high hopes for his group, but the enterprising Ashburn also took notes on The Soul Dukes. "I met Benny several times over the years following the Cheetah gig," said Daniels. "He always said, 'you guys have got that raw power and we're going to get together some day.'"

Before the year was out, The Soul Dukes added Larry Williams on keyboards. "I learned that The Soul Dukes were influenced by The Commodores' Milan Williams and they wanted to add a keyboard player," said Williams. "Fortunately, that keyboard player was me."

The Soul Dukes were given a week-long contract to play at a club in Springfield, Massachusetts. "But it was late December and we drove up there in two vehicles, one was an old Volkswagon bus," explained Williams to me in 2014. "I remember you driving the bus and occasionally stopping to clear the ice from the windshield with a beer can. We didn't get up there until the second day of the contracted gig."

The group returned to the recording studio on March 18. "Soul-69" and "Jellyfish," a pair of original instrumentals, was released on the indie label Highway Records, but it failed to chart.

"Besides some area sales, it didn't do much without lyrics," laughed Daniels. Surprisingly, "Soul-69" was eventually released thirty-eight years later on *Funky Hot Pants: 14 Super Rare Original Funk Monsters from the Late 60s to the Early 70s*, which was produced by Soul Patrol Records, a French company.

The Soul Dukes continued to play various venues in the greater New York area and were featured on local television programs. On February 27, 1969, the band appeared on PBS television's *Soul*, which was hosted by Ellis Haizlip. The nationally broadcast program was a major showcase for talent and the band expected that a record deal would finally be forthcoming; however, no major label approached the band with a serious offer.

Despite the lack of a charted recording, the band's TV appearances generated enough attention for them to be invited back to Palisades Park on July 5 and 6. The Soul Dukes were also asked to be the opening act at the Cavalcade of Stars concert at Shea Stadium on July 21, 1969. The show was actually a benefit for the United Negro College Fund.

"That Shea concert featured every Soul recording artist you could think of," said Daniels. "We were the only act not to have a record out or a national following at the time." The concert roster listed Lloyd Price, The Moments, Thelma Jones, Howard Tate, The Barkeys, Kim Weston, Johnny Nash, The Delphonics, Sam and Dave, Joe Tex, and James Brown. Some concert posters even stated: "Special Guest Appearance: Jimi Hendrix."

All of the participating male artists were assigned the visiting team's clubhouse and each one was given a locker; the female performers were provided with some other accommodations inside the stadium. The atmosphere in the clubhouse was friendly and convivial—and then James Brown entered. For a moment, everything quieted down, but the King of Soul started greeting everyone and the place quickly filled with banter. "I remember seeing James Brown walking through the dressing room area," said Williams. "That was special, especially for me, a kid at the time."

The Soul Dukes were called out from the visiting team's dugout and the band walked towards the stage, which was constructed at second base, the same place where The Beatles had performed in 1965 and 1966. We were walking on sacred soil. It was a wonderful moment, but then reality set in.

Hendrix was a no show, and so was the crowd. It appeared that there were fewer than 10,000 people in the stadium, and the producers of the show didn't even provide a custom sound system. Instead, all of the artists had to use the Shea Stadium sound system, which was only suited for baseball and football announcements. Due to the cavernous size of the ball park, fans heard the sound of the instruments a second or two before they heard the vocals. It was a sonic disaster.

"It was a real problem for us to handle that constant echo sound," laughed Williams. "Every act used the stadium system, but some of the more established acts like James Brown and The Delphonics didn't seem to have too much trouble with it. Still, it was a big deal to play there."

I left the band at the end of the 1969 summer to attend college full time. Other bassists followed. "First, Joel Utterbach, then Tommy Davis, and then Clarence [Clay] Drayton, who was suggested by our drummer, Paul Cutner, who later replaced Steve Daniels," said Nesbitt. "Shortly after Clay joined The Soul Dukes in the summer of 1970, there was more of a push to leave The Soul Dukes management."

"We were increasingly having discussions in the band about what new material we should play," said Williams. "I remember Stag Ford was always mentioning that we should do more Rock material in order to expand our sound and our audience. But we didn't. And, as a result, some of us started talking about breaking off from The Soul Dukes."

Eventually, The Soul Dukes split up. "The break up occurred when I was sent to Fort Leonard Wood in Missouri for basic training in the

National Guard in 1970," said Daniels. A conflict arose over ownership of the van and the sound system, which underscored the dissolution of the band.

"I think it was in August of 1970, we had booked a job in Montclair on our own," said Nesbitt. "That was the first time we officially appeared under our new name: Parkway North."

"It sucked," said Daniels about the band's breakup. "But I completed my basic training and when I got back to New Jersey I started looking around for other musicians who would be interested in doing something special."

Parkway North underwent more lineup changes. "By the end of 1970, Clay decided to leave to work for Motown," said Nesbitt. "We replaced him with Romeo Williams, Larry's brother, and we brought in Paul's brother, Bernard Cutner, as lead singer. That lineup lasted for a few years, but like most groups we had several replacements from 1973 through the end of 1978."

"We had no established lead singer at the time so we booked Timothy Wilson, who had a Rhythm and Blues hit with 'Baby Baby Please' in 1967, to be the night's featured vocalist at one show," said Williams, who, along with The Soul Dukes, had backed the singer several years earlier at a few concerts.

Parkway North remained together for several years. "But Romeo went to California in 1976 or 1977," said Nesbitt. Romeo Williams became a highly regarded bass player, who performed with such diverse artists as Elton John, Patrice Rushen, Brian Eno, Steven Van Zandt, and War, among others.

"Richard started performing with Sonny Fortune a few months before his [Richard's] death in November of 1978," added Nesbitt. "I played with Carl Harris from East Orange, New Jersey from the summer of 1979, until I retired from music in February 1982."

Daniels kept The Soul Dukes name after his former sidemen formed

Parkway North. "I had no idea if I would ever be able to put together another group of guys that I liked playing with," remarked Daniels. But he did.

Daniels recruited new musicians and led his latest incarnation of the band halfway around the world, playing everywhere from Mexico and the Caribbean islands to Canada and the Mediterranean Riviera. "I can remember my first couple of gigs with The Soul Dukes," said Robin David Corley, who was recruited to join the band as a saxophonist. "The most memorable one was at against our nemesis Parkway North."

"It was either the late fall of 1970 or early 1971, at the Rutgers-Newark campus," recalled Nesbitt. "This was an awkward time between us. Remember, we had just split in the late summer of 1970. I started at Rutgers the fall of 1970 and had befriended a fellow student, who was a member of a Black student fraternity that was organizing a dance on campus. He recognized me from The Soul Dukes. I explained to him that we were now called Parkway North. He hired us for the dance. However, another fraternity member also hired Steve's new Soul Dukes for the dance. Now, it became the battle of the bands atmosphere. We knew we had to bring our best game."

Both bands arrived and set up their equipment. "The place was packed," said Nesbitt. "I forget who went on first, but we put on a good show and so did Steve's new Soul Dukes. I do remember a gimmick they used at the end of their set that impressed me. They were grooving on their theme song and one by one they started walking off stage while the music was still playing. They had a tape recorder playing while they walked off. It got a really good reaction from the audience. I think that performance kind of broke the ice between us going forward. I remember going to see the new Soul Dukes perform around the Newark area a few times. When they became Platinum Hook, Steve got Parkway North an audition with Benny Ashburn in New York for one of his shows. Benny said we did not fit the mold for his show, but would consider us for his Jazz label."

Unfortunately, Ashburn didn't sign Parkway North. The Soul Dukes headed south.

"In 1971, we got an offer from our agent, Johnny Jackson, to perform at the Los Globos Club in Mexico City for six months," said Daniels. "We shared the stage with the Banditos. Both bands provided continuous music at Los Globos. But they were fantastic! The lead singer sang David Clayton Thomas of Blood, Sweat & Tears better than David Clayton Thomas himself, and he didn't speak a word of English."

"Many, many stories happened here," remarked Daniels. "Most notable was the night an American was asking to speak to anyone in the band. That American turned out to be Jim Brown." The NFL Pro Football Hall of Fame running back was in Mexico City working on *Slaughter*. "He was in town shooting a movie and had left his wallet back at his hotel. I paid his bill for him and he invited us back to his hotel to kick around. I think he really wanted to kick somebody's ass in a few games of chess – and he beat me in three moves. He then invited us out to the movie set the next day. We had a great time over two days around Jim."

After performing south of the border, The Soul Dukes headed to Canada. "Johnny Jackson also arranged for us to play at Le Coq Dor in Toronto," said Daniels. "He told us that we could play our stuff but we had to back up Solomon Burke who was the headliner there at the time." Burke, the so-called King of Rock 'n' Soul, was a Rhythm and Blues legend who sang such hits as "Got to Get You Off My Mind" and "Everybody Needs Somebody to Love." The Soul Dukes were prepared for the assignment.

"We got in town two days early to set up and rehearse with him," Daniels pointed out. "But he never showed up at the club. We went to his apartment the second day, very concerned about what we would be doing on stage and he just told us not to worry about it. 'Look, just follow me,' he told us. That gig actually turned out to be a great learning experience and a lot of fun. We became regulars there on our own in the following years."

However, on one occasion Canada proved to be a nightmare for the band, especially for Daniels.

"As The Soul Dukes, we played Montreal for the first time at Rockhead's Paradise, a Blues club off of the main strip," explained Daniels. "Mr. Rockhead was a spry old man, who spoke as though he was still on the island he came from – Jamaica. He shouted, 'Where are girls?' at us while we were setting up, and 'What am I going to do with eight hard boys?' It was a great show place and we played there many times. However, at the end of the night, the last time we performed there, he asked me to see him in the morning to get paid. This was unusual, but I didn't think twice about it. The next morning we got up very early and argued about who should drive first before we headed out. We were all extremely tired from the night before, and I ended up driving. I swung by the joint for the dough before heading on to our next gig in Albany. I did notice that the club was dark, but again I didn't expect that the place would be fully lit as it was closed. The wind up is that I received the money and didn't pay anyone because we needed to get moving. We were stopped at the border and this time the border patrol did a thorough search of our van and persons. They confiscated the roll of money I was holding. There had been a rash of counterfeit cash flooding into Canada and the money I had turned out to be just that. I was sent directly to jail! The guys spent the night at a nearby hotel but pushed on to Albany after hearing on the radio that an arrest was made in the counterfeit money case."

Daniels was desperate. "I reached out for my then girlfriend, Sylvia Hoffman," he said. "She contacted our agent, Johnny, who was able to convince the border authorities that the only money I had on me had just been given to me from the club in Montreal. I was released the next day and had to charter a single engine prop to get me to Albany in time to play the next night. It was a tiny one-seater, piloted by a man who went right from his wheel chair into the pilot's seat! It was really hairy."

Daniels and the band didn't find peace, love, and harmony in upstate New York. "The last time that we played in Albany – at the Shack – we were packing up on the final night and the owner called me into his office to pay me," said Daniels. "He owed us $1,600.00 dollars but only put $800.00 on the table. Because it was not what we were owed, I refused to accept it. That's when he pulled a gun out from the desk he was sitting at and demanded that I accept the money. I stood up, raised my hands and said loudly, 'Okay, he's got a gun!' The guys in the next room were stunned and didn't move. I backed away slowly while talking to him. 'Is this how you want to be remembered?' I asked him, 'for shooting the drummer?' He didn't follow me or come out of the office and we quickly got our stuff out of there and left. I must say after all we went through, Johnny Jackson was a great agent. He wired me the money in full as he had done for the Montreal counterfeit situation. Needless to say we never went back to either establishment."

The band wasn't approached by any major management company or record label. Daniels was disappointed but he refused to give up. Then along came Benny Ashburn. He took The Soul Dukes under his management wing and introduced the band to a gathering of record executives at the Cellar in Manhattan in 1977. A Motown record deal soon followed.

The band – Stephen Daniels (drums and lead vocals), Tina Renee Stanford (lead vocals), Robert Douglas (keyboards and vocals), Elisha "Skip" Ingram (bass and vocals), Victor Jones (guitar and vocals), Robin David Corley (saxophone, flute and vocals), and Glenn Wallace (trombone and vocals) – changed its name to Platinum Hook. According to a fanciful Motown bio, "... the group met and discussed their goals. Of course, they wanted to be stars. What does it take to have a hit? A hook. And if you've got the hook, why not shoot for the best and go platinum."

Although Daniels and his fellow musicians had been playing for over a decade, they were the new kids on the musical block at Motown.

Platinum Hook needed to established its identity and separate itself from the rest of the Rhythm and Blues, Soul, Disco, and Funk crowd. "I hope we don't sound like everyone else," said Daniels at the time. "We have our own style."

Daniels was optimistic about the band's debut album, which was produced by Greg Wright, a veteran Motown writer-arranger-producer, who had worked with such established artists as The Supremes, Jermaine Jackson, and Thelma Houston, among others. On *Platinum Hook*, Wright co-wrote two songs: "Bittersweet" and "City Life."

"Once the album is distributed around the country, we'll follow with a national tour," said Daniels after the recording session was completed. "I know it's being on the old grind again – I've done it before – but this time there's a feeling I've got that goes deep. I'm sure we'll make it. We've put in the time and we've put in the effort. It's all got to fall in place."

But it didn't fall into place. "My expectation was that Motown would support Platinum Hook as a marketing force with Rhythm and Blues and Pop elements," Daniels pointed out. "Looking back at our time with Motown, it is clear that Motown was just placating Benny Ashburn. I don't believe that they ever had the intention of supporting *two* of his bands – Platinum Hook and The Commodores – since they both might possibly pull from the same fan base."

Still, Platinum Hook played on. In its self-titled debut LP in 1978, the group displayed a tightly crafted roster of danceable Pop-Funk tunes frequently embellished with punchy horn salvos and catchy rhythmic lines. "Standing on the Verge (Of Getting It On)" was the album's single release but it failed to chart. A strong contender for another single release was "Hotline," a powerful restrained ballad that demonstrated Daniels' strong emotional vocal skills, but Motown didn't issue it.

A lineup problem developed when Tina Renee Stanford wanted out. "Simply put, Tina had demonstrated on a number of occasions that being just a member of a band was not where she wanted to go," said Daniels. "It became crystal clear when she showed up at a show in Cincinnati without her Platinum Hook outfit."

Stanford was out and Kevin Jasper was in. "I had known Kevin Jasper from a few local bands I had seen playing at Sparky J's in Newark," said Daniels. "He looked good, had good energy, a decent voice, and played the trumpet."

In 1979, Platinum Hook released its follow-up LP, *It's Time*, which was again produced by Greg Wright. Among the seven tracks, Wright co-wrote two songs, "Time" (with Daniels and Victor Jones) and "Love Makes Me Feel Good." The band promptly went on the road. "Early on we played at the Apollo," explained Daniels. "We also played at two Kool Jazz Festivals, one in St. Louis and one in Cincinnati."

Platinum Hook returned to New Jersey when it played at the Capitol Theater in Passaic, opening for the Philadelphia-based Fat Larry's Band and the headlining Kool and the Gang on October 27, 1979. At the time, Kool and the Gang had successfully made the move into the mainstream Pop market on the strength of their best-selling *Ladies' Night* LP.

"As I recall, there was not a lot of fraternizing between the bands," said Daniels. "They were there to work and we were, too. They had set up guys and we had our sound guy, Will Lewis, and ourselves. In fact, I don't think I ever had a conversation of any consequence with another band member. But I was happy for Kool and the Gang's success. The business has always been 'catch as catch can' or being in the right place at the right time with the right look and the right song."

The band continued to seek its "right place at the right time."

"We also appeared at Studio 54; Carnegie Hall, opening for Kool and the Gang and Peaches and Herb; and at the Hyatt in Los Angeles, opening for Marvin Gaye," said Daniels. "In addition, we also opened for The Commodores at Nassau Coliseum on Long Island, and Stephanie Mills at Symphony Hall in Newark, New Jersey."

It was an exciting time for the band. "We were meeting superstars, such as Smokey Robinson, Marvin Gaye, Quincy Jones, and Michael Jackson," said Corley.

It's Time was a chart disappointment, and the band moved on from Wright. Platinum Hook returned to the studio under the supervision of successful producer Eumir Deodato, the Brazilian pianist who transformed Richard Strauss' "Also sprach Zarathustra" into a memorable Jazz-Funk creation on the 1972 LP *Prelude*. Expectations were high for the Deodato-Platinum Hook association.

Motown pressed the band's "Words of Love" track as a promo single in 1980, but did not distribute it commercially. The 45-rpm disc's label, which spelled the producer's name incorrectly as Deodator, noted that the song was included on the group's forthcoming LP titled *Ecstasy Paradise*. The unreleased title track was a rhythmically classy dance tune that featured Daniels' evocative vocal delivery, fine backing harmonies, and a pulsating beat, but production on the album slowed when Deodato started another project that, ironically, involved Platinum Hook.

"Some of us were working on his album, *Night Cruiser*, at the same time," said Daniels. "The fact that Deo was working on his album at the same time as ours had Benny very upset. He was hammering Deo for the finished Platinum Hook product, but Deo felt that it shouldn't be rushed, and I agreed with Deo. But I'm sure Benny was being pressured to produce a finished product."

The production process was occasionally slowed by social time outs fueled by alcohol. "There were always libations available, and at that point, Deo started drinking more and more," said Daniels. "The whole thing seemed to fizzle out."

Ecstasy Paradise was never completed, but *Night Cruiser* was released in 1980, and Deodato's album lists Platinum Hook and some of its members by name – including Daniels, who contributed drums, vocals, and conceptual ideas – on the credits. But Platinum Hook's days with Motown were numbered.

The band expanded its geographic and cultural boundaries when Daniels and his fellow band members wrote and recorded an album, *Made In Italy*, in 1981 for Italian Rock vocalist Loredana Berte. "We toured Italy in support of the album as her backup band," said Daniels.

Returning home, Platinum Hook teamed up with Sister Sledge of "We Are Family" fame. "We did a short concert tour as the backup band for Sister Sledge and participated in the video *An Evening with Sister Sledge – Live at the Roxy* in Los Angeles," said Daniels.

Platinum Hook eventually left Motown. "The association between Motown and Platinum Hook ended when Benny felt he could do better for us at RCA after Motown did not show interest in promoting Platinum Hook in the manner that they had done for The Commodores," noted Daniels. "We just got lost in the shuffle over there. There were a lot of big name acts over at Motown, but I thought that we would be a part of it all one day. But it didn't happen."

In 1982, the group began work on a new album, *Watching You*, at Conway Recording Studios in Los Angeles. Early session work produced such sophisticated Funk compositions like "Wonderful World" and "What You Want," which featured Daniels' soulful vocal acrobatics. "We've got a Funk sound, but without the capital F," explained Daniels at the time. "And we would like to think that we include more heart in some of our dancier numbers than some of the British synthesizer bands."

Daniels had concerns about the production process, especially on "What You Want."

"Yes, I really like my vocal performance on that tune, but the song was left absolutely barren," he pointed out. "There was no treatment to the tracks at all. When you're being produced by someone who has already had success in the field, you have to trust what they hear. My guess is that it's much like reading a book versus watching the book in movie form."

August 16, 1982 was a day that Platinum Hook would never forget.

"We were in the middle of mixing the *Watching You* album with the same producers of the Dazz Band when we got the word that Benny had died of a heart attack," said Daniels. "He was at home in Fort Lee, New Jersey, and passed away after eating Chinese food and going to bed. Benny was gone and we no longer had a friend at RCA. I remember going to the RCA offices in New York over three days trying to find out where we stood and when the album would be released. As I recall I never got an appointment to see the A&R person. I remember hearing second hand from Benny's office that the person responsible for the release didn't hear a hit. All our efforts with RCA died with Benny."

RCA finally released *Watching You* as a five-song mini LP in 1983. Daniels wasn't pleased. "I was very unhappy about it," he remarked. "I remembered it as a non-release. It was released with no fanfare, no push, no marketing plan, much like a stillborn child."

Despite the setback, Daniels and the band kept on playing. "We didn't intend to give up," said Daniels in a 1983 interview with me. "I've questioned myself many times. But knowing that it *can* happen keeps us going. We look around and see that success doesn't belong to just one band or one singer; it belongs to anyone willing to make the sacrifice. Sure, it's sometimes frustrating, but it's no longer a factor in what we do or how we do it. I look at every day as a learning experience, whether it's good or bad. You've got to remember that talent pays off in the end. Even luck can change things around in a way that you didn't think possible. But, in the end, each step is a step forward. That's my philosophy."

Although Daniels refused to give up, some of the other band members did. "In 1986, we lost a few members and picked up a few more and went on to tour Canada," said Daniels. "At that time only Victor, Robin, and I were left from the group. It was shortly after that when added Drexel Anderson on guitar and vocals, Cee Cee Rogers on keys and vocals, and a new bassist, Jerry Dalce, who was from Haiti."

The new lineup returned to the studio and recorded an original song, "I Walk The Line." The catchy rhythmic tune was replete with zesty instrumentation and Daniels' expressive voice. "I felt that finally we had a good vocal treatment on this one." The band shopped the song to potential producers, but no one was interested. "It was a one-shot effort," said Daniels. "We had limited funds and needed to give it our best shot."

Platinum Hook's next sojourn to Canada provided more drama. "Our manager at the time was Bob Durdin," explained Daniels. "He was Robin's brother-in-law, who had an office-cleaning business. His son, actor Gary Dourdan, played Warrick Brown, one of the main characters in the original *CSI* series. We worked out a show to take on the road to Canada, but the girl we originally worked out with backed out at the last minute."

However, help was on the way. At least that's what Daniels and the rest of the band thought. "Anyway, Drexel – Boots, as he was called – told us the he knew of a female vocalist named Mavis Gumbs who could make trip," said Daniels. "It was the last minute so we went with it. I had spoken to all members about what would be needed at the border since we had made the crossing many times. We get to the border and Jerry has no identification at all! He brought some mail that was addressed to him here in the states. I had no idea he was not a citizen. We had to leave him at the border. He had to get back the best way he could. I never spoke to him again so I have no idea how he got back. In order to make it to the first gig we had to push on."

Guitarist Drexel Anderson was designated to fill in on bass. But the band had no bass guitar for him to use. "We stopped in Montreal and picked up a bass for Boots to use and pressed on," said Daniels. "It was not until we set up at the first gig and rehearsed that we found out that Mabel couldn't sing a lick! It was way too late to make any other arrangements, so we made due. Her voice was so weak that the volume on her microphone had to be pushed to the max, but the sound system picked up my drums through her mike so we had to turn her volume down. Mabel was just window dressing and recreation for Boots. Just like he planned it! Still, we had a great time."

Corley remembered the many artists the band met and shared stages with. "We met the most wonderful people during those days," remarked Corley. "We were hanging out with George Clinton, meeting Grover Washington and Chuck Mangione, and backing up Bo Diddley."

Platinum Hook also worked with Change, the Italian group that launched the career of Luther Vandross. "We were working on a new venture with the folks from Change," explained Daniels. "We created a song titled 'I'll Take My Chances,' and I felt that the vocal treatment was much better and this was not even a completed mix." Unfortunately, "I'll Take My Chances" only got as far as a studio pre-mix.

"We played as Platinum Hook right up until 1988," said Daniels. It had been twenty years since Daniels and The Soul Dukes had cut their first recording, "Don't Leave Me Girl."

The band members finally went their separate ways. Keyboardist Robert Douglas became a highly-regarded session and touring musician, who provided his skills to such artists as Aretha Franklin, Madonna, Luther Vandross, and Keith Sweat, among many others. Douglas also recorded his own material and served as an A&R director for an independent record label.

"I was returning to college to pursue a teaching career," explained Corley.

Although the band officially dissolved, a few years later Daniels teamed up with former bandmates Victor Jones and Robin Corley occasionally under the Platinum Hook name. "We recruited a few more guys from around town and started playing once again," said Daniels.

By the late 1990s, Daniels was leading Share The Wealth, another Progressive-Funk band. "Once again, I sang and played the drums," said Daniels. "But I got a chance every now and then to sing out front by using a drum machine. I enjoyed that. However, things just didn't work out with the band, and I returned to the world of work at CATV. I stayed there until 2006 when I was pushed over to the manufacturing industry – my section was out-sourced – by joining up with Rotor Clip Company in Somerset, New Jersey, where I have stayed to date."

In 2011, The Soul Dukes' obscure Highway Records single, "Soul-69," was released again, this time as part of *Feeling Nice: A Collection of Super Rare and Super Heavy Funk 45s From The Late 60s & Early 70s Vol. I*, an effort organized by Daniel Wanders and Tobias Kirmayer on Germany's Tramp Records.

Daniels couldn't stay away from performing, so he got back into the music business by joining another group of performers. "Robin Corley, who became the maestro at University High School in Newark, and I continued to perform for weddings and other gatherings with Eddy D Orchestras in association with The Blast, a talented group of musicians," noted Daniels. "But it was rough, working during the day and playing again at night."

In 2014, Corley reflected on his forty-plus-year association with Daniels. "Steve really knew how to deal with people," said Corley. "He was as comfortable speaking to an obnoxious drunk as he was to a top record executive. We've traveled to many far away places and dealt with all kinds of situations, but Steve has always been the rock upon whom we could all depend. Steve is a great man, and he had a real command of his instrument. I consider him my brother."

Although Platinum Hook never achieved national stardom, the band left its mark. "At least fifteen years ago, I sang background and played percussion for the Village People when they performed on *The Tonight Show with Jay Leno*," said Daniels. "The piano player for *The Tonight Show* band at the time recognized me as being in Platinum Hook from the days when we played at the Cellar up on 96th Street in the City, and he let me know that he was inspired by us. I appreciated that."

It's been nearly fifty years since Daniels starting performing. "I would not trade my time as a professional musician for anything in the world," explained Daniels. "Did I achieve great notoriety? No, not very much. Am I independently wealthy? No. But it's been a fantastic journey and I'm still on it."

Chapter 11

The Ramones

"I Wanna Be Sedated"

The Ramones were probably the most influential act in Rock history that never made it big – *really* big.

That bothered the quartet's front man, Joey Ramone. All he ever wanted was a Top 10 hit in the United States – just one huge hit record on the *Billboard* Hot 100.

Formed in Queens, New York in 1974, the band included Joey Ramone (real name: Jeffrey Hyman), lead vocals; Johnny Ramone (John Cummings), guitar; Dee Dee Ramone (Douglas Colvin), bass; and Tommy Ramone (Thomas Erdelyi), drums.

The band ignored the elaborate, multi-tracked arrangements of progressive Rock and the genre's predictable essentials of lofty and lengthy instrumental passages and solos. Instead, The Ramones delivered a no-frills, hurry-up Rock and Roll offensive that was short (most of the band's tunes clocked in at less than two minutes), heavy, fast, fresh, and to the point.

Inspired by the likes of The New York Dolls and the Big Apple's underground music scene, The Ramones set out to establish their own unique profile among other street rockers. The band played anywhere they could but found a home of sorts at CBGB, a gritty club in lower Manhattan that became a meeting place where raw original music thrived and flourished. Besides pounding the drums in the group's formative years, Tommy Ramone also served as the band's manager and producer.

Joey Ramone's distinctive vocal delivery, which recalled the purist joy of someone singing along with reckless abandon to tunes on a car radio, accentuated the group's overall sound. Dressed in black leather jackets, T-shirts, torn blue jeans, sneakers, and sporting mop top hair cuts, the band members didn't look like any other musical lineup either. In particular, Joey was tall and ungainly; his pale countenance was shrouded by a face full of hair and a large pair of sunglasses. Audience members couldn't keep their eyes off of him.

A deal with Sire Records generated the band's self-titled album in 1976. The LP contained an innovative assortment of rockers from the uncomplicated chant-a-long ("Hey ho, let's go") power of "Blitzkrieg Bop," the record's first single, to "Now I Wanna Sniff Some Glue" and a frantic version of Chris Montez's 1962 hit, "Let's Dance." Although *The Ramones* album failed to break the Top 100, it managed to power the embryonic Punk music scene – especially in England, where the band first performed in Europe on July 4, 1976. The date was symbolic: 200 years earlier, the United States declared its political independence from England; in 1976, The Ramones displayed their musical independence *to* England. A Punk explosion followed in the UK. Thanks to The Ramones, no band since The Beatles had inspired so many to create Pop music on both sides of the Atlantic.

The group's second album, *Leave Home*, which was released in early 1977, was a commercial disappointment, but later in the year the band produced *Rocket To Russia*, which was more successful, thanks to the riveting "Teenage Lobotomy" and the catchy "Sheena is a Punk Rocker," among other tracks. The LP eventually broke the Top 50 and one of its singles, "Rockaway Beach," maxed out at #66 on the *Billboard* Hot 100. The band toured constantly, gaining fans at every venue.

Road to Ruin, which featured new drummer Marky Ramone (Marc Bell), followed in September 1978. The LP's dozen tracks featured "I Wanna Be Sedated," a manic mantra that would become one of the band's most identifiable songs.

The Ramones appeared in Roger Corman's teen musical comedy *Rock 'n' Roll High School* (1979), performing the film's title track, "I Wanna Be Your Boyfriend," and "Sheena Is a Punk Rocker," among other selections. The low-budget film didn't pretend to be anything more than a goofy, fun-filled musical. Interestingly enough, Riff Randell, one of the film's lead characters played by P. J. Soles (she was one of Michael Myers' victims in *Halloween*), ironically comments on The Ramones' first LP: "That's The Ramones' best album; it's #1 with a bullet."

The band's fifth studio album, *End of the Century*, was released in early 1980 and featured a more mainstream Pop direction, thanks to veteran producer Phil Spector, who added keyboards and saxophone to his multi-tracked mix. "Do You Remember Rock 'n' Roll Radio?" was the record's lead track and clearly displayed The Ramones' new delivery in a more carefully crafted Spectoresque manner. But the song was more than just a new offering to the masses: the tune's nostalgic lyrics paid homage to such classic 1960s Rock music TV shows as *Hullabaloo*, *Upbeat*, and *Shindig*, programs that the members of the band viewed regularly when they were younger. The song also gave credit to TV host Ed Sullivan and disc jockeys Murray the K and Alan Freed for promoting Rock and Roll music. Moreover, "Do You Remember Rock 'n' Roll Radio?" acknowledged Rock and Roll's heritage as the genre was about to enter a new decade.

Spector also had the band record "Baby, I Love You," a song he had co-written in 1963 for the Ronettes. However, the entire band didn't play on its version of the Ronettes' Top 40 hit; other musicians filled in. Some punk purists were upset at the "new" Ramones sound, a style that seemed to counter the band's original non-conformist approach to offbeat Pop, but Joey wasn't too concerned. He was just trying to score his first Top 10 hit. No single from the album charted in the United States; "Baby, I Love You," though, became a Top 10 hit in Great Britain.

I first interviewed the band in 1980 before a taping of *The Uncle Floyd Show*, a local New York metro area entertainment television program that later went national on NBC during the 1982-83 season. Uncle Floyd is the professional name of Floyd Vivino, a pianist-music historian-actor-comedian, who resurrected the classic kiddie show format in the late 1970s, but with a tongue-in-cheek twist and the wink of an eye. *The Uncle Floyd Show* was filled with comedic bits, zany cast members and puppets, off-camera banter, and inside jokes that made it regular viewing for young, hip adults.

Although Vivino specialized in playing early twentieth century tunes on his upright piano (his knowledge of the time period's music catalog was particularly impressive), he frequently had current musical performers on his show, from local bands to such established Rock and Pop artists as Cyndi Lauper, Peter Tork of The Monkees, Gary U. S. Bonds, Bon Jovi, Paul Simon, and The Ramones.

"I had them on my show twenty-seven times," said Vivino. "And then I had various members of the band appear separately from time to time. They knew I enjoyed different kinds of music – Dixieland jazz, Louis Prima, more traditional stuff. But they also knew I respected the passion of the Punk artists. That's why I first had David Johansen on my show. The most important thing about The Ramones personally was that they were so down to earth and friendly. And they were fun to be around, especially Joey. All Joey wanted to talk about was cowboy movies, the Three Stooges, food – you name it."

At the time of *The Uncle Floyd Show* taping, The Ramones had a new album in the works, and Joey and Johnny Ramone stopped by to promote the disc. Both were eager to discuss the new record, although Joey displayed a shyness that seemed the antithesis to his on-stage persona. "It'll have a lot more variety," explained Joey. "Yeah, variety."

"We've written ten tracks for it so far," remarked Johnny. "We'll be writing more songs than usual for this album. Usually, we go in with one extra song, but this time we might have four or five extra songs to work with." Upon its completion, the album would be titled *Pleasant Dreams*.

Johnny and Joey Ramone admitted that the band's hectic tour schedule was seemingly more frenzied than ever. "We played seven weeks in Europe, twice," noted Johnny.

"Yeah, and Japan, Australia, and New Zealand, too," added Joey, who explained one of the cultural aspects of Japan's Pop music preferences.

"The most popular acts in Japan are not Kiss, Cheap Trick, or The Ramones," stated Joey. "The most popular acts are Japanese. If you're not Japanese, you have to go over there and carefully develop a following. You've got to work at it – constantly."

How had The Ramones' hard work paid off? I diplomatically asked what the band's members did with their money. Did they buy real estate, perhaps a new car or two?

"I've been buying monster magazines and movie posters lately," said Johnny without hesitation. "And baseball cards, too! I'm trying to complete the set of *Famous Monsters of Filmland*, but I'm missing a few issues, including number seven with Zacherley on the cover. I've got some good movie-monster posters, mostly recent stuff, like *Zombie*."

Johnny's response was a breath of fresh air, to be sure, but then again, the band had always been honest and forthcoming. There was no artificial veneer beneath those well-worn leather jackets, and the band's collective truthfulness helped underscore its growing success among punkdom's fan base.

Joey Ramone explained that a number of factors contribute to any band's achievement. "To each his own," stated Joey about the musical choices bands make. "If you've got the right chemistry, you'll make it. You can't fool the public. If you want to survive, you have to have substance. We haven't had a hit record but we still pack 'em in. Audiences know what they're coming for – and they get it!"

"Joey and the band had a great relationship with their fans, who were very literate," Vivino pointed out. "And Ramones fans were loyal, that's for sure."

The Ramones released *Pleasant Dreams* in the summer of 1981. The album avoided the simple production techniques of earlier records and featured only Ramones-penned originals, a first in the band's vinyl history. However, such pounding tracks as "We Want the Airwaves" and "The KKK Took My Baby Away," didn't help elevate the recording on the LP charts. It stalled at #58.

In 1982, the band was marking a turning point of sorts in its history. Since its creation eight years earlier, the group had released five studio albums, one live album, and sixteen singles, and none of them had been a huge hit. The quartet's highest ranking album was 1980's *End of the Century*, which peaked at #44. The Ramones' quest for a big hit continued. The band members believed that the best way to achieve record chart success was to combine an aggressive lineup of gigs with a new record.

"We've just finished doing a number of local gigs," said Joey. "You know, in places like Providence, New Haven, and Virginia Beach. But we're ready to go back into the studio to start work on another album."

Joey Ramone was pleased about the band's role in elevating Punk to popular heights but he was concerned that some observers thought that The Ramones were caught in a creative rut. "We definitely inspired a whole bunch of bands over the years," said Joey. "But many people fail to see that we've progressed and expanded musically. The one thing about this band is that we've always continued to expand and try. And every member of this band wants the same thing: we want to make it! But we want to make it in our own way. That's why we didn't go Disco in '76 or Reggae now."

He noted that the band's audience was also evolving. "We're seeing a whole lot of new people at our shows," explained Joey. "Sure, we still see those familiar faces – and we want to *keep* on seeing those familiar faces – but we like getting newer fans as well. Look, we're even getting a lot of hard core fans these days. I guess some of them are not getting satisfied musically these days either."

Joey remained determined to make a hit record despite music company demands and mainstream radio limitations. "You've got to care," he stated firmly. "In this business, money isn't everything – it *shouldn't* be everything. But that's the way it is right now, and that's why the music business sucks. It's an emphasis on quantity over quality. Yeah, as I said before, the music business sucks. Everything about it sucks, even radio. Imagine, even *radio* sucks!"

Joey lamented about the early days of Rock and Roll when disc jockeys had more freedom to play whatever they wanted. "Definitely, those were the days," said Joey. "But now, radio, like everything else, is part of a large brainwashing process. It sucks! But, I tell you what: I'm somewhat optimistic about some of these new radio stations starting up in this country."

The singer explained that he enjoyed a number of new bands. "I like Def Leppard and Van Halen, to name just two," he said. "As a matter of fact, Van Halen is very entertaining. They make it fun and exciting to get into their music, and that's what all good Rock and Roll bands do."

Joey pointed out that he was getting desperate for that high-ranking vinyl release. However, he was unwilling to compromise in order to achieve his elusive goal. "I just don't want to see the band exploited," he said. "But I tell you, all I want is an American Top 10 hit! And our next album, produced by Richie Cordell, might just be the one. We've got thirty songs down to seventeen as of now. And we'll be recording a final fourteen songs which will which include some originals and some older songs like some 1901 Fruitgum Company stuff and maybe even the Music Explosion's 'Little Bit O' Soul.'"

Joey Ramone remained optimistic. "You know, the more I think about it, I'm sure we're *already* making it," said the vocalist. "It's not that we're going to stop what we've always been doing and it's not going to mean that we're going to start taking ourselves seriously or something. But we're still making music, and that's still something that's important to us. Still, we've always enjoyed what we've been doing. Sure, it's more than just music: it's entertainment as well."

The band released *Subterranean Jungle* in early 1983. True to Joey Ramone's word, "Little Bit O' Soul" appeared on the album; however, the quartet's studio version of a 1910 Fruitgum Company song – "Indian Giver" – would not be released until years later until it appeared on various compilation albums. Though lively and as upbeat as ever, *Subterranean Jungle* failed to crack *Billboard's* top eighty albums. Another lineup change followed: Marky Ramone was out and Richie Ramone (Richard Reinhardt) was in.

I named the band's "Psychotherapy" video as the year's best in 1983 due to its blunt and chilling depictions of the institutionalized. The video's story line, powered by the band's relentless musical assault, concludes with an attempted lobotomy that results in a challenge for the institution's staff.

The group continued its breakneck schedule of touring, writing, and recording. *Too Tough to Die* (1984), *Animal Boy* (1986), and *Halfway to Sanity* (1987) followed. Richie Ramone left and was replaced briefly by Clem Burke, Blondie's accomplished drummer, who adopted the name Elvis Ramone. However, after a few gigs he was quickly replaced when Marky returned to the band.

In 1985, Joey was involved with Artists United Against Apartheid

(AUAA), a group organized by Steve Van Zandt and music producer Arthur Baker to protest racial policies in South Africa. The Ramones' front man participated in AUAA's song and video "Sun City" in which he sang the line "Constructive Engagement is Ronald Reagan's plan," a criticism of the president's non-punitive policy toward the South African government. The single reached #38. Ironically, it was the highest-charting *Billboard* Hot 100 chart single Joey ever was a part of.

The "Sun City" single and the subsequent album was not the only time Joey was critical of President Reagan: The Ramones' 1985 song "Bonzo Goes to Bitburg" criticized Reagan's visit to a cemetery in Bitburg, Germany where some Nazi soldiers had been buried. However, due to Johnny's influence (the guitarist was a political conservative), the American release was re-titled "My Brain is Hanging Upside Down (Bonzo Goes to Bitburg)." Joey's liberal point of view ignored Reagan's 1987 challenge to tear down the Berlin Wall, which had kept East Berliners under the Soviet yoke for decades. When the wall was destroyed three years, Joey remained silent. The political differences between Joey and Johnny remained, but the pair tolerated each other – onstage only.

The group earned its first RIAA-certified gold album in 1988 when *Ramones Mania,* a compilation album, reached the precious metal threshold. However, band membership changes continued when Dee Dee left the band during the recording of *Brain Drain* in 1989. C. J. Ramone (C. J. Ward) became the new bass player.

The Ramones left Sire Records and carried on into the 1990s, but the group failed to score any record chart successes with the likes of *Mondo Bizarro* in 1992 and *Acid Eaters* in 1993. On October 21, 1993, The Ramones appeared as characters on *The Simpsons* episode "Rosebud," a laughfest that included references to a host of classic Hollywood films. The episode was well received by both fans of the program and the band.

The quest for a big hit record continued. The band's fourteenth studio album, ¡Adios Amigos!, in was released in 1995. The album's twenty-song lineup was kicked off by "I Don't Want to Grow Up," a strong catchy rocker that was lyrically filled with the fears of adulthood. The tune, co-written by Tom Waits and Kathleen Brennan, managed to reach *Billboard's* modern Rock list, but it failed to break *Billboard's* Hot 100. The album was one of the band's best offerings in years with guitar-driven rockers like "I'm Making Monsters for My Friends" and "Born to Die in Berlin," but it turned out to be another commercial disappointment. More bad news was on the way.

In 1995, Joey was diagnosed with lymphoma, and his bandmates eventually found out. The group called it quits the next summer, but Joey didn't disappear from the limelight. He made an appearance on *The Drew Carey Show* in an episode titled "In Ramada da Vida" on September 30, 1998, in which he portrayed one of a number of musicians who audition for Carey's local band. "But where are we going to get somebody to play on one day's notice for only $10?" asked Carey. Joey's backyard audition followed unsuccessful efforts by the likes of Slash, Guns N' Roses' former guitarist; Rick Nielsen of Cheap Trick; Dusty Hill of ZZ Top; and Matthew Sweet. After a few simple chords, Joey smashed his guitar and asked: "Hey, what ya think?" Carey quipped back with: "Sorry, we already have a tall skinny guy." Joey shrugged with "Oh man, that really sucks," and then accidentally tripped over his guitar cord as he left the yard. It was a funny scene, but few knew that Joey's health was worsening.

Despite Joey's medical concerns, interpersonal relationships deteriorated, especially between the singer and Marky Ramone. The pair avoided each other for over a year. "There were animosities that started a long time ago, and I guess it got to a head," explained Marky on *The Howard Stern Show* on July 20, 1999. Stern raised a question about Joey's health; as a matter of fact, he asked the singer if he had cancer. Joey dismissed the inquiry with a laugh, but never denied that he had the disease. Marky diplomatically avoided answering the question, too. But it was true.

The lanky lead singer died on April 15, 2001, a month short of his fiftieth birthday. He family, friends, and fellow musicians planned to celebrate his birthday anyway. On May 19, 2001 – on what would have been Joey's fiftieth birthday – Jeffrey Hyman's life was remembered in grand style at the Hammerstein Ballroom in Manhattan. An all-star lineup of artists appeared and performed, including Cheap Trick, The Damned and Blondie. Other performers delivered video messages. However, other than Tommy Ramone, none of the other band members attended.

"I escorted Joey's mother, Charlotte, at the event," recalled Vivino. "It was wonderful. We were both cheered, but it was really a tribute by the audience to Joey. The Ramones were great to me; they really boosted my audience. And I was grateful to them. Surprisingly, the very last act I had on my show, back in April of 2001, was Marky Ramone with his current band at the time, M-80."

The next year, The Ramones were inducted into the Rock and Roll Hall of Fame, along with Brenda Lee, Gene Pitney, Talking Heads, Tom Petty and the Heartbreakers, and Isaac Hayes.

On March 18, 2002, at New York's Waldorf Astoria hotel, the band was formerly introduced by Pearl Jam's Eddie Vedder, who sported a Mohawk hair cut as way to protest "world events." Vedder, who also wore a black leather jacket and a Ramones T-shirt, noted that The Ramones "... obliterated the mystique of what it was to play in a band." In his remarks, which lasted longer than The Ramones' acceptance speeches, Vedder noted that the band never had a Top 10 record, despite working with Spector. He also questioned why C. J. Ramone, who played bass with the band from 1989 to 1996, was not invited to be in the Hall of Fame. "For whatever reason, the Rock and Roll Hall of Fame chose not to include him with those being inducted," said Vedder. "It's a Hall of Fame thing; I wouldn't understand." But C. J. was in the audience. Vedder asked him to stand and be recognized. It was a nice gesture.

Johnny, Tommy, Marky, and Dee Dee represented the band at the ceremony. Johnny and Tommy expressed their thanks, and Dee Dee noted: "I'd like to congratulate myself." Tommy's acceptance was much more heart felt. "The honor of our induction into the Hall of Fame means a lot to us," he said. "But it really meant everything to Joey." Later in the ceremony, Green Day honored the band by performing "Teenage Lobotomy," "Rockaway Beach," and "Blitzkrieg Bop."

In 2002, Dee Dee died of a drug overdose, and Johnny died two years later from prostate cancer.

A 2004 documentary, *End of the Century: The Story of The Ramones*, was released in the United States. Additional compilation and live albums were released over the next several years. *Opus Collection: Rockaway Beach*, a fifteen-track collection, was released in 2012. It failed to break into the Top 100 album ranks. However, the band's debut album finally topped the gold plateau in April 2014, thirty-eight years after its release.

Tommy Ramone died of cancer on July 11, 2014. He was the last member of the band's original lineup.

Despite the lack of that elusive Top 10 hit, the music of The Ramones has been fully integrated into mainstream American culture. "Blitzkrieg Bop," in particular with its captivating "Hey ho, let's go" intro, has been featured in commercials, TV show promotions, video games, and live sports events.

The Ramones left an enduring mark that still resonates among those who embrace free expression, nonconformity, and the inherent joy of Rock and Roll. Not a bad legacy for a bunch of working-class punks from Queens.

Chapter 12

Van Halen

"Runnin' With the Devil"

David Lee Roth was suspended upside down on an exercise rack, looking like Richard Gere's character, Julian, in *American Gigolo*, when we were introduced backstage at Philadelphia's Spectrum prior to Van Halen's May 7, 1980 concert. The band – Eddie Van Halen (guitar and vocals), Alex Van Halen (drums), Michael Anthony (bass and vocals), and Roth – had returned to the popular venue after making their initial appearance at the historic city on May 19, the year before.

Once his feet touched the ground, Roth explained the reason for his awkward positioning. "I hang that way ten minutes at a time before each show," explained the flamboyant vocalist. "The hanging actually reverses the spine-compacting process that occurs throughout the day. It also helps to reduce the impact of my jumping around onstage."

Roth's conditioning routine kept him in top shape. "He'll maintain his twenty-nine-inch waist for the entire tour," stated Nancy Grossi, the band's costume designer. "Designing for him is a breeze."

Dressed in skin-tight, black-and-wine striped pants and a strategically-torn Van Halen T-shirt, Roth looked more prepared for the second round of some kind of martial arts challenge.

"Look, Van Halen is a very physical band both on and off stage," he pointed out. "We've even got a roller hockey team! As a matter of fact, we're in better shape than most sports teams. We compete night after night for eight months at a time. But don't get me wrong; we don't mind it one bit. We love to perform. I love to jump from the drum platform. Hell, anybody can jump off something five or six feet off the ground. But I jump *up* from the platform some ten or twelve feet in the air. And there's a point, that split second when you are actually up there flying! It's quite a buzz. Then you start falling, like a re-entry back to earth. That's why I need my ankles taped."

At that time, Roth, then twenty-four years old, was Rock's quintessential front man. Onstage, he was as poetically graceful as Baryshnikov, as high stepping as any Rockette, and as captivating as any pop idol. And yet he was more: he possessed a charismatic quality that was uniquely genuine in a business that prided itself in artificial hype. Of course, his antics were garnished with chutzpah, and he would be the first to admit it.

But Van Halen was more than David Lee Roth. I recalled the first time I had heard the band's riveting self-titled debut album on Warner Bros. Records in 1978, which featured Eddie Van Halen's earth-shaking guitar track, "Eruption," the powerful "Ain't Talkin' Bout Love" and "Runnin' with the Devil," the mega-watt version of the The Kinks' "You Really Got Me," and Roth's acoustic-meets-electric Blues rocker "Ice Cream Man."

Guitar Player magazine quickly crowned Eddie Van Halen with a Best New Talent award, and fans quickly embraced the band's pyrotechnic energy, verve, and flair. However, many music critics dismissed Van Halen as just another hard Rock/Heavy Metal band. But Van Halen was different. The band members displayed a devil-may-care attitude, confidence, musical prowess, hedonistic muscularity, and a sense of style. They were serious about their craft but they never avoided the joys associated with being professional Rock and Rollers, and they wanted to world to know it and be a part of it. Utimately, Van Halen helped revive the hard Rock genre in the late 1970s.

I saw Van Halen for the first time on August 11, 1979, at Convention Hall in Asbury Park, New Jersey. It was a hot and steamy Jersey Shore evening, and the band's electrifying performance turned the seaside venue into a rocking sauna room. Eddie Van Halen demonstrated impressive rapid-fire dexterity not witnessed since Jimi Hendrix, and Roth's animated posturing was augmented by occasional end-of-song acknowledgments to the audience, which delighted the fans and forged a bond between them and the band.

By the time Van Halen released its second album, the multi-platinum *Van Halen II,* which reached #6 on the *Billboard* LP chart in 1979, the halls and theaters that the quartet had played in the past were being replaced by larger venues and sports arenas. The band's third successful album, *Women And Children First,* which contained such memorable rockers as "And The Cradle Will Rock" and "Everybody Wants Some!," fueled Van Halen's fan base.

"We've come a long way," said Roth. It was an understatement to say the least.

The band formed in California in the mid-1970s after the Van Halen brothers, who were born in the Netherlands, joined forces first with Anthony and later Roth. After a brief time when the quartet was known as Mammoth, the band assumed its Van Halen moniker. The band played at local gigs displaying a diversified set list that include songs by the likes of Cream, James Brown, The Isley Brothers, The Ohio Players, Deep Purple, and K. C. and the Sunshine Band, plus a handful of originals. Despite its motley song roster, the band developed its own style characterized by the disciplined heavy-bottom rhythms of Alex Van Halen and Anthony, the creative wizardy of guitarist Eddie Van Halen, and the look-at-me vocal dramatics of Roth.

Occasionally, the band landed one-night opening assignments for such acts as Aerosmith, Bob Seger, UFO, Santana, Journey, Montrose, and Nils Lofgren. Gene Simmons of Kiss heard Van Halen and paid for the band's first demo tape. While gigging the greater Los Angeles club circuit in 1977, the band was signed to a Warner Bros. recording contract by Ted Templeman, who later produced the band's first six albums.

Roth explained that the studio albums have a live feel to them because of the production techniques that the band and Templeman utilize – or actually don't utilize.

"Overdubbing, when it's used is always used sparingly," said Roth. "On certain songs, two channels are used, but only because it may sound better; it's not that complicated."

The band follows a certain creation-to-recording process. "Basically, I'll write the music along with Mike, and then Dave will write the lyrics," explained Eddie Van Halen. Alex develops the rhythm structure with Mike, and that's about it. It's not a perfect system; I know I've made a few mistakes, but Rock and Roll wasn't made to be perfect."

The guitarist pointed out that the band doesn't like to waste time in the studio. "Before we go into the studio, we've already rehearsed the material," he noted. "Studio time is very expensive, but we don't end up recording everything we bring with us. I think we had about fifty songs with us when we went in to cut the first album. Still, we save time by only doing two or three takes per song, and we usually end up taking the first run through. 'And The Cradle Will Rock' was done just that way – in one take."

"And The Cradle Will Rock" features one of Eddie Van Halen's classic riffs: a slow-scratching, locomotive-like chording that had been featured before on "Atomic Punk" from the band's debut LP and "D. O. A." from *Van Halen II*. Thanks to the rhythmic teamwork that Alex Van Halen and Michael Anthony provided, the song established an incredibly deep bottom that allowed Eddie Van Halen's instrumental fireworks to achieve maximum effectiveness.

"That tightness of sound comes, simply enough, from working with Alex over the years," said Anthony, who grew up listening to the bass artistry of Jaco Pastorius, Cream's Jack Bruce, and Led Zeppelin's John Paul Jones. "It really comes out on that number."

The third album also featured the contribution of an uncredited additional vocalist, Nicolette Larson, a fellow Warner Bros. artist, on "Could This be Magic." The California-based singer, who scored a Top 10 single in 1978 with "Lotta Love," told me during an interview several months earlier that she was brought in to add her vocal contribution to the track. Larson described the Van Halen recording process as "very much of a boys club" that was lacking in social pleasantries.

"It's not that we're a closed, secretive club or anything like that," countered Anthony, who was decked out in his concert attire: black military khakis and jungle boots. "But we are aware of studio costs and the need for the just the band to concentrate on our tasks without any distractions."

Nearby, Eddie Van Halen zipped up his blue jump suit and nodded in agreement with Anthony's comments. "Hey, we didn't even plan on having a chick's voice on the album," said Eddie. "But it turned out all right."

As show time approached, Roth and Anthony got their ankles taped as if they were about to play in a football game. "I sprained my ankle on the last night of rehearsal before this current tour while leaping off of Alex's platform," confessed Anthony. "So I have to get them taped like Dave every night we play."

"I go through about a case of athletic tape every three weeks," explained Ed Anderson, the band's trainer and security officer. "And each case contains thirty-two rolls of one-and-a-half-inch tape at fifteen yards of tape per roll."

Like Anthony, Eddie Van Halen confessed that he wasn't completely healthy. He explained that he suffered from blood poisoning after repeated stage slides on his knees, and had utilized knee pads to ease the suffering. "I thought the pads would help, but they didn't," said the guitarist.

Before the band left the dressing room for the stage, the members discussed the negative comments that some critics directed towards their work. "Critics are different from the average music fan," stated Roth. "They see so many concerts and hear so many albums that they define their tastes in a much broader sense, sometimes forgetting that the common fan is a thinking individual, too."

Alex Van Halen disliked being categorized, a favorite activity of critics. "We realize that in the music business you have to be called *something*," said Alex as he flashed a grin. "But don't call us Disco."

"If anything, Van Halen is high impact Rock and Roll," stated Roth. "We play Van Halen music, not Heavy Metal or New Wave. You've got to play with a certain emotion, a certain passion. Rock and Roll, for all it's worth, makes you feel like an animal. New Wave doesn't necessarily do that."

Eddie Van Halen pointed out that New Wave's earlier incarnation still had merit. "I do, however, prefer Punk to New Wave," said the guitarist. "Punk has rough-edged energy, but New Wave is much more predictable. Imagine, Blondie doing 'Heart Of Glass' – a Disco record!"

The band disappeared for a private moment before emerging onstage to a thunderous reception. Part of Van Halen's success was based on Roth's ability to create pledges of allegiance with his audience by re-emphasizing the city's name to the faithful. After concluding one song, Roth paused and shouted: "Philadelphia, you blow my fuckin' mind!" The crowd went wild. To be sure, Roth used the same line in cities around the world, but his delivery seemed more sincere than many other performers.

At the time, Van Halen's stage show was free of fireworks, flame-filled mortars, fog machines, and video sideshows. There were plenty of lights; in fact, lots of them: 850,000 watts of brightness augmented by 40,000 watts of sound. Of course, all the equipment had to be broken down, organized, and loaded for the next concert. Van Halen's road crew didn't wear the indentured servant look that so many other crews displayed. "We're all family, the band and the road crew," stated Eddie Van Halen. "They don't work *for* us, they work *with* us."

The Philadelphia show marked the end of the band's tour of the United States (the group had opened its 1981 concert lineup in Canada) and the beginning of its next string of concerts. "We'll be covering some European countries we've never played in before, like Greece, Italy, Spain, and Denmark," said Alex Van Halen. "We all enjoy touring."

"Touring is part of the good life of Rock and Roll," noted Eddie Van Halen. "Sometimes it gets hectic, but it's something that I always wanted to do ever since I stood next to a stage from the audience, looking up at the guitarist. I won't forget those early days when we began."

"We'll also be playing Japan again," said Anthony. "But then we'll backtrack across Europe, play the southwestern United States, Hawaii, with a probable finish near our homes in southern California."

"We're living a Rock and Roll fantasy," added Roth. "We're doing all the things we only dreamed of when we were Rock fans like everyone else years ago."

Roth also looked ahead ten years and shared an interesting observation about how he viewed his career at that time. He described it as if he were reading a novel: "David Roth rolls towards the curb in New York City, stares up at the buildings and contemplates: 'What the fuck went wrong?'"

The next year, Van Halen released *Fair Warning*. The multi-platinum album included such power rockers as "Unchained," "So This Is Love," and the melodramatic "Mean Street."

The band hit the road again. I caught up with them in the City of Brotherly Love on a late afternoon on July 22, 1981. I was standing outside David Lee Roth's hotel room at the Stadium Hilton Hotel in Philadelphia, not far from the Spectrum where Van Halen was scheduled to play later that evening, the concluding night of a three-day concert schedule.

From the hallway, I heard music in his room – music from the 1920s! It was Al Jolson's "Toot Toot Tootsie! Goodbye." Go figure. Then again, it was Roth, the over-the-top frontman, the daring musical master of ceremonies, who was leading rockdom's version of Dante's Inferno with the flair of three-ring circus' lion tamer.

I knocked on the door and he promptly opened it. "Interview time!" exclaimed Roth, who was wearing a shower-soaked bath towel. "Lemme dry off and I'll be with you in a minute." He closed the door and I waited for him to return. A few minutes later, the vocalist opened the door, popped out the cassette tape of Al Jolson's classics, and updated me about the band's latest album and concert tour. Roth sat at a table and ate a modest salad as he reflected on the band's recording studio process.

Roth explained that Van Halen recorded its first four albums – *Van Halen* (1978), *Van Halen II* (1979), *Women and Children First* (1980), *Fair Warning* (1981) – in three weeks or less because of the band's live-studio style which he identified with an action-inspired name.

"The idea is to get there and lean into it where it's a little out of control," said Roth. "We call it 'screaming sports.' You can do this at a typewriter; you can play screaming sports on skis or you can do it in a car. Let's take a car to illustrate: when you're coming into the corner full blast, the radio is real loud and the car starts to slip a little bit out of control, you know you should hit the brakes – instead, try screaming! It doesn't always work, but when it does the feeling and the whole spirit of the event is so much better. And that's what you do – you were out of control. Yeah, maybe you hit a flat note. Maybe that was lousy driving, but what a feeling!"

Roth was the band's chief lyricist, but he didn't place that much importance on his role; in fact, he considered lyrics to be merely part of the song, not some significant element of the composition. As a result, the band didn't reproduce lyrics on the album's sleeve or back cover.

"It's not poetry," Roth pointed out. "If you write it down it reads more like dialogue from a script. It's just stream of thought with high impact music. I make it the lowest common denominator. I figure our music is built from the neck down. You can feel it, you can dance to it. To me, Rock and Roll is far superior to other types of music. That's because there's a whole lot more to it than notes, octaves, and sounds. It's a whole style, man!"

Roth pointed out that there are no hidden messages or debatable interpretive passages in his straight-forward lyrics. "I write this shit while I'm watching television," laughed Roth. "For example, people ask me about 'Mean Street.' They go, 'Dave: what do you really *know* about 'Mean Street?' Dave: have you really been down and dirty? I mean *Dave!*' This is not an autobiographical text. Everybody always writes songs about falling in love, and that's great; I've written a couple. Some people write songs about falling out of love; some people are happy they're in love; some aren't happy they're not in love; some are happy they're breaking up; and some are very unhappy that they're breaking up. I just wanted to write a song about robbing a liquor store – that's 'Mean Street.' To me, that's a very simple concept. I'm not trying to prove *anything* with that tune."

Roth said that he enjoyed recording but he liked performing live even more. "It's the high point of my evening," he stated with a large grin. "As a matter of fact, it is *the* point! Why do you go on the road? Why do you go through all the time zone changes, the food problems, and this and that? Let me give you an example why: I got to New York City at 6:30 in the morning. We had just come in from New Haven, and we pull into the hotel. I walk into the hotel. The first thing I see and hear is this security guy. He's looking at me and I'm looking at him, and just as I get to the elevator, he goes, 'Hey, fuck you!'" Roth laughed as he shrugged his shoulders. "Why do you put yourself through that? Because it's how much do you want to play. It's how much do you actually like to make music!"

Later, I caught up with Roth and the rest of the band at the Spectrum after their sound check. Everyone seemed relaxed. Alex Van Halen was sitting on a sofa, but he didn't look particular upbeat. "I've got this bronchitis," he said. "But it's no big thing. "I've just got to take a little nap before showtime."

Before the drummer took his rest, he stood up and popped a Rush cassette into his portable player. He plopped back on the couch and began his snooze listening to the lullaby flourishes from Rush's Neil Peart. A half hour later, he was up and feeling much better; in fact, he starts telling jokes as fast as a drum roll: "This guy walks into a bar...."

During a conversation about the band's recording style, Alex Van Halen echoed Roth's sentiments about studio fundamentals. "We go in and play like it was a show for the most part," said Alex Van Halen. "I think the results justify our methods."

In another room – one that looked more like a guitar warehouse – Eddie Van Halen was putting finishing touches on a homemade instrument. "It's tuned," he said as he sat down, played a few riffs, and finished off a piece of blueberry pie. Although he had completed his sound check, the gifted musician wanted to play a bit more. "It's a way to get ready for later," he said.

Michael Anthony strolled around, laughing and joking with just about everyone. He seemed like the antithesis of his recent alter ego onstage, where he performed an aggressive solo while drenched in red spotlights. Alone onstage, Anthony dazzled the crowd with his four-string skills. He didn't merely play the bass: he kicked, stomped, and simulated shooting his instrument as if it were some futuristic bazooka – and then played a concluding passage with his teeth. "The solo just sort of developed during this tour," he said. "I enjoy doing it, and surprisingly my bass doesn't easily go out of tune."

Anthony not only provided Van Halen's bottom end, he also contributed high end harmonies to Roth's vocals. And Roth quickly offered his praises. "He's the most valuable player," said Roth. "Somebody's got to be at the mike at the time. You get guys like me and Edward – a bit too energetic – but he's solid, a solid sender every night, every time."

Despite the casual atmosphere backstage, Roth pointed out that the business aspect of Van Halen is carefully orchestrated. "We control everything," he said firmly. "We control the vertical; we control the horizontal. Don't touch the set! And that means everything, from the crew to what we eat backstage. No, we do not have brown M&Ms. It's down to that fine of a detail." Indeed, the designated M&Ms restrictions are stipulated in the band's contract rider. However, the forbidden candy clause is not the pompous demand of over pampered performers; rather, it's an inserted reminder that goofy fun has a place in the business world of Rock and Roll.

"From the album cover to what hotel room I'm going to be sleeping in that night is up to the band," explained Roth. "And somehow or other we manage to get together often enough to decide these things. And then it comes out like you want. You're not being closed in by other people; you're not being bossed around or told what to do. You work closely with other people, but you're in control."

Van Halen was certainly in control a few days earlier when it performed in the Big Apple. The band's appearance at New York City's Madison Square Garden on July 17, 1981 was the first time that Van Halen played at the legendary venue. It was an important event in the band's history. "If you don't make it in New York, you stink!" exclaimed Roth. "You can make a terrific living and have a good time around the rest of the world, but until New York gives you that validation, you haven't made it yet."

The band delivered its power-packed show to the sold-out crowd with hedonistic flair and dazzling showmanship, and the enthusiastic audience's reactions removed any doubts that Van Halen had yet "made it." I attended the after-concert party, which featured such celebrities as Kiss members Ace Frehley and Eric Carr; teen movie idol Matt Dillon; Mitch Weissman, who played Paul McCartney on Broadway's *Beatlemania*; and Valerie Bertinelli of TV's *One Day At A Time*, who had married Eddie Van Halen earlier in the year on April 11.

Bertinelli held her husband's hand as he caught up with Ace Frehley, who had been staggering around the party singing "Popeye the Sailor Man." The two ax men sat down together and chatted while Mrs. Van Halen stood by. "We'll be spending some time together when this tour is over," she told me as she displayed her infectious smile. "We did manage a short honeymoon in Santa Barbara, though."

Roth spoofed the couple's marriage several days after the Madison Square Garden gig when the band performed during its third night at Philadelphia's Spectrum. At the end of one song, Roth picked up a straw hat that had been thrown on stage and read a note that was tucked inside it. "Hey, Eddie, it says his girl wants to fuck you after the show!" shouted Roth. Sitting next to Bertinelli in a special seating area, I noticed her head shaking back and forth in a "no way!" motion. She seemed to have heard such Rothisms before and diplomatically shrugged it off.

Though Roth was playful with his guitarist and new wife, he once again exhibited genuine contempt for most Rock music journalists – and he would frequently mention them during concerts. He had a well-worn line that stated that most Rock critics preferred Elvis Costello over Van Halen because most critics *looked* like Elvis Costello. "There's a tremendous love-hate relationship going on between Van Halen and the press," said Roth with a devilish grin. "The more personal people take it and the more they antagonize over this whole thing, the more dramatic it becomes. And I just fuckin' love it!"

Criticism of the band also came from another performer: Roger Daltrey of The Who. In a national magazine, Daltrey compared bands from the early 1980s with bands from the late 1960s. "Led Zeppelin were great, but then we get all the soundalikes – Van Halen, I mean, the worst load of shit I've ever heard in my life."

Roth responded to The Who's front man with uncharacteristic restraint. "The more complex the idea, the more simple the opposition comes," he said. "Hey, I've got a lot of respect for The Who, but what can you say? In a way, his comments remind me of pro wrestling, you know, how one wrestler threatens and taunts the other."

Roth was more concerned with how the fans, not other bands, reacted to Van Halen. The group's followers purchased albums by the truckload, but singles sales were another matter. Prior to 1982, the band only had two Top 40 hits: the Van Halenized version of The Kinks' "You Really Got Me" reached #12 on the *Billboard* Hot 100 in 1978; "Dance the Night Away" topped out at #15 a year later.

"It's always neat to have that kind of acceptance, and it's always neat to have your song on the radio," said Roth. "But in fact, none of us really care about that. We don't raise singles; we raise albums!"

I crossed paths again with Van Halen when the band returned to the Meadowlands Arena in East Rutherford, New Jersey for two concerts on November 14-15, 1982 (the group had performed a pair of shows at the venue a month earlier). The quartet's concert tour coincided with its latest best-selling album, *Diver Down*, which included spirited re-workings of such classic tunes as Roy Orbison's "(Oh) Pretty Woman" and Martha and the Vandellas' "Dancing in the Street."

"We've never made a conscious effort to make a commercial album, even the new album," said Roth. "We've never viewed it as anything but a Rock LP, a *hard* Rock LP. But Van Halen plays tight, and that's where it's at. For us, it's always been a question about just wanting to play music our way."

Van Halen was playing it much bigger on its 1982 tour. According to the band's management, Van Halen's stage setup featured 1 million watts of lights. "And 107 tons of equipment!" exclaimed Roth with a confident laugh. The singer explained that stage lighting and special effects have to be properly balanced with the music. "Look, a band can really go to extravagance with a lot of moving lights and lasers and what have you," he said. "And what results some of the time is that the audience will watch the *lights* rather than what the lights are trying to illuminate. In the end, the basics are always the best way to go."

The band's "basics" were augmented by the Great Wall of Amps, a stage-wide barricade of stacked guitar and bass amplifiers that warned the fans about what was going to happen to their ears over the course of the next hour and a half. And once again the band delived its performance set in grand style.

After the concert, backstage access was difficult since special passes were issued only to working personnel, security, catering, production, operations, and VIP guests. Additional passes were issued to friends and the press, but no one was allowed to see the band until after 11:30 p.m. I chatted with Roth as the midnight hour approached. He was particularly pleased at the enthusiastic reception the band received from the audience.

"I don't know what it is, but I do know that we're getting better at what we do," he explained. "And, perhaps most of all, we try and push everything we do to the limit!"

True to his word, the band went beyond the limit with its video for "(Oh) Pretty Woman." The audio-visual production was initially pulled from MTV's video rotation when complaints were raised about the story line: a transvestite is captured and molested by a pair of malevolent midgets until the costumed band members – Anthony as a Samurai warrior, Alex Van Halen as a Tarzan-like character, Eddie Van Halen as a cowboy gun slinger, and Roth as a Napoleon clone – come to the rescue and save the day.

According to Roth, the video was not designed to be offensive. "Hey," chuckled the singer, "all we wanted to do was something shocking, but in a serious way. Look, every band does videos one of two ways: either they play the song straight or they act out the song. I mean, if somebody did a song about trees, you'd expect to see some trees in the video. But we wanted to do something completely different, yet in a Hollywood-type style."

Roth later appeared on MTV during a late night airing of the video. The interview evolved into a typical David Lee Roth monologue, complete with one-liners, philosophical descriptions of the band and its music, lots of bleeped-out curses, and salvos of laughter. Despite the minor uproar about the video, Roth was as relaxed as ever. He seemed to enjoy life at its fullest and took pleasure in explaining his situation. But the stud rocker's larger-than-life answers sounded almost pre-programmed, and they seemed to create a kind of artificial barrier which separated the man from the performer.

When I explained my observation about his MTV interview, Roth paused for quite some time. His Cheshire cat grin evaporated into a more serious look. "Well, you have to remember there are a number of facets to everyone's personality," he said. "I guess, in a way, that I'm like a five-sided coin. To date, I've shown three of those sides, but two of those sides are yet to be shown. And if you think I'm going to tell you about them, well, fuck, no way." His smile returned. "I'll tell you, though, nobody's every asked me about that before."

The atmosphere of camaraderie among the members of the band that was so identifiable years earlier seemed to be missing somewhat following the Meadowlands performance. "We go our separate ways when we're not playing," said Roth. "But when we get back together again, everything is refreshing, even the arguments. We're four individuals first and we all have our different interests. One of mine is Tahiti, a beautiful place thousands of miles away from all of this. To me, there's something to be said about a forty-eight-hour Tahitian thunderstorm with the sky lighting completely up every seven seconds or so."

After over 100 concerts, the 1982-83 tour came to an end on February 18, 1983, in Lima, Peru, although Van Halen made an appearance at the California US Festival on May 29, 1983. The band members soon went their separate ways until they got together in the studio to record their next album.

The new record, *1984*, was released in January and featured several hit singles which were made into entertaining videos. Once again, the band went on tour. I flew to Atlanta, Georgia to interview Van Halen during the band's two nights at the Omni Arena on February 22-23, 1984. It was an historic time for the band members: they had just been informed that their first single, "Jump," from the new album was going to be the next #1 single in the nation.

"The *1984* album was basically created in my brother's home studio," explained Alex. "It's given the entire band a new kind of freedom to write and develop more of what we want to do."

"That's the idea," added Roth. "To do what you want to and be successful at it as well."

The singer continued his discourse with a wide grin as he began a series of pre-concert stretching exercises. "All musicians take great pains to tell people – and I will, too, later – how they would be playing even if it was still only in bars, how they would still enjoy playing even if it was just studio work," laughed Roth. "Well, bullshit! I'm content. I never have to work another day in my life. I've got three beautiful musicians to play with. I'm having a ball; as a matter of fact, I'm having a better time now than ever. It's louder than ever and my pants are *tighter* than ever!"

After the band went through its soundcheck, Eddie plopped down in an oversized chair. "I haven't been feeling that well," he said. "I had a fever, my stomach was upset, and I still feel a little messed up."

The band, of course, was doing much better. Alex put the band's commercial status in perspective. "Sure, it's nice to have a best selling record, five tour buses and nine equipment trucks, but those are only means toward one end: playing our music," noted Alex. Those non-musical means added up to 150 tons of equipment and 2 million watts of lights arranged by a seventy-man road crew that was supplemented by thirty additional workers from the arena.

"Look, Rock and Roll shows are events in which everybody – the band, the fans, everybody – plays a part," explained Alex. "What Van Halen tries to do is create a musical situation that also duplicates the feeling of stealing your father's car or your best friend's girlfriend."

Roth explained the band's position atop the Rock world's summit. "Yeah, Van Halen's eleven-year overnight success story," quipped the singer. "It's not like we just put out our first record, you know."

After the initial interview, the band members disappeared into separate rooms or other parts of the backstage area. An awkward quietness set in. The backstage area seemed quite different from my earlier encounters with the band. The atmosphere was more sedate and businesslike. Gone were the carefree gregarious interactions among the members of the band; as a matter of fact, I didn't see any two of them together again until they walked to the backstage area.

Instead of viewing the concert from the seats, the band suggested that I see the performance from a pit area between the front of the stage and the first row of fans. The area was secured thanks to a makeshift barrier and a platoon of security personnel. It was a prime location, but my ears would pay the price with a ringing sensation over the next few days.

The lights lowered and the band emerged from a temporary stairway situated below the stage. The lights went up and Van Halen cranked out "Unchained," a semiautobiographical anthem from *Fair Warning*. "Hot For Teacher, from the quartet's new album," followed as Roth added a healthy dose of sex-tinged vocal yells and assorted bumps, grinds, and thrusts. At the conclusion of the song came the first salvo of bras from the audience. It seemed like a tornado had slammed into Fredericks of Hollywood, and Roth loved every minute of it. "If it wasn't for people like you, there wouldn't be people like us," exclaimed the vocalist to the audience.

Alex Van Halen contributed an impressive drum solo that was followed by "On Fire" and "Runnin' With the Devil," two magnetically powerful selections from the band's debut LP. As the bras continued to litter the stage, Roth picked one up and said: "It's too big to be Valerie's!" The auditorium went wild. "Jamie's Cryin'" and "Everbody Wants Some" were delivered with confidence and authority.

Michael Anthony and Eddie Van Halen stepped up to keyboard platforms that anchored the opposite sides of the stage. The two initiated the opening passages of "I'll Wait," one of three novel keyboard-flavored tracks from *1984*. After performing "Girl Gone Bad" and the title track from the new album, Van Halen played "Jump" to the delight of the enthusiastic crowd; however, a nondescript keyboard solo by Eddie Van Halen was no substitute for the blistering guitar passage he performed on the recording. He made up for it later in the show when he delivered a memorable guitar solo as the other band members stood aside. His guitar was supported by a homemade rack that allowed Eddie to play his instrument in a near horizontal position. He weaved a series of impressive extemporaneous runs that reflected Flamenco, Blues, Psychedelic, and gut-crunching hard Rock styles.

As the rainfall of bras continued, the band completed its set with "(Oh) Pretty Woman" and "Panama." The foursome returned for an obligatory encore: "You Really Got Me." A second encore produced "Ain't Talkin' 'Bout Love," which included a brief chorus of "Happy Trails."

Immediately after the concert, Roth had a staff assistant place a large towel around him and we sat under the stage and talked for a while. I presented him with a fan letter from Hillary Broas, one of my high school students. He read it and kindly autographed a photo of him which I had also brought along. The next Monday in school, I made a special presentation to Hillary, who was pleasantly shocked.

Roth was appreciative of the band's first number one single. "It's a very special feeling," he said. "As I said before, it's Van Halen's eleven-year overnight success story. But we weren't working towards number one. But it's damn nice to be there. However, when we first came down with the keyboard tunes and the first people started hearing it, there was a lot of beleaguering by our colleagues. 'Oh man, you're going to *keyboards*! You're going to lose your following! Hey, that's not Rock and Roll! You guys have sold out, and this and that!' So don't come to the show."

Roth explained the band's philosophy between sips of beer. "I think the integrity of the band lies in the phrase 'to thine own self be true.'" He said, "I've got a little poster on my wall that's got two chickens looking at a turkey and it says 'to thine own self be true.' My father gave me that poster in seventh grade. I don't get the connection, but the phrase fits."

The front man shifted into a higher gear of verbosity. "Van Halen is one of the few acts which plays, writes, composes, and records *exactly* what we want to," he stated. "Van Halen is like a recombinative drug. There are four separate chemicals at work here. You put them together and who knows what you end up with! The fact is, though, it's good for you. Take it! Van Halen has bred a legion a disciples or imitators or copycats or mimics, whatever you wish to call them. Many use Van Halen as a primary source of inspiration and then begin to innovate from there. There are people with Dave Roth haircuts, people with Eddie guitar licks, people with Alex drum sounds. But much more important than all of *them* are the people who are *disgusted* by my posture and the way I do interviews. There are many who *refuse* to keep our records in their possession. Hence, those people were forced to come up with a substantial alternative musically – and that's why we have New Wave!"

Roth used his wall poster philosophy to assess other performers. "What happened to Queen and Elton John?" he asked. "They maintained their integrity up to a certain level. They wrote the music *they* enjoyed. To themselves, they remained true. Then greed struck! Mercedes-Benzs! So they found that if the fourth cut on the second side didn't make it commercially, well, the good life was over. So Elton John says, 'I'm gonna whip up a little "Crocodile Rock" on these babes and see if they swing into it.' And it came to pass that they bought the shit out of it and they adored him. But the rest of his fans, who were with him up to that point, threw up their hands and said, 'you sold out! You made a Pop hit!'"

Roth took another sip of beer and evaluated Queen. "They did the same thing," remarked Roth. "They played Rock, they played this, they played that. They had hits. 'Bohemian Rhapsody,' for example. But to thine own self be true! Then they said, 'we're gonna make some Disco music!' They tried to do another form of music specifically to sell, I would imagine. So their 'Another one Bites the Dust' becomes like Kahlua: you have to have it on your shelf or nobody comes over that week."

I reminded Roth about his Ohio Players-inspired yelps and the commercialism-tinted sounds of "Jump." I questioned why those connections didn't apply to him. "Because I'm holier than thou," he laughed. "Look, 'Jump' was *not* a commercial move. We arrive at our songs the same way we do our videos: in a simple direct way. 'Jump' was shot on one hand-held 16mm camera, nothing fancy. When it was time for me to say 'jump,' I just stuck my face in the camera and said 'jump.' Then I pulled my face out, ran around to the other side of the camera and stuck my head in again."

Roth admitted that he enjoyed the playful and sometimes goofy nature of Van Halen's video, but he was critical of some other artists' audio-visual productions – and one in particular: Pat Benatar's "Love Is a Battlefield."

"All of Pat's songs are based on 'hey-fuck-you-if-you-don't-want-me-'cause-I'm-the-best-thing-you-ever-had-and-I-can-cook-too-but-now-I'm-throwing-your-ass-out-'cause-you-did-me-something-wrong-so-think-about-it-later-'cause-I'm-gone,'" noted a breathless Roth. "So, in this video she turns into a quasi-hooker who confronts this Latin guy with a gold tooth. She's closing in on him. We expect a slow motion shot of her throwing a glass of whiskey in his face. But no! We expect a left hook to the jaw to be delivered by Pat. But no! We expect her to body slam the guy like Andre the Giant would. But no! Instead, she takes four steps back and shakes her *tits* at him! She ends up sending women's lib back five years in the space of three seconds."

I smiled but quickly brought up humility. "I'm not great enough to be humble, Bill!" he proclaimed with a laugh.

We finished our beers and joined the rest of the backstage crowd. After a short while, I departed. Before I left the area, I counted seventeen attractive girls standing in line, each wearing a Van Halen backstage pass affixed to their respective thighs. They had been hand-picked by the band's security personnel before, during, and after the concert. It appeared that another performance would soon be underway.

Despite the festive backstage festivities that followed every Van Halen concert, a major change was about to take place. Internal conflicts – primarily between Roth and Eddie Van Halen – resulted in the lead singer's dismissal from the band. However, Roth rebounded nicely. While still a member of the band, he had released an extended-play solo recording, *Crazy From the Heat*, in late 1984 that included his version of The Beach Boys' "California Girls." Supported by a surfside-flavored video that was in heavy rotation on MTV, the tune reached #3 on the national singles chart; another selection from the EP, "Just a Gigolo/I Ain't Got Nobody," was a Top 20 hit.

During the next few years, Roth scored with several hit albums, including *Eat 'Em and Smile* in 1986 and *Skyscraper* in 1988, but his former partners in musical mayhem topped him on the charts when they recruited Sammy Hagar. "Van Hagar," as the band was sometimes called, generated several #1 albums over the next ten years: *5150, OU812, For Unlawful Carnal Knowledge,* and *Balance.*

However, conflicts between Hagar and the Van Halen brothers resulted in the new lead singer's departure. Gary Cherone, the former lead singer of Extreme, replaced Hagar and was featured on *Van Halen III*, which reached #4 on the album charts, but Cherone and Michael Anthony were soon gone from the band and Van Halen remained relatively inactive for years until Roth reunited with them permanently. Roth did provide new vocals on *Van Halen Best Of Vol. I* in 1996, which also featured previously recorded tracks by Hagar. Another greatest hits album, *The Best of Both Words,* featuring Roth and Hagar vocals, was released in 2004, the same year that Hagar rejoined the band briefly for a second go-round.

Eddie Van Halen's son, Wolfgang, became the band's new bassist in 2007, and the band hit the road with Roth handling the lead vocals. On March 12, Van Halen was inducted into the Rock and Roll Hall of Fame, but only Anthony and Hagar attended the event.

With Roth back, Van Halen's 2008 tour generated over $90,000,000, an all-time record gross for the band. The group – the Van Halen brothers, Wolfgang Van Halen and Roth – returned to the studio in early 2011.

A Different Kind of Truth, which included a number of reworked originals from years past, was released in 2012 with nostalgic fanfare and the album reached #2 on the charts. It had been nearly twenty-eight years since Roth had been featured as the band's lead singer on a new album. The quartet hit the road for nearly four dozen concerts from February to the early summer. Then Eddie Van Halen was diagnosed with diverticulitis, an inflammation of the intestines, and the remainder of the tour was postponed. After he recovered, the band went out on road.

Van Halen's concert activities in 2013 were limited, but the band performed a handful of dates in the United States and overseas. The next year marked the 30th Anniversary of its *1984* album, which included the band's first #1, "Jump." 2014 also signaled the 40th Anniversary of the band's most famous lineup: the Van Halen brothers, Anthony, and Roth. It had been quite a Rock and Roll ride.

Chapter 13

Stevie Ray Vaughan

"Pride and Joy"

On July 6, 1983, I met Stevie Ray Vaughan at Asbury Park, New Jersey's Convention Hall, where the gifted Blues guitarist and his band, Double Trouble, were the opening act for Marshall Crenshaw and The Dave Edmunds Band.

It was late afternoon, and inside, the venue workers were placing the final floor-level audience chairs in their respective long horizontal rows. The only other person in the hall was Vaughan, who was walking around his equipment that had been temporarily placed on the floor in front of the stage. At first, he carefully examined each amplifier and guitar case as if he was one of his band's road crew. As Vaughan periodically looked up at the stage, he appeared to be thinking where the equipment should be placed for his show. Of course, as the opening act, he would be limited as to where he would be able to set up. After several minutes, Vaughan paused, put his hands on his hips and nodded his head in approval. He stared at the stage like a painter who had just completed a canvas; however, in this case, the artist's creative work had yet to begin. There was a Zen-like quality to this ritual of examination, and I stood aside, not wanting to interrupt.

The relative silence was broken when three roadies emerged from behind the partially closed curtain and quickly placed the amps, drums, and guitar cases in position on the stage. Although, his sound check with Double Trouble – drummer Chris "Whipper" Layton and bassist Tommy Shannon – had yet to take place, Vaughan seemed satisfied and ready to perform the concert that was scheduled for later that night. He sat down on one of the concert's front row seats and once again stared at the stage for a few moments and seemed deep in thought.

At the time, Vaughan was on the upswing of a brilliant career, and his third-billing status at small arenas would soon be a thing of the past; as a matter of fact, in a few more years, the native-born Texan would be considered one of the top electric guitarists of all time.

His debut album, *Texas Flood*, had just been released on Epic Records a few weeks before his Asbury Park concert appearance. On the recording, Vaughan's passionate playing seemed to be reviving the Blues Rock genre almost single-handedly. In concert, he displayed even higher levels of energy and intensity.

While conducting his sound check, Vaughan appeared relaxed. Still, he was serious about his craft. He expressed a sense of purpose as he approached his instruments and equipment with the same confidence John Wayne exhibited walking down a Western movie street. He strapped on his guitar and began to play, and he didn't disappoint. Vaughan played as brilliantly for me and his crew as he did for the audience later in the evening.

"I've been with him since I was kid," said Cutter Brandenberg, who along with Jim "J. B." Burlage and Byron Barr, took care of the band's equipment – a no-frills collection of rag tag-looking instruments and amplifiers. Vaughan played through two small amps, a Fender Super Reverb with four ten-inch speakers, and a Vibroverb with one fifteen-inch speaker. "It doesn't seem like much," admitted Burlage. "But it's enough for Stevie."

As Vaughan played inventive riff after riff in the empty hall, each flurry of notes conjured up comparisons with the great guitarists of Rock and Blues, but Vaughan dismissed the judgments; in fact, he confessed to being intimidated by one of his heroes.

"Let me tell you something," he said after the sound check. "I've had the opportunity to play with a lot of the people I admire and respect, like Albert King and Buddy Guy. But you know what? I played some rhythm guitar with B. B. King one time. Well, he stood up, hit one of those incredible notes of his and gazed right over at me. I damn near died. He's the only guy who scares the shit out of me! He really does."

Joined by Double Trouble, Vaughan opened the concert with a short forty-five minute set that featured such *Texas Flood* tracks as "Love Struck Baby" and "Pride and Joy."

Onstage, Vaughan was a commanding presence with his familiar hi-roller flat-brim hat, music motif shirt, jeans, and snakeskin boots. He demonstated his vibrant style without excessive visual flash, although he did play his guitar behind his waist and head at times, and during one song he even stroked his guitar's neck palm down as if he were petting a domestic cat. He was dazzling, to say the least. Vaughan's uniqueness came from his ability to combine lead and rhythm elements into crystal clear shuffle patterns of fluidity, all dripping with Texas roadhouse Blues. His right hand occasionally weaved rhythmic circles while his left hand's fingers bent, pressed, and caressed the strings with a sense of splendor.

Vaughan, though, followed no exact plan on stage; as a matter of fact, there was an improvisational quality about his playing that sometimes reflected more Jazz than delta Blues. Vaughan was also noted for not remaining content to stay within the basic structure of the Blues. For example, instead of returning to the first chord after reaching the fifth on a standard one-four-five progression turn around, Vaughan might remain on the fourth for an additional measure. As such, Layton and Shannon constantly watched and listened to him as he played in order that all three musicians would stay in step. His veteran side men were never unnerved by Vaughan's extemporaneous solo flights.

"We never play everything the same," said Vaughan with a Texas-sized grin after completing his set. "As a matter of fact, we've never even made up a set list before we play."

He grabbed a chair, sat down, and removed his sweaty musical note-covered shirt that exposed a peacock tattoo on his chest. He pointed to the ink work. "I got this one some years ago at Wild Bill's in Corpus Christi," explained Vaughan. "It's actually a square tailed peacock. It's a kind special conversation piece."

So was Vaughan at the time. The twenty-eight-year-old singer-songwriter-guitarist had contributed his tasty six-string talents to David Bowie's "Let's Dance" single and had received praise from the likes of The Rolling Stones, Jackson Browne, Ted Nugent, and other artists. Furthermore, Vaughan was frequently being called the "next Clapton" or the "next Hendrix."

Vaughan dismissed the comparisons. "You know, you can't believe all the things you read, especially when it's about yourself," he remarked. "I'm just me. I really don't know what to think when people start comparing me to all those other great guitarists. After all, I'm just a guitar player from Texas."

Vaughan wasn't just another axman from the Lone Star State: he was at a stage in his career where he could hold his own against anyone.

Vaughan was born in Dallas in 1954. He received a toy guitar as a birthday gift in 1961. He told me that he got his first "real guitar," a Gibson Messenger, in 1963, due to the influence of his older brother, Jimmie, who later went on to join the Fabulous Thunderbirds. His brother also had a large collection of Rhythm and Blues records by such artists as B. B. King, Otis Rush, Magic Sam, Albert Collins, and Albert King, among others. Young Stevie listened with devoted admiration and attention to all of his sibling's vinyl discs.

As a pre-teen, Vaughan started buying his own records. He was particularly influenced by Lonnie Mack, who created such inventive, Blues-flavored instrumental rockers as "Memphis" and "Wham." In 1967, Vaughan heard Jimi Hendrix's extraordinary playing on the *Are You Experienced* album and quickly embraced characteristics of his psychedelic Blues style.

Two years later, Vaughan purchased his first Fender Stratocaster – a 1963 version with a maple neck – and set out to join the Texas bar circuit with his band, Blackbird. In time, his hourly investments in music cut so sharply into his high school studies that he was forced to decide between academics and the Blues. He quickly made his choice: Vaughan left his secondary school education behind and moved to Austin in order to play guitar in a professional setting. Blackbird evolved in Krackerjack, which included Tommy Shannon on bass. However, in early 1973, Vaughan left the band and joined The Nightcrawlers, a band that generated enough attention to secure an album deal with A&M Records. The LP was never released. Vaughan left the band and joined the Cobras, an established rocking Rhythm and Blues band.

Armed with everything from Les Pauls and Barney Kessel hollow bodies to various vintage Stratocasters, Vaughan kept working at his craft. "Back in those days, I just played and played, and then played some more," he said with a laugh.

Vaughan left the Cobras and created Triple Threat (aka the Triple Threat Revue), which morphed into Double Trouble, (which was the title of an old Otis Rush composition). The new band went through a few lineup changes until it became the Blues power trio of Vaughan, Layton, and Shannon.

Double Trouble performed all over Texas. One night at an Austin gig, producer Jerry Wexler saw the band and invited the trio to appear at the summer Montreaux Jazz Festival in Switzerland. Vaughan and his sidemen performed at the festival in July. Their appearance was viewed by David Bowie, who was in the process of organizing his *Let's Dance* album. The British vocalist, like so many others, was so impressed by Vaughan that he greeted the Texan backstage and conversed with him for a few hours. Before long, Bowie invited Vaughan to appear on the album.

Singer-songwriter Jackson Browne granted Vaughan and company the opportunity to record a demo at Down Town, his Los Angeles studio. Things were happening for Vaughan very quickly, but he didn't mind the exciting pace.

"Some people say that we cut it all in two days," said Vaughan. "That ain't too far from the truth, but what we did was record the *tracks* in two days. We did the vocals in another two, mixed it in two, and mastered it in another day or two. And we even did some changing of the music after that. But we still did it pretty fast. We thought it sounded all right." And so did the highly regarded producer John Hammond, who had previously counseled and developed such artists as Billie Holiday, Bob Dylan, and Aretha Franklin, among others. Hammond ended up as the executive producer of *Texas Flood*.

"More than anything, Hammond kept us on the right musical course," explained Vaughan. "He kind of steered us back on the right track when we strayed a bit. It was a good thing, too. After all, the release of the album was very important to us."

Texas Flood was a solid debut hit. It reached #38 on the *Billboard* LP chart and achieved double platinum status from to the Recording Industry Association of America. Two songs were nominated for Grammy Awards: the title track was nominated in the Best Traditional Blues Performance category, and "Rude Mood" received a nod for Best Rock Instrumental Performance. However, *Texas Flood* won Album of the Year recognition from the Austin Music Awards, which had inducted Vaughan into its Hall of Fame in 1982.

The album reflected Vaughan's sonic intensity, passionate manner, and eclectic incorporation of various styles, including one aspect of Hendrix's artistic manner. On "Lenny," for example, which was dedicated to Vaughan's wife, Leonora, listeners can recall the haunting guitar textures that Hendrix delivered on "The Wind Cries Mary."

"Above all, Hendrix was a great *musician*," said Vaughan. "He just happened to play guitar, if you know what I mean. As for my playing, well, I've never tried to get his *sound*. What I've attempted to do a number of times is to get his *tone*. The fact of it is, tone is the *whole* thing in music. B. B. King's got it! Technique is something else, something secondary after tone."

Besides his exceptional guitar work, Vaughan exhibited an earthy, no-nonsense vocal style that delighted fans and critics alike. He sang with obligatory Blues sincerity but added a touch of Lone Star State confidence that elevated his delivery. Above all, Vaughan maintained a Soul-powered vocal approach that easily worked within the band's overall sound. Vaughan's phenomenal instrumental skills were unmistakable, but his singing style was an ideal, though underrated, complement to his six-string expertise.

Vaughan was soon in demand by concert promoters, festival organizers, and other artists. Bowie wanted Vaughan to join him on the singer's forthcoming Serious Moonlight international tour. It appeared that it was going to happen, but Vaughan's label issued a statement on May 27, 1983: "Due to mutually separate interests, Epic Records' Stevie Ray Vaughan will not be joining the David Bowie tour. Vaughan, who played lead guitar on Bowie's new album, *Let's Dance*, had been asked to perform the same duties with Bowie's band. Because the six-month tour would have interfered with his contractual agreements with Epic

Records in regards to his upcoming album, *Texas Flood*, Vaughan decided that it would not be possible to complete the tour and also devote the amount of time necessary to promote his own album."

There was more to the decision than just a conflict over time. It was alleged by someone in Vaughan's camp that Bowie's management wanted control of media access to the guitarist during the duration of the tour. Furthermore, there was a discrepancy about Vaughan's compensation. Later, Bowie's publicist stated that the singer had no objection to the guitarist conducting interviews that promoted Double Trouble and *Texas Flood* as long as the media sessions did not interfere with his work on the tour. Nevertheless, Vaughan did not participate with Bowie on tour. The rest of 1983 belonged exclusively to Vaughan and his band.

Later in the evening after the Asbury Park concert, Vaughan seemed even more confident and relaxed. He explained that the only thing he was concerned about was the consistency of his band's performance. "We're having fun at what we're doing," he said. "And we're just going to keep doing what we're doing. It's as simple as that. Fortunately, the only thing on my mind is maintaining our ability with our musicianship. You know, I've never questioned what I've done musically. The only thing I've ever questioned was the way to go *about* doing what I wanted to do. I once thought that if I ever lost an arm that I'd still try and play some kind of musical instrument."

In 1984, Double Trouble released *Couldn't Stand the Weather*, an eight-song collection that included the band's interpretation of Hendrix's "Voodoo Child (Slight Return)" and contributions from Vaughan's brother, Jimmie, on a pair of tracks. The album was successful and reached #31 on the *Billboard* LP chart. A world tour followed, including a memorable headlining performance at New York's Carnegie Hall. The Austin Music Awards named *Couldn't Stand the Weather* Album of the Year, and Vaughan was one of a number of artists who contributed to the *Blues Explosion* album, which won a Grammy in the Best Traditional Blues Album category.

The next year, Vaughan and Double Trouble became a quartet with the addition of keyboardist Reese Wynans. The group released *Soul to Soul*, a ten-track assortment of originals and refueled Soul rockers, such as Hank Ballard's "Look at Little Sister." The LP did well enough to reach #34 on the charts. The band also earned its third Album of the Year award from the Austin Music Awards, and Vaughan received W. C. Handy Awards as the Entertainer of the Year and Instrumentalist of the Year.

The band returned to the Montreaux Jazz Festival on July 16, 1985, where the group's performance was recorded and released the following year as *Live Alive*. However, the album only made it to #52 on *Billboard's* roster of long-playing discs. It was a minor chart setback but it foreshadowed a personal problem that would later surface.

Vaughan got a chance to acknowledge the influence of Lonnie Mack when Double Trouble was joined onstage in Memphis in 1986 by the guitar great. Vaughan told the audience that Mack was "the baddest guitar player I know," and then both launched into a rousing version of "Wham."

By the mid-1980s, Vaughan struggled with substance abuse issues. His condition worsened and he was hospitalized in Germany, yet he fought back. Vaughan entered a rehab facility in the United States. He later departed clean and sober and remained that way for the rest of his life. In part, he maintained his sobriety by joining Alcoholics Anonymous and sharing his experiences with fellow members who supported him wherever he traveled.

The band hit the road again and dazzled audiences around the world. Vaughan also delivered messages to his audiences about substance abuse. He described his addictions and expressed hope that everyone would adhere to his warnings regarding drugs and alcohol.

The guitarist appeared with his band on television, performing on such shows as *Saturday Night Live* and *The Arsenio Hall Show*. On *MTV Unplugged*, Vaughan displayed his incredible talent on acoustic guitar. He also performed in a handful of films, including TV's *Farm Aid '86* and the big screen's *Back to the Beach* (1987).

In 1989, Vaughan and Double Trouble released *In Step*, an album that reflected the band leader's recent struggles with addiction. *In Step* peaked at #33 on the *Billboard* album charts, went double platinum, and earned a Grammy for Best Contemporary Blues Recording.

One of Vaughan's most memorable performances took place on October 10, 1989, when the guitarist and his band appeared on *Austin City Limits*. He kicked off the set with a blistering rendition of "May I Have a Talk With You," a punchy Blues rocker. The band followed with a restrained but funky version of "Mary Had a Little Lamb," and then launched into the soulful "Look at Little Sister," which resulted in a broken guitar string. Vaughan kept singing and removed the instrument as a roadie handed him another guitar, just in time for him to pick up the tune. An intense "Couldn't Stand the Weather," which included solos by everyone, was next on the band's play list. "Voodoo Child (Slight Return)," with Vaughan resurrecting Hendrix-like riffs, completed the half-hour set. It was an exceptional display of his artistry.

The following year, Vaughan and his brother, Jimmie, joined forces on an album project that was later titled *Family Style*. Under the supervision of producer Nile Rodgers, the brothers delivered ten Blues rockers, including "Hillbillies from Outerspace" and "Brothers," which were written by the siblings.

On the road again in 1990, Vaughan and the band toured the United States and Canada. On August 24, the group performed at Kalamazoo County Fair, and on the next two days the band played at the Alpine Valley Music Theatre in East Troy, Michigan, sharing the stage with Robert Cray and headliner Eric Clapton. After the second show, Vaughan and three members of Clapton's support staff boarded a helicopter for a flight to Chicago. Just before 1 a.m. on the foggy morning of August 27, the helicopter crashed into a hillside. All those on board perished. In six weeks, Vaughan would have turned thirty-six.

Vaughan's funeral service on August 30 in Dallas was attended by thousands, including such musical performers as Buddy Guy, Eric Clapton, ZZ Top, Bonnie Raitt, and Stevie Wonder.

Despite his death, Vaughan's artistry lived on via new album releases. *The Sky is Crying*, which contained previously unreleased Double Trouble tracks, was issued in 1991. The album's production was shared by Vaughan's brother, his bandmates, and others. The Austin Music Awards acknowledged the recording as its Album of the Year, which marked the tenth time that Vaughan was recognized by the organization.

On October 3, 1991, the day that Vaughan would have been thirty-seven years old, Texas Governor Ann Richards proclaimed it "Stevie Ray Vaughan Day."

A recorded 1980 Texas concert was released a year later as *In The Beginning*. Additional albums were released over the years, including *Live at Carnegie Hall* and *Live at Montreux 1982 & 1985*, among others.

On November 21, 1993, Austin, Texas erected a statue of Vaughan on Lady Bird Lake Trail near Auditorium Shores, a place where he had performed a number of times. Vaughan's eight-foot-tall bronze image, created by Boston sculptor Ralph Helmick, depicts the performer with a guitar in hand and wearing his familar hat and a serape. Without the guitar, Vaughan's statue could be mistaken for a life-sized scultpture of one of the Republic of Texas' founding fathers.

After his death, Vaughan also received accolades from a number of sources. He was named one of the top guitarists of all time by *Rolling Stone* and *Guitar World* magazines, and he received additional Grammy Awards including Best Contemporary Blues Album for *The Sky is Crying* and Best Rock Instrumental Rock Performance for "Little Wing," a Jimi Hendrix tune from 1967.

In 1995, Jimmie Vaughan co-wrote and recorded "Six Strings Down," a touching acknowledgement to his late brother and other Blues guitarists who had died. On May 11, 1995, a special *Austin City Limits* concert honored Stevie Ray Vaughan when Bonnie Raitt, Eric Clapton, Buddy Guy, B. B. King, Dr. John, Robert Cray, Art Neville, Jimmie Vaughan, Double Trouble, and the Tilt-A-Whirl Band joined musical forces.

Over the years, other artists have paid their respects to Vaughan in song, album dedications, and tribute concerts. October 5, 2014 marked the 20th annual Stevie Ray Vaughan Remembrance Ride & Concert in Dallas. Proceeds benefit the Stevie Ray Vaughan Memorial Scholarship Fund, which is designed to assist students at the Greiner Middle School in Dallas "who demonstrate a strong interest and ability to pursue a college education." Martha Vaughan, Stevie Ray's mother, has been an active participant in the scholarship program.

On June 12, 2014 the Grammy Museum in Los Angeles opened Pride & Joy: The Texas Blues of Stevie Ray Vaughan, a year-long exhibit which featured guitars, stage-worn clothing, photos, and assorted concert memorabilia. Jimme Vaughan, who served as the exhibit's guest curator, said, in a prepared statement for the museum, that Pride & Joy "will remind people of the incredible musician he was and all the music and love he gave to the world."

In 1983, at the end of one of his concerts, I had asked Vaughan about the importance of remaining true to himself artistically. His answer seemed somewhat prophetic.

"The thing for me is to play my own kind of music in my own kind of way," he said with a smile. "If I couldn't do it that way, I'd die – or go nuts!"

Chapter 14

The Who

"The Kids Are Alright"

I first discovered The Who in my college Western Civilization course during the 1965-66 academic year. The band, though, was not included in the course of study. My Who orientation came from another student in the class.

Fellow Bloomfield College freshman Mark Greenberg, who would later become the drummer of Richard and the Young Lions (the band scored a minor hit, "Open Up Your Door," in 1966), managed to acquire copies of *Melody Maker*, a British tabloid that was filled with interesting articles about the diverse UK music scene. Unfortunately, there were no music publications of importance in the United States at the time. Instead, various teen magazines, like *16*, concentrated on performers' "likes and loves" not their music. Another magazine, *Hit Parader*, published song lyrics and brief artist profiles. That was about it. Of course, major newspaper music columnists avoided Rock and Roll like the plague.

Greenberg, who later dubbed himself "the Twig," shared copies of *Melody Maker* with me in class. Instead of learning about ancient Greece and Rome, we read about such up and coming British acts as

The Yardbirds, The Spencer Davis Group, and The Hollies, among others, and we read about The Who.

The band – Roger Daltrey (lead vocals), Pete Townshend (guitar), John Entwistle (bass), and Keith Moon (drums) – was formed in 1964 (the quartet, minus Moon, had originally been called The Detours). Like so many other British bands in their formative years, the group's repertoire was heavily based upon American Rhythm and Blues tunes. The Miracles' "I Gotta Dance to Keep From Crying," Eddie Holland's "Leaving Here," Jesse Hill's "Ooh Poo Pah Doo," and assorted James Brown and Chuck Berry songs were in the band's early set list.

Quickly generating a local following, the band members secured the services of publicist-manager Peter Meaden, a proponent of the "mod" culture-fashion trend. Meaden changed the group's name to The High Numbers and ushered them into a recording studio.

By the summer of 1964, the band released its first single, "I'm the Face" and "Zoot Suit," a pair of original songs that were based on American Rhythm and Blues tunes. "Zoot Suit" was essentially a modified interpretation of The Dynamics' "Misery," and "I'm the Face," written by Meaden, was a reworked version of Slim Harpo's "I've Got Love If You Want It." However, the single failed to enter the British record charts.

The group reconfigured classic Rhythm and Blues material into something quite different from other British bands that were also exploring the nuances of American Soul music at the time. The High Numbers added a stronger guitar sound and an aggressive rhythmic punch – to say nothing of Daltrey's intense vocal delivery – to create "maximum R&B," a phrase that would soon be incorporated as the band's promotional musical signature.

The next month, Meaden was replaced by Kit Lambert and Chris Stamp. Despite the management change, the quartet continued performing as The High Numbers. On August 16, the group appeared as a support act for The Kinks and The Beatles at Blackpool, a popular seaside resort. Eight days later, the band made its debut on BBC-TV's *The Beat Room*.

Lambert arranged an audition session for EMI Records, but the label wasn't impressed. In a letter dated October 22, 1964, John Burgess, an assistant to Norman Newell, EMI's Artistes & Repertoire manager, told Lambert that he still couldn't decide whether or not the band had "anything to offer."

Later in the autumn, the group dropped its High Numbers identity and became The Who once again.

As a live act, The Who reinforced its musical identity with a calculated mix of instrumental power, demonstrative vocals, and uncontrolled onstage mayhem. Each member of the band was a singular force that commanded attention. Daltrey served as the animated front man; Townshend delivered powerful windmill-like arm sweeps across his guitar's neck; Moon thrashed away on his battered drum kit; and Entwistle, like The Rolling Stones' Bill Wyman, solidly anchored the music with a reserved stance. Unlike Wyman, Entwistle's vocals were an important element in the band's stage shows, particularly in the early days. The group's appearance was complemented with mod-art touches from bull's eye targets on its shirts to the fashionable use of the British Union Jack banner on everything from clothing to amp covers. They were a sight to see.

Unlike the staffers at EMI, producer Shel Talmy was impressed. He signed The Who to a production deal and secured a label contract with Brunswick Records in Great Britain. The band's albums in the United States would be released on Decca.

On its first album, *My Generation*, which was released in Great Britain in December 1965 (the U. S. release came in April 1966), the band presented a collection of Townshend originals and Rhythm and Blues classics including Bo Diddley's "I'm a Man" and James Brown's "Please, Please, Please" and "I Don't Mind." The LP's title track became the group's anthem with its bold lyrical posturing ("I hope I die before I get old"), Entwistle's captivating bass lines, and its chaotic instrumental conclusion.

"My Generation" wasn't the only song that displayed the band's musical vandalism and carefree expressionism in concert. On occasion, Pete Townshend threw guitars and battered amplifiers on other songs, including "Anyway, Anyhow, Anywhere." And more than once, Townshend's extended wind-up power chording resulted in bloody fingers that dripped onto his guitar and clothing. Clearly, The Who was creating a new musical path, both on record and in concert.

Every live performance contained its own memorable highlights, but replacing destroyed guitars and damaged drum kits was costly. Some compromise had to be reached between the band's artistry and the scheduled destruction of instruments at each show. A temporary solution was found when Townshend started using multiple amps on stage. His road crew placed a broken amp within the stack of functioning encased speakers and the non-working one became the designated piece of equipment that Townshend was *supposed* to spear or knock over with his guitar.

Although Daltrey was the band's lead singer, all the members of band contributed vocals. Townshend was essentially a co-lead vocalist, while Entwistle and Moon added occasional backing vocals and harmonies. On The Who's in-concert version of the Regents' 1961 hit, "Barbara Ann" (also popularized by The Beach Boys), Moon handled the lead vocals.

Despite the band's rapidly growing profile in Great Britain, The Who remained relatively unknown in the United States. The British Invasion was in full force stateside with The Beatles, Peter and Gordon, The Animals, Manfred Mann, Petula Clark, Freddie and the Dreamers, Wayne Fontana and the Mindbenders, Herman's Hermits, The Rolling Stones, and The Dave Clark Five scoring chart-topping hits between February 1964 and December 1965. Yet teen magazines were still unaware of The Who, and only a few record stores carried European Rock imports.

Somehow, the Twig secured a copy of The Who's "I Can't Explain" from a contact he had in Great Britain and lent it to me. From the first jagged power riffs of Townshend's guitar, the song demonstrated the raw energy of the band. The Twig subsequently acquired the band's next single, "Anyway, Anyhow, Anywhere," another captivating rocker. The Who's powerful "My Generation" was released next. The song's immediacy was accented by Daltrey's deliberate stuttering through some of the lyrics and the band's slam-bang instrumentalism. It marked the band's third British Top 10 hit, but the record managed to only reach the #74 position on the U.S. charts. The band's next five singles failed to break *Billboard's* Hot 100. The Who needed some publicity on this side of the Atlantic Ocean, and I intended to provide it.

In my June 4, 1966 "On the Record" column in the *Newark Evening News*, I wrote: "For Pop fans who want to be one step ahead of the crowd, get *The Who Sings My Generation*. This great LP features 'Out in the Street' and 'Please, Please, Please.'" However, the album failed to break the American LP charts.

On December 24, 1966, I wrote: "Always one step ahead of the in-crowd, The Who play it strong on 'Happy Jack.'" The single was eventually released in the United States four months later. "The U.S. scene ignores such British ravers as The Who," I lamented in my January 14, 1967 column. I was determined to continue spreading the word.

The first leg of The Who's 1967 tour began in Great Britain on January 6 and ended on February 20. A quick four-day concert swing in Italy followed; the band resumed touring in London on March 2 and continued for another eighteen days.

On March 18, 1967, I wrote: "The Who, one of England's greatest groups, will appear at Murray the K's Easter Show at The RKO [Radio

Theater] in New York." The event (actually a series of shows that ran from March 25 to April 2) marked The Who's first American concert. The band's performance coincided with the release of its latest stateside single, "Happy Jack." The concert – full title: Murray the K's Music in the Fifth Dimension – included appearances by such acts as The Young Rascals, Wilson Pickett, Mitch Ryder, Cream, and The Blues Project.

In the band's brief time onstage (the group played several songs in no more than fifteen minutes), The Who displayed more energy and reckless abandon than any of the other performers, and that's saying a lot considering the sweltering performances delivered by Mitch Ryder, the show's headliner, and Wilson Pickett. From the first sight of Keith Moon's double bass drum kit to the final destructive moments of "My Generation," The Who's American debut was memorable. Moon's percussion skills were extraordinary: a mix of rapid, maniacal rolls occasionally interrupted by selective delicate taps on his ride and crash cymbals. Most of all, he seemed to be genuinely enjoying himself.

In my April 8 column, I noted: "The Who from England were, by far, the most exciting act" of the concert. At the time, the band was performing in Germany until April 19. Two days later, The Who were back onstage in Great Britain

In the April 22 column, I wrote: "Finally, the most exciting Pop performers on the scene, The Who, are catching on in this country with their unimitative sounds on *Happy Jack*," the group's American debut LP. A week later, I wrote: "The Who's *Happy Jack* is, by far, one of the top trend-setting LPs on the market. A definite must for the connoisseur of contemporary Pop music." The band's single managed to reach the #24 position on the *Billboard* Hot 100.

Happy Jack's collection of songs flowed well together. The LP's most unique work was its final second-side track, "A Quick One, While He's Away," which consisted of six distinctly-titled, progressive Rock tracks that were accented by serene and airy Western passages, pub-like harmonies, unexpected structural changes, and diverse time signatures. In nine minutes and ten seconds, The Who redefined Rock music's creative potential; in fact, the elaborate creation was a challenge of sorts to other artists to expand beyond the limits of the traditional sub-three minute Rock and Roll song that had been a staple of Pop radio for over a decade.

From April 30 to June 12, 1967, The Who toured Finland, Norway, Sweden, Great Britain, and Belgium. On June 14, the band crossed the Atlantic Ocean once again.

On its second-leg tour of the United States, The Who were elevated to rockdom's forefront thanks to its performance at the Monterey International Pop Music Festival on June 18. Displaying the organized destructive chaos that characterized its Murray the K shows months earlier, The Who mesmerized the west coast audience. The band's animated performance of "My Generation," which concluded their set, became a singular moment of Rock theater that some artists would emulate in one form or another over the subsequent decades. The concert was filmed by D. A. Pennebaker and released as *Monterey Pop*, a documentary, on December 26, 1968.

Finally, The Who arrived in New Jersey on August 12 at Asbury Park's Convention Hall – but not as headliners. The band was scheduled as the second act on a Herman's Hermits bill; The Blues Magoos opened the concert. In fact, with few exceptions, like the Monterey show, The Who's summer concert run was in support of Herman's Hermits, a band that had generated over a dozen Top 40 hits since 1964 in the United States.

Although my tenure with the *Newark Evening News* had ended, I managed to secure tickets for the first of the day's two scheduled shows at Convention Hall. I had no idea that before the night was over I'd be hanging out with The Who.

The Blues Magoos – Ralph Scala (keyboards and vocals), Emil

"Peppy" Thielhelm (guitar and vocals), Ron Gilbert (bass), Mike Esposito (lead guitar), and Geoff Daking (drums) – kicked off the first show with an enjoyable set of tunes from their debut 1966 LP, *Psychedelic Lollipop*, which included the Top 5 hit "(We Ain't Got) Nothin' Yet," and their latest album, *Electric Comic Book*. Dressed in matching outfits that featured pulsating circles of light, the quintet dazzled the young crowd with its interesting play list.

Following The Blues Magoos' set, the curtain closed, the venue's lights went up, and the stage was rearranged for the next act. The backstage workers moved quickly, and within several minutes, Convention Hall's lights started to lower. Some mild applause erupted and a few isolated cheers rang out.

Then, The Who took the stage – not like the next act on the bill but more like conquering heroes from another land. Of course, the band members' instruments were as much tools of destruction as they were music-making devices during the performance. They shocked many in the audience with combative salvos of power chords, thunderous percussion slams, chunky bass lines, and screeching vocals. When Townshend and Moon destroyed their instruments and equipment at the end of "My Generation," gasps were heard throughout the crowd.

With the stage littered with instrumental debris, The Who walked off the musical battlefield. Most in the audience were gleefully stunned, and the small cadre of Who fans were in a state of delirious satisfaction. Clearly, what was to follow next on stage would be more like the calm after a typical Jersey Shore storm.

One could almost expect that the British bubble-gum Rock of Herman's Hermits would not be well-received by some in the crowd. However, Herman's Hermits were warmly greeted and promptly performed hit after hit with innocuous posturing. When lead singer Peter Noone delivered the spoken word segment of "I Understand (Just How You Feel)," and old standard that had been re-recorded by the G-Clefs in

1961, a handful of Who and Blues Magoos fans shouted out some assorted cat calls. Though only nineteen years old at the time, Noone was a seasoned professional, and he carried on without missing a beat.

After the concert, I walked to my car, a 1956 Volkswagon that had seen better days, but before I could reach it, I heard a commotion outside the Wonder Bar, which was located across the street from Convention Hall on Fifth Avenue near Ocean Avenue. A handful of young Who fans had gathered outside the watering hole's entrance hoping to get a glance at the band members who had gone inside for a drink between shows. Since I had turned twenty-one, I entered the bar. Surprisingly, the place was nearly empty except for several British visitors.

Sitting at the bar (from left to right) were John Entwistle, manager-producer Kit Lambert, Pete Townshend, and Keith Moon. For some reason, Roger Daltrey remained backstage. I walked up to Lambert and introduced myself. "I know of you," remarked Lambert, who acknowledged my Who write-ups in the *Newark Evening News*. It was a very satisfying moment. "Let me introduce you to the boys," he said courteously. Lambert gave me his seat and he moved one seat to the right, bumping Townshend and Moon to the right.

Everyone in the band drank whiskey and beer. I quickly wondered what kind of shape they were going to be in for the second show. Lambert, seated to my right, bought me a beer; Entwistle sat to my left. As a bass player, I wanted to know how Entwistle executed that chunky sound of his, especially on his own offbeat composition "Boris the Spider." So I asked him. "I turn the treble all the way up and the bass down," he replied as he lifted his drink from the bar. "That's all it is, really."

Moon was polite, quiet, reserved, and friendly, and he explained that he was enjoying the tour; as a matter of fact, he was the antithesis of the mad drummer who less than an hour before had destroyed most his drum kit, but he wasn't quite that reserved, as I would discover later.

Townsend was the most talkative and gregarious. Genuinely

friendly, he told me that the band was trying to expand its creative boundaries in a "different way." His mini-Rock opera, "A Quick One, While He's Away," was going to be followed in the future by something "more elaborate." Townsend was true to his word, but the music world would have to wait another two years until the Rock-opera *Tommy* made its vinyl debut.

We continued our conversation and our drinks. I bought a round and they bought a round. This went on for about a half hour. Although the beers cost less than $1 each at the time, I returned home nearly broke that night. Fortunately, I had just enough money for the tolls on the Garden State Parkway.

"Well, we'll be getting back for the next show," said Lambert. I secured a small piece of paper and asked the band members to autograph it, which they did without hesitation. (The signed paper still rests inside my *Happy Jack* album.) Townsend ordered a large cardboard container of beer to go, and then Lambert said to me: "Coming back with us?" Wonderfully surprised, but trying to act as cool as possible, I casually remarked, "Yeah, sure." The five of us left the Wonder Bar, crossed the street, and entered one of Convention Hall's side doors. The few fans that had waited outside the bar closely trailed behind us until we walked past a security guard.

By the time we got backstage, the second show had already begun; The Blues Magoos were performing their version of the Nashville Teens' "Tobacco Road." When The Blues Magoos' set was over, I talked with some of the New York-based band members (I had seen them a number of times a year earlier when they were regulars at the Night Owl in Greenwich Village). I had a brief conversation with guitarist "Peppy" Thielhelm before rejoining The Who. But Daltrey was still missing. I noticed Townshend's broken guitar from the first show lying next to a trash can. I contemplated picking it up, but I didn't. I've regretted the missed opportunity ever since.

Daltrey finally appeared as if out of nowhere and the band took the stage. Moon walked over to his drum kit and placed his beer container on one of his floor tom toms; Townshend was still drinking his beer as he walked out into position. He looked over at me, lifted the container as if he were leading a toast, nodded with a smile, and chugged the rest of the brew. The empty beer container went flying and then all kinds of musical hell broke loose on the second audience. The Who, no doubt powered by alcohol, managed to top the intensity of the first show. In the crowd were fellow Abstraction bandmates drummer Mike Byrne, guitarist Ed DeRosa, and their dates. I peeked out from the side of the stage at the edge of the curtain, and Byrne and DeRosa noticed me. They couldn't believe I was standing there, and either could I at the time.

Decades later, Byrne remembered the concert. "The audience, which was definitely a young Herman's Hermits crowd, tolerated The Blues Magoos, who opened up both shows," said Byrne. "Maybe it was because The Blues Magoos had a couple of hit singles and The Who didn't. But after The Who went on and finished, something seemed to change in the audience, at least in part of the audience. The Who, of course, were great, and people in the audience knew it. I had never seen a band dominate a stage like they did, and the speed of Keith Moon's drumming was unbelievable. I'm still amazed thinking about after all these years."

Byrne described the change in the audience after The Who performed. "Yeah, after they finished their set, I remember a lot of people walking out during Herman's Hermits' set," noted Byrne. "I don't know whether they were Who fans or Blues Magoos fans or both, but to them the music of Herman's Hermits seemed immediately dated and out of place. It seemed like music for little kids and young girls, and some in the audience didn't want to be a part of it."

"One thing that I do remember," remarked DeRosa with a smile. "After The Who finished their show, Mike and I wanted to leave but our dates wanted to stay and see Herman's Hermits. It was absolute torture."

Although the second concert was over, the backstage high jinks were just getting started, but I didn't learn about until years later when I interviewed Peter Noone while he was promoting his new band, The Tremblers. Noone explained that the legend of Keith Moon's outrageous behavior had its start, perhaps, at the New Jersey Shore.

"Keith wasn't as wild back then as he would become, but that night after the show, the both of us dove off the back of Convention Hall into the ocean," said Noone. At the time, there was no rock jetty that protected the back of the facility; the ocean waves slapped against the hall's concrete pillars. Although it was dark at the end of Convention Hall, except for lighting that originated from nearby boardwalk concession stands, the two performers plunged into the dark Atlantic.

Following shows in Hawaii in September, The Who returned to Great Britain and quickly returned to the road starting with a gig in Nairn, Scotland on October 6. That same month, The Who released "I Can See For Miles," an advance single from the band's forthcoming LP, *The Who Sell Out*. The rousing Rock tune scored well in both North America and Europe: it reached #10 on the British charts, and #9 on the *Billboard* charts in the United States. In fact, "I Can See for Miles" became The Who's highest-charting record in America and the band's only Top 10 single. They continued their British concert tour until November 11, and then they flew back to the United States for more shows.

Starting on November 17, The Who performed at a diversified lineup of concert venues, from high schools in Kansas and New Jersey to California's Hollywood Bowl. I saw the band in concert again on November 25, 1967 at New York's City's Village Theater, which would later be renamed the Fillmore East. On the concert lineup were such varied acts The Vagrants, a Long Island-based band that featured Leslie West on guitar, and the quirky Tiny Tim, who played his ukulele and sang obscure tunes from the early twentieth century. The band returned to Great Britain and played several December concerts through the last day of the year in support of its new album, *The Who Sell Out*. By the time New Year's Eve arrived, The Who had played over 200 concerts worldwide. Their extensive concert pace continued the next year.

In 1968, Townshend began writing *Tommy*, the Rock opera that elevated The Who into the top echelon of Rock bands. After the double-disc LP's release in May 1969, positive reviews by the developing Rock press and an enthusiastic reception from the record buying public, *Tommy* reached the #4 position on the *Billboard* top albums chart and spawned several hit singles, including "Pinball Wizard" and "I'm Free."

The band's appearance at Woodstock in August 1969 – and its featured segment in the motion picture *Woodstock* the following year – cemented The Who's reputation as one of Rock music's best groups. The *Live at Leeds* LP in 1970 captured the essence of the band's powerful concert dynamics and set a standard for live recordings that would be rarely matched by any band in the decades that followed. The album strengthened the quartet's popularity, and in the wake of The Beatles' breakup, only The Rolling Stones remained to challenge The Who as the world's most popular Rock act.

Throughout the rest on the 1970s, The Who continued to expand its musical boundaries with innovative albums like *Who's Next*, which spawned such classic tracks as "Baba O'Reilly" and the powerful "Won't Get Fooled Again," the imaginative Rock opera *Quadrophenia*, and *The Who By Numbers*. *Who Are You*, which was released on August 18, 1978, was the last LP recorded by the four original musicians: Keith Moon died of a drug overdose on September 7, 1978, five weeks after the death of the band's first manager, Peter Meaden. Kenny Jones of The Faces replaced Moon and the band played on; however, The Who's most creative and memorable years were over.

During the decade, Townshend occasionally branched out on his own teaming up with other artists on a number of album projects including *Happy Birthday* with Ronnie Lane in 1970; *I Am* and *With Love*, a pair of tributes to Indian mystic Meher Baba; and *Rough Mix*, again with Lane, in 1977.

In the December 26, 1979 issue of *The Aquarian Weekly*, I wrote an article titled "The Music of the '70s," and noted: "The Who shared superstar billing with Fleetwood Mac, the Stones, the Doobie Brothers and, for a joyous while, with Peter Frampton, but the quartet (after the death of Keith Moon) became part of one of the decade's worst tragedies when eleven fans were killed outside a Cincinnati concert arena during the last months of the '70s." On December 3, young concert goers had rushed a narrow entrance which resulted in some of them being trampled to death. Over two dozen other fans were injured.

Despite Moon's death, the Cincinnati tragedy, and the rise of Punk and New Wave, the popularity of The Who continued. A writers' poll in *The Aquarian Weekly* – "The Best Moments, Music & Musicians of the 70's" – favored The Who. Keith Moon was voted the decade's best drummer; John Entwistle was named the second best bassist (Stanley Clarke was #1); Pete Townshend took top guitarist honors; and Roger Daltrey took fifth place among the vocalists (following Mick Jagger, Bruce Springsteen, David Bowie, and Al Green). The Who's 1974 Madison Square Garden concert was named one of the decade's best (following shows by The Rolling Stones, The Clash, and Bruce Springsteen), and the band's *Who's Next* was voted the second best album of the 1970s (Springsteen's *Born to Run* was first).

With Jones on the drums, The Who released *Face Dances* (1981), which generated the Top 20 hit "You Better You Bet." The single benefited from the band's promotional video which aired on MTV. *It's Hard* (1982) spawned two singles: "Athena," the band's last Top 40 American hit, and "Eminence Front," which became a mainstay in the group's concert set list. However, the video version of "Eminence Front" wasn't particularly memorable, as I noted in my *Aquarian Weekly* column, "Video Report Card." The production was nothing more than some hand-held footage of an arena sound check.

Townshend provided a reminder of his musical independence when he released a solo LP in 1981, *All the Best Cowboys Have Chinese Eyes*. He would leave the band within two years.

In 1982, the 15th Anniversary of The Who's memorable Jersey Shore concert, I wrote an article in *The Aquarian Weekly* titled "The Who in Asbury Park: A Hot Night in '67." Once again, the passage of time seemed to escalate. A couple of reunion concerts – notably the Live Aid event in 1985 – followed by a more permanent association in 1989, maintained The Who's profile as an active Rock act, although the unpredictable power of its early days had been diminished. A 25th Anniversary The Kids Are Alright Tour was financially successful, but the band seemed to be going through the motions. Augmented by other musicians and caught up in the excesses of stage production, The Who seemed a bit dated, at least to the band's first generation of fans. In all fairness, though, the members of one of Rock's most aggressive acts were all now in their mid-forties.

In 1990, the group was inducted into the Rock and Roll Hall of Fame. Five years later, Enwistle joined Ringo Starr's All-Starr Band and performed "Boris the Spider" to concert fans in the United States and Japan. The band performed infrequently in the 1990s, although Daltrey headlined some concerts on his own. In 1996, the band presented a number of *Quadrophenia* shows in Great Britain and the United States. At the end of the decade, The Who returned to the concert scene and continued a more regular schedule.

On November 5, 2000, The Who joined the ranks of other rockers who became characters on *The Simpsons*. In the episode, "A Tale of Two Springfields," the band – in its classic lineup with Keith Moon on drums – cranked out a part of "Won't Get Fooled Again." Entwistle had provided his own voice for the project. Sadly, Entwistle died on June 27, 2002. The bassist was fifty-seven years old.

After Entwistle's death, Daltrey and Townshend maintained the band's identity primarily as a live act, utilizing a number of different musicians on drums, bass, keyboards, and horns.

The Who's *Endless Wire* CD release in 2006 marked its first studio album since 1982. It was the band's eighth studio album to place on the American Top 10 roster. *Endless Wire* may have lacked the punch of the band's early albums but the CD contained some of the group's more interesting songs, especially those which reflected religious themes like "A Man in a Purple Dress," "Two Thousand Years," "God Speaks of Marty Robbins," and "Unholy Trinity." However, another 2006 album, *Live From Toronto*, recorded in 1982, did not chart.

On February 7, 2010, The Who performed selections of several hits at Super Bowl XLIV's halftime show in Miami where the New Orleans Saints defeated the Indianapolis Colts, 31-17.

Tapping the nostalgia market, Geffen Records released *Live at Hull*, a live recording from 1970, in November 2012. On December 12, 2012, Daltrey and Townshend performed in New York City's Madison Square Garden at the Concert for Sandy Relief, a musical fundraiser to help those residents along the Jersey Shore and parts of New York who were devastated by destructive powers of super storm Sandy two months earlier.

One of the Jersey Shore communities affected by the storm was Asbury Park, the place where I had met the band in 1967. Convention Hall and the Wonder Bar had survived the storm, and Daltrey and Townshend had endured nearly a half century of "maximum" Rock and Roll. Sadly, Moon and Entwistle did not.

Daltrey, who had first proclaimed Townshend's most famous lyrical line, "I hope I die before I get old," in 1965, turned seventy on March 1, 2014. Townshend had his sixty-ninth birthday on May 19.

Chapter 15

The Young Rascals

"People Got to Be Free"

As The Beatles departed from their historic Shea Stadium concert on August 15, 1965, an electric scoreboard sign in the outfield turned on and proclaimed "The Young Rascals Are Coming." From my seat beyond first base along the right field line, the message was easy to see but difficult to understand. Just who were The Young Rascals? Where were they coming from? And when?

The answers came in a few months.

The Young Rascals – Felix Cavaliere (keyboards and vocals), Eddie Brigati (percussion and vocals), Gene Cornish (guitar and vocals), and Dino Danelli (drums) – emerged from the New York-New Jersey club scene in late 1964. Three of the band's members – Cavaliere, Brigati, and Cornish – had spent some time in Joey Dee and the Starliters, the group that had a number of chart hits including "Peppermint Twist," which reached #1 in early 1962 during the height of the international Twist craze.

Not content to be a backing band for Joey Dee, the trio joined forces with Danelli, an accomplished musician, and created a group that specialized in blue-eyed Soul, mixing energetic Rhythm and

Blues-flavored vocals and punchy rhythms with Rock and Roll earthiness. Without a bass player, Cavaliere played most of the songs' bass lines with his left hand on his Hammond B-3 organ; he also utilized the instrument's foot pedals to add some bottom to the band's sound. Danelli complemented his keyboardist by delivering syncopated drum lines that provided a bass-like foundation to the tunes. It was a unique rhythmic arrangement, and it worked.

In February 1965, The Rascals made their debut at Ferarro's Club Choo Choo (popularly known as the Choo Choo Club) in Garfield, New Jersey, the town where Brigati and Danelli resided. The band members quickly established themselves as first-rate entertainers. As a club act, the quartet put on an exciting show characterized by Cavaliere's powerfully rich play on the organ, Brigati's energetic stage presence, and Danelli's flamboyantly thunderous drum work. Cornish added just the right amount of flair with his guitar and backing vocals.

"Danelli and I had attended high school together, and he was well-known from his work in an earlier band, Ronnie Speeks and the Elrods," said former Choo Choo Club house guitarist Rich Blake, who almost became The Rascals guitarist but was rejected because of his demonstrative stage presence. "They wanted a guitarist who wasn't featured but could meet their needs in terms of playing and personality. Oh well, I kept going. Dino, though, was the best – his style, his unorthodox way of playing. He was really an innovative creator."

The Rascals remained at the Choo Choo Club until the summer of 1965, when the band got booked at the Barge, a floating club located in Westhampton Beach on Long Island. Like the Choo Choo Club, the Barge was packed at every Rascals show. The enthusiasm generated by the New York crowd created a buzz in the entertainment industry.

Sid Bernstein, the promoter who contracted The Beatles to perform at Shea Stadium, heard and signed the band. He also provided them with their Young Rascals moniker to avoid legal hassles with another act that used "rascals" in its title. A month after the Shea concert, which had announced the band's future arrival, Bernstein had the band in the Atlantic Records recording studio. The established label was the musical home of such Soul artists as Carla Thomas, Rufus Thomas, Solomon Burke, Don Covay, King Curtis, Ben E. King, The Drifters, Joe Tex, and Wilson Pickett, among others. Atlantic Records was a perfect fit for the blue-eyed Soul brothers.

In the studio, the quartet was joined by vocalist Dave Brigati, Eddie's brother, who had also been a member of Joey Dee and the Starliters. They recorded over two dozen tracks, including both originals and versions of other artists' compositions. By the autumn of 1965, the group released its first single, "I Ain't Gonna Eat Out My Heart Anymore." On December 27, the band performed the song to a national television audience for the first time when it appeared on NBC-TV's *Hullaballo*. Despite the song's hook-laden chorus and shock-powered guitar work by Cornish, it failed to break the Top 40, stalling at #52 on the *Billboard* Hot 100. The band was on the rise, and its unique sound and style, especially Cavaliere's pronounced Hammond B-3 playing, helped spawn countless local bands around the country that quickly joined The Young Rascals bandwagon.

The group's self-titled album was released in March 1966, and its next single, "Good Lovin'," started its climb up the charts, thanks in part to the band's March 20 appearance on *The Ed Sullivan Show*. As a live act, The Young Rascals displayed a collective energy that few bands possessed, although their somewhat goofy costuming of short pants, wide-colored shirts, and mini-ties didn't promote their edgy soulful posture. In time, those outfits would be replaced by more conventional Rock attire.

On April 30, 1966 "Good Lovin'" replaced The Righteous Brothers' "(You're My) Soul and Inspiration" as the nation's #1 song. Despite the popularity of their chart topper, local bands in the New York area embraced a number of other tunes on The Young Rascals' debut LP, especially the group's reworking of two Wilson Pickett hits: "In The Midnight Hour" and "Mustang Sally."

One month after "Good Lovin'" reached #1, the band released its next single, "You Better Run," which eventually reached the #20 position on the *Billboard* Hot 100. "Come On Up" followed but managed to only reach #43. Still, it was yet another tune that became part of many local bands' playlists.

The band also traveled to Great Britain, where it performed a number of concerts and made appearances on *Top of the Pops* and *Ready Steady Go*, two popular television programs.

The Young Rascals began 1967 with a new album, *Collections*, which featured the hit single "I've Been Lonely Too Long," and a few reworked Motown tunes, "Mickey's Monkey" and "Too Many Fish in the Sea." One of the most impressive vocals on the album was delivered by Brigati on the band's interpretation of Buddy Johnson's "Since I Fell For You," which had been a hit for Lenny Welch a few years earlier. Brigati displayed a spiritual soulfulness on the song – especially when he sang it live – that resonated among the quartet's multi-racial fans.

The quartet's New York metro area base served the band well. The multiculturalism of the city and its outer boroughs and suburbs provided the group's music with elements of Latin, urban Soul, and Afro-Cuban styles, and The Rascals' music was embraced in Canada, where they scored more higher-charting hits than in the United States.

The band was booked to appear at Murray the K's Music in The Fifth Dimension spring concert in New York, an event which also featured Cream, The Who, Wilson Pickett, and other acts. Unlike the other performers who played only a handful of songs at the show, The Young Rascals played an entire concert set, which included the band's next single, "Groovin." Sitting in the audience, I thought the tune was a bit unusual for the hard-rocking quartet – after all, the song didn't even have any drums. Nevertheless, "Groovin'" became the band's next #1 single and the title of its next LP. *Groovin'* also generated a few additional hit tracks: the punchy rhythmic "A Girl Like You" and the eternally romantic ballad "How Can I Be Sure."

I saw the band in concert later that summer in Central Park, but the quartet was upstaged by the opening act: Jimi Hendrix. After the concert, I ran across the members of the Left Banke of "Walk Away Renée" fame, who kept talking about Hendrix's dynamic performance. They didn't say a word about The Young Rascals.

Over a decade later, I reminded Danelli of the Central Park concert. "You remember that?" he said with a laugh. "Hendrix blew us off the stage." Interestingly, the 1967 concert marked a reunion of sorts for Danelli and Hendrix, who had briefly played together as pick-up musicians backing up various artists in the New York club scene years earlier.

In 1968, the band officially dropped the "Young" from its name and released its *Once Upon A Dream* album, a kind of Sgt. Pepper-meets-Hudson-River-Soul concept collection that included lead vocals from Dave Brigati on "(Finale): Once Upon A Dream." The times had been a changing, and The Rascals were caught up in the evolving anti-establishment posture of maturing Baby Boomers. The band started to look different, too. The old look was discarded; beards and longer hair became symbolic of the new Rascals.

The group's "It's a Beautiful Morning" reached #3 on the singles charts, and its follow-up release, the powerful "People Got to Be Free," which featured socially-relevant lyrics about racial intolerance in America, topped the charts on August 17. It remained there for five weeks. At the same time, *Time Peace: The Rascals Greatest Hits* was released and it reached #1 on the *Billboard* album charts. There was no bigger year in the history of The Rascals than 1968, although no one knew it at the time.

The band's *Freedom Suite* LP, which included "People Got to Be

Free," was a successful Top 20 album in 1969, but most of its other tracks strayed from the classic Rhythm and Blues power that characterized the group's previous hits. Their follow-up LP, *See*, only managed to reach #45 on album charts. One of the single releases from *See*, "Carry Me Back," an uptempo rocker featuring Brigati on lead vocals, was a Top 30 hit in 1969, but the next single release, "Hold On," was not successful. Despite its lack of chart achievement, "Hold On" was a fascinating recording. The rocking Soul tune featured spirited shout outs by Cavaliere and Brigati, solid rhythm lines and lead fills by Cornish, and Danelli's sophisticated New Orleans-flavored drum licks. The recording concluded with a jam-like rave-up, as all four Rascals seemed to push the limits of their artistic intensity. However, "Hold On" stalled at #51 on the *Billboard* Hot 100. Nevertheless, the song remains one of The Rascals' most unappreciated compositions.

The Rascals' hit-making machine was slowing down and interpersonal relationships among the members of the band were deteriorating over financial issues and other matters. The band's collapse as one of the nation's most successful acts had begun.

On August 6, 1970, The Rascals made their last appearance together at Shea Stadium's Festival For Peace concert, an anti-war lineup of Pop, Rock, Soul, and Jazz performers that included Janis Joplin, Johnny Winter, Poco, Dionne Warwick, and many others. Despite the concert's theme of peace, love, and harmony, a civil war had commenced in The Rascals camp. Later that month, Eddie Brigati left the band.

The situation worsened. A single release, "Right On," a psychedelic Funk tune from a soon to be released album, failed to break the Top 100. Cornish departed the group shortly after Brigati left.

In early 1971, the group – Cavaliere, Danelli, and a platoon of studio musicians – released *Search and Nearness*, an interesting and well-written ten-song collection that included contributions by Brigati and Cornish. But the album was missing those catchy, rhythmic songs that most of the band's fans had come to expect. *Search and Nearness* spent a week on the LP charts at #198. One of its single releases, "Glory Glory," only managed to reach #58 on the charts. It was the band's last LP on Atlantic.

Two more Rascals' albums were released by Columbia Records – the Jazz-flavored *Peaceful World* and *The Island of Real,* which contained "Lament," one of Cavaliere's best Jazz-Funk compositions – but they failed commercially. The Rascals were history, or so it seemed at the time.

Cavaliere eventually formed his own group called Treasure, which included guitarist Vinnie Vincent, who would later replace Ace Frehley in Kiss. Treasure never proved commercially successful despite first-rate playing by Cavaliere and Vincent's soaring six-string solos. Brigati remained in semi-retirement; Cornish and Danelli formed Bulldog, a short-lived, uptempo Rock group.

In 1978, Cornish and Danelli teamed up again, this time in Fotomaker, a five-piece band that included guitarist Wally Bryson, a former member of The Rasberries; keyboardist-vocalist Frankie Vinci; and guitarist-vocalist Lex Marchesi. The band specialized in a kind of hybrid Rock that incorporated progressive fundamentals, Rhythm and Blues, and post-British Invasion styles.

While working for *Entertainment Spectrum*, I met the band during a sound-check break at South Mountain Arena in West Orange, New Jersey. After playing parts of a few songs, Cornish, Danelli, and I walked into the venue's seating area and discussed the duo's musical past and present. Cornish was quick to comment about the most important item on his musical resume. "We're proud of what we did in the past," he said. "The Rascals did nothing musically that I'm ashamed of." He quickly altered the discussion to his new band. Cornish believed the Fotomaker's musical mix was an asset. "We not only had a Rhythm and Blues background, but we were into English Rock, as well," he noted.

Unfortunately, the band's style on record was nothing more than other typical Pop-Rock creations. Fotomaker's self-titled LP on Atlantic failed to chart, and the group's concerts were not enthusiastically received by audiences; polite applause is all the band could generate. Frequently, Fotomaker was booked as the opening act for such bands as Southside Johnny and the Asbury Jukes, The Ozark Mountain Daredevils, and Pure Prairie League.

"It is difficult in opening up for shows whose headliners are in a different musical category," said Cornish. "But I really don't care at this stage of our new career, as long as we don't get booed off the stage."

Instead of being booed off the stage, Fotomaker was ignored.

The band released two more unsuccessful LPs, *Vis-a-vis* and *Transfer Station*. By the end of the decade, Fotomaker was finished. Cornish, however, remained active in the band G. C. Dangerous, but the group didn't generate any attention from producers and soon folded.

Coincidentally, at about the same time, Felix Cavaliere was attempting a solo comeback. He was also well aware about being the member of a former hit-making machine. "When you've been up at the top, there's only one place to go, and that's down," explained Cavaliere to me in an April 1980 interview. Echoing the sentiments of Cornish and Danelli in Fotomaker, he pointed out that "after the years go by, you take a look at the weekly lists of the Top 200 albums and think to yourself that one of those slots *has got* to have your name on it again."

Cavaliere was hoping that one of those coveted LP chart slots would be reserved for his latest album, *Castles In The Air*, a ten-song assortment that featured some of the artist's most soulful vocal efforts. The album also included contributions made by Eddie and Dave Brigati, who had recorded their own LP, *Lost in the Wilderness*, a few years earlier. Although Eddie Brigati and Cavaliere were once again sharing space on a vinyl platter, the keyboardist shook his head when I raised the question about the possibility that the two former bandmates would be working together again.

Cavaliere stated that he was glad to see and end to the 1970s. "I didn't fit into the 1970s," he explained. "Those great community vibrations of the '60s ended and so did the freedom to make music. The *business* became the most important thing with the music considerations secondary."

Castles in the Air generated a Top 40 hit, "Only a Lonely Heart Sees," and included a well-received track that Rascals fans embraced: a reworked version of "People Got to Be Free," which originally wasn't going to be included on the album.

"The recording of it in the studio just seemed to happen," he explained. "The studio musicians – The 24th Street Band – felt that they *had* to play at least one old Rascals song. And 'People Got to Be Free' seemed to fit the bill. It's been nearly twelve years since that song was released. A lot of things have changed. The '60s had music for the heart; the '70s were more computerized, without those good feelings. Yet I think the '80s can combine the best of both decades if the right forces are combined."

Again, I asked Cavaliere if there was any chance that he would one day rejoin his former Rascals band members. He paused for a moment. "Seriously, though, I don't think it would work," said Cavaliere. "I would rather not do it. I'd like to keep it as it was: a nice memory." I also reminded him that The Rascals still had many fans, especially in Canada and Great Britain, who would support a reunion, and I added that a popular Blues revival was underway once again in Great Britain.

"I really wasn't aware that it was that big over there," admitted Cavaliere. "But I can understand it since the British always appreciated music that was done well."

Cavaliere stated that he looked forward to continue to perform as a solo artist. "All I really want to do is maintain a good standard of living for myself and my family," he said. "But, of course, I'd like having my music played again. If there's going to be a renaissance of the '60s, I'm going to be a part of it."

Despite Cavaliere's rejection of The Rascals reunion idea, he did join Cornish and Dinelli one more time. The trio got together on May 14, 1988 at New York's Madison Square Garden for the Atlantic Records 40th Anniversary Celebration (Brigati did not participate). The record label's party coincided with the 20th Anniversary of "People Got to be Free," which had been a fast-climbing chart hit in May of 1968. Introduced by Dan Aykroyd and Bill Murray and backed by Paul Shaffer's band, The Rascals launched into spirited and extended versions of "Good Lovin," "Groovin," and "People Got to be Free." The three Rascals later appeared on ABC-TV's *The Morning Show* with Regis Philbin and talked about the band's summer Good Lovin' Tour. However, once the 1988 tour ended, the musicians again went their separate ways.

A few years later, Cavaliere was touring with his new act: Felix Cavaliere's Rascals, which consisted of new sidemen. Cavaliere also did a stint as a member of Ringo Starr's All-Starr Band in 1995, performing "People Got to be Free," "Groovin," and "Good Lovin" to concert audiences in the United States and Japan. Meanwhile, Cornish and Danelli went on the road as the New Rascals. However, Cornish later underwent quadruple bypass surgery and stopped performing for quite some time.

Finally, the original members joined musical forces once again when The Rascals were inducted into the Rock and Roll Hall of Fame on May 6, 1997. Steven Van Zandt introduced and inducted the band. "In the real world, in the center of the universe – New Jersey – The Rascals were the first band," stated Van Zandt. "Which is why I don't understand why it took so long [for them] to get into the Hall of Fame."

Each member of The Rascals delivered a few sincere remarks. Felix pointed out that the group wanted their music "to be more than Pop:

we wanted it to reach across races, and social barriers, and to help all of us understand each other a little better." But Brigati's words were the most touching. "We thank the creator, we thank our families, we thank all our fans," he said. "We had a lot more magic. And . . . we had enough. Thank you."

At the event, The Rascals played a few of their hits, but it wasn't the band's best performance. Cornish was physically challenged; Brigati's vocals were a bit off, although they were protectively shrouded by his brother's on-stage harmonics; and Cavaliere didn't look like he was having the time of his life, although his voice was as impressive as ever. Danelli, however, was his usual focused self, still in total command of his drum kit. The band's showing was well received.

Twenty days later, as a member of the recreated 33rd New Jersey Volunteer Infantry, a Civil War living history unit, I participated in a special Memorial Day ceremony in Boonton, New Jersey. The ceremony saluted all veterans but acknowledged Charles Hopkins, a Civil War Medal of Honor recipient, who later became mayor of Boonton. Later, a number of local residents looked on as members of the 33rd New Jersey paid their respects at Hopkins' grave in the town's Greenwood Cemetery. Afterwards, I noticed someone in attendance who looked very familiar: it was Eddie Brigati, the only member of The Rascals I had never met or interviewed. I promptly walked up to him in my Civil War uniform, introduced myself, and congratulated him on his induction to the Rock and Roll Hall of Fame. He was appreciative and gracious, and he invited me back to his house which was nearby. For several hours we talked about The Rascals, contemporary music, and spirituality. Brigati was particularly interested in discussing the plight of nature, Native American beliefs, and faith. The entire experience was something like meeting Henry David Thoreau at the Choo Choo Club. I returned the conversation to music and asked him if the band's appearance at the Rock and Roll Hall of Fame might lead to a reunion of sorts. He explained that his association with the other members of The Rascals was a one time thing. Brigati told me that he had "had enough." Nevertheless, the four band members got together once again for a benefit in 2010, in which Van Zandt and Bruce Springsteen joined The Rascals for a rousing rendition of "Good Lovin.'"

Van Zandt, though, wasn't satisfied with two Rascals reunions taking place over a three-year period; he wanted something more. Much more.

In late 2012, Van Zandt wrote and organized *The Rascals: Once Upon A Dream*, a multi-media production that featured Cavaliere, Brigati, Cornish, and Dinelli performing together again. Van Zandt and Marc Brickman, an accomplished lighting technician, directed the production, which traced the band's story within the context of American history. After a week of performances in New York State, the show opened at the Richard Rodgers Theatre on April 16, 2103.

Reviews were generally favorable. "A show you can't miss," proclaimed the *New York Post*. "Luckily, the play isn't the thing here," stated New York's *Daily News*. "The music is, and it never sounded better."

After its limited Broadway run concluded in May, *The Rascals: Once Upon A Dream* went on the road in the summer of 2013.

"The tour was an amazing healing process," explained Cavaliere. "It was gratifying to be with guys that had made music together reunite and still have the magic that was there many years ago."

The Rascals were scheduled to return to Broadway at the Marquis Theatre on December 16, 2013, and continue playing until January 6, 2014, but the group backed out when a "scheduling conflict" was cited. It was probably more than that. Perhaps the original band members simply needed a rest after their hectic return to the stage after so many years, or possibly unresolved issues which caused the band to originally splinter may have resurfaced.

In any event, Cavaliere was back in action in 2014. On January 23, 2014, Cavaliere was inducted into the Hammond Hall of Fame's first class at the National Association of Music Merchants show in Anaheim, California. According to the Hammond makers, the criteria for induction were based on the company's slogan: "The Sound, the Soul, the One." Cavaliere's distinctive style on the Hammond B-3 organ was recognized along with over two dozen other legendary keyboardists, including Booker T. Jones, Billy Preston, Gregg Allman, Jimmy Smith, Keith Emerson, and Steve Winwood.

"I was very happy to be part of the first Hammond Hall of Fame class," remarked Cavaliere. "The instrument is not a popular one, like guitar or drums, and does not get a lot of press. However, everyone knows it's one of the coolest ever invented."

Felix Cavaliere's Rascals were on the road, too. His lineup performed at the Suncoast Hotel and Casino in Las Vegas on March 22-23, 2014. There's also more music in the works.

"I am currently planning a Christmas album and am back to writing here in Nashville," said Cavaliere in the spring of 2014. "There should be a solo album in the near future, as well. I am and will be forever grateful for the opportunity to create and perform music in my lifetime."

Chapter 16

ZZ Top

"Gimme All Your Lovin'"

During the summer of 1980, ZZ Top – the self-proclaimed "little 'ol band from Texas" – was touring the northeastern United States as MTV, the round-the-clock music-video cable station, was being planned. MTV debuted on August 1, 1981.

At the time, neither the band – Billy Gibbons (guitar and vocals), Dusty Hill (bass and vocals), and Frank Beard (drums) – or the developing music network had any meaningful knowledge of each other, but within a few seasons ZZ Top would be one of MTV's most popular acts, performing in some of the most entertaining videos of the '80s and winning several Video Music Awards along the way.

Until the MTV-ZZ Top hookup, the Texas threesome was slugging it out on the road. The trio wasn't struggling financially, by any means; in fact, the band was doing quite well with respectable record sales and a loyal fan base that stretched from coast to coast. However, ZZ Top wasn't a high profile mega-act at that time, and it certainly wasn't one of those charismatic bands whom the media gravitated to with blind devotion. Yet in a way, the group seemed to prefer it that way.

I met the band for the first time when the veteran trio rolled into

Asbury Park, New Jersey's Convention Hall for a concert on July 17, 1980. The veteran British group Humble Pie, which had reformed the previous year following a lengthy breakup, opened for the Texas power trio at the show. After a dozen years on the road, ZZ Top was playing in a venue that held only 3,600 fans. Yet, six years earlier, the band played before nearly 100,000 fans at its "First Annual Texas Size Rompin' Stompin' Barn Dance and Bar B. Q." at the University of Texas in Austin. To some, it appeared that the band had peaked and was beginning the downside of its career. Still, it had been a good run since the three musicians first got together.

As a young teenager, Gibbons first picked up the electric guitar and was soon listening to such Blues masters as Jimmy Reed, Muddy Waters, Albert King, T-Bone Walker, Freddie King, and B. B. King, among many others. Like his future Texas mates, he was also exposed to the Lone Star State's diverse musical culture which included everything from Country and Gospel to Texas Swing and Rock-a-billy.

Gibbons' first claim to fame was in a Houston-based psychedelic Rock and Blues band, Moving Sideways, which released "99th Floor" and a few other regional hits during the late 1960s. In 1969, the guitarist eventually teamed up with Hill and Beard, who had been in a band called American Blues. Hill and Beard's heavy rhythm section and Gibbons' extraordinary Blues-guitar wizardry merged to form an arresting Boogie-Rock style that was enhanced by gritty vocals and suggestive lyrics that sometimes bordered on being crude. The band played at clubs, halls, and honky tonks, and was subsequently signed to a London Records contract.

The band debuted with *ZZ Top's First Album* in early 1971, but the Bill Ham-produced LP failed to chart. The group's first single, "(Somebody Else Been) Shakin' Your Tree," fared no better. The following year, the group's *Rio Grande Mud* LP charted but didn't break the Top 100 albums list. A tour in support of the album was unsuccessful, too, but they never stopped performing.

In 1973, ZZ Top's third album, *Tres Hombres*, was a break-through recording. It reached #8 on the charts and earned a gold record from the Recording Industry Association of America. Furthermore, the band nearly cracked the Top 40 with "La Grange," which peaked at #41 on the singles chart. In addition to the band's growing chart success, fans, and critics were tuning in to Gibbons' spectacular guitar work, which incorporated many classic Blues styles.

"We didn't hit our stride until *Tres Hombres*," Beard told me after the concert. "In a way, I'm glad we didn't go platinum right away like some other groups because there's added pressure on your second album and your third. Because people didn't catch on quickly to us, we were able to grow at our own pace."

The band's "own pace" resulted in *Fandango* in 1975, and *Tejas* in 1976; both albums went platinum. One *Fandango* track, "Tush," became the band's first hit. The single, with its sexually suggestive lyrics and captivating rhythm section, reached #40 on the *Billboard* Hot 100 and became an essential tune on the band's live set list.

By 1976, ZZ Top became a major Rock act. The trio's worldwide concert tour that year grossed $11.5 million – on ticket sales of 1.2 million – and *Fandango* went platinum and remained on the *Billboard* LP charts for an impressive eighty-three weeks. However, life in the fast lane had its price.

"It just got too hectic," said Beard. "Billy's got a good saying for it."

Gibbons turned to Beard, stroked his long whiskers and leaned into the conversation with a smile. "Either unsaddle that pony or shoot him; just don't ride him into the ground," said Gibbons. "At the peak of the summer of 1976, the tour had reached such ridiculous proportions that it was time to do something."

"Or *not* do something," added Hill.

The three musicians stopped playing and departed to places unknown. It was supposed to be a three-month break, but it lasted longer – much longer. From time to time, ZZ Top's management headquarters in Houston received postcards with postmarks from Paris, the Virgin Islands, Mexico, and other international locations. Management staffers wondered how long the three members of the band were going to remain inactive. The trio's hiatus lasted for a couple of years.

Well-rested and eager to pick up where they left off, the musicians recorded a new album on a new label (Warner Bros.) in late 1979: *Degüello*. The LP's title was the same name as the no-quarter bugle call played by Mexican soldiers during the Battle of the Alamo on March 6, 1836.

When I mentioned the Alamo connection, Gibbons became animated. As a Texan, he appreciated the Alamo as the most important historical site in Texas, but he was displeased with the inappropriate commercialism and cheap souvenir shops that bordered the Shrine of Texas Liberty in San Antonio. "It's kind of a shame how it looks today," said Gibbons. "But the Alamo's got its history." Beard and Hill nodded in agreement.

The band members were also aware of Alamo Village, the reclaimed movie site in Brackettville, Texas, where John Wayne filmed his 1960 big-screen epic, *The Alamo*.

"Yeah, that's Happy Shahan's place," noted Hill about the movie location's owner. Then all three briefly engaged in conversations about John Wayne's Western movies. They shared a laugh or two about Texas history on film and then shifted their focus to the future.

ZZ Top was looking to expand the horizons of its fan base in a unique way.

"A while back, NASA, based in Texas, declared that it would accept applications for a trip on the proposed space shuttle," explained Gibbons. "So we wrote NASA a letter – a very formal one – saying that ZZ Top would like to be the lounge band on the first trip."

The band thought its tongue-in-cheek message would be ignored. "Well, we got this letter back, explaining that only certain scientists and engineers would be allowed to make the trip," said Gibbons, "But they said that they would keep our request on file. So there's still a chance that ZZ Top will be on one of those future space-shuttle flights."

My interview with the band took a pause when the three performers took a break to eat their post-concert meal – grilled steak, which had been prepared by a chef backstage, and some cold beer.

Backstage Gibbons and Hill were wearing baseball caps, similar to the ones they wore during their performance. Long gone were the ubiquitous ten-gallon cowboy hats that were part of the ZZ Top uniform for years. "We've been getting that *Urban Cowboy* feedback," laughed Hill, who was referring to the popular John Travolta film that had been released the previous month. "Everybody's wearing Western clothes and hats these days, so we've been giving our ten-gallon hats a rest."

"But we haven't given up on them," countered Gibbons, as if to reassure the band's Lone Star State fan base. "We just don't wear them everywhere we go. We let our music identify us more now."

Of course, the long beards that Gibbons and Hill wore were more identifiable with ZZ Top than any hat or cap could ever be. Ironically, Beard, the un-bearded band member, sported a mustache. "I don't think our fans mind what we wear or how we look as long as we can keep playing the music they like to hear," said Beard.

"That's for sure!" added Gibbons between sips of beer.

"And one thing about our fans: they're a real loyal bunch," noted Beard. "There were faces in the audiences of this current tour that I remember before we took time off in 1976. I don't know 'em by name, but the faces were real familiar to me."

The band's 1980 stage show was a no-frills, freewheeling Rock-a-thon that usually included such classic ZZ Top tunes as "La Grange," "Heard It on the X," "Tush," and a Texanized version of Sam and Dave's "I Thank You," a Top 40 hit off the *Degüello* LP.

Next on ZZ Top's schedule was a European concert tour. "I'll admit that we're kind of a cult band in Europe," said Hill. "I'd say that our reputation has spread slowly by word of mouth, you know, by mutual friends, not by the media. But we do all right in the United States."

"It seems that no matter what we do or where we play, we always relate back to Texas," said Gibbons. "We seem to stick to our Texas image."

The band's image got a Texas-size boost courtesy of two albums: *El Loco* in 1981 and *Eliminator* in 1983. The first of the two LPs, which was once again produced by Bill Ham, spun off a few hit tracks including the devilish "Tube Snake Boogie" and the punchy "Pearl Necklace." One track, "Groovy Little Hippie Pad," featured a synthesizer intro that reflected Gibbons' psychedelic heritage and an acknowledgement to New Wave instrumental quirkiness. It was a signal of things to come.

Eliminator's appealing Blues-Rock tracks were enhanced with synthesizer and other techno-touches, and the result was a best-selling, multi-platinum recording that produced such Top 40 hit singles as "Gimme All Your Lovin'" and "Legs." Both songs were made into memorable videos that featured the musicians (with their signature choreographed windmill arm motions), sexy story lines, New Zealand sheepskin-covered guitars, and a bright red 1933 Ford coupe hot rod – the "Eliminator." MTV championed the videos and helped elevate ZZ Top to the top rung of the Rock world's most popular acts.

The band reinforced its top-of-the-commercial-heap status in 1985 with *Afterburner*, another multi-platinum release that spawned a number of synthesizer-flavored hit singles, including the Top 10 "Sleeping Bag." The album was essentially an extension of *Eliminator* except for "Rough Boy," a restrained but powerful tune that featured a hauntingly morose vocal by Gibbons and superb guitar work. The eye-catching video for "Rough Boy" was inventive and recalled ZZ Top's aspiration to perform in outer space.

"Velcro Fly," another track from *Afterburner,* was a Top 40 hit in 1986; however, it was the band's last single to score on the upper echelons of *Billboard's* Hot 100.

After extensive touring, ZZ Top released its next studio album, *Recycler,* in early 1990. Despite being recorded in Memphis, the album didn't fully reflect the city's vibrant soulful flavor. Nevertheless, like the band's two previous long-play recordings, *Recycler* was a Top 10 smash, but it lacked the mega-sales and the catchy singles that *Afterburner* and *Eliminator* produced. As a result, the band's contract with Warner Bros. ended. That same year, the trio made an uncredited cameo appearance in *Back to the Future III*.

The band signed with RCA Records and followed a more back-to-basics approach to its musical delivery. ZZ Top created three more studio albums in the 1990s – *Antenna* in 1994, *Rhythmeen* in 1996, and *XXX* in 1999 – but each of them sold fewer copies than the previous one; in fact, *XXX* only managed to reach #100 on *Billboard's* album chart.

Another RCA album followed in 2003: *Mescalero,* which included a rough-edged, pedal steel-flavored version of "As Time Goes By." But *Mescalaro* failed to generate satisfactory sales figures.

After many successful years, another kind of recognition was on the way for the band. In 2004, ZZ Top was inducted into the Rock and Roll Hall of Fame, along with Jackson Browne, The Dells, Prince, Bob Seger, and the late George Harrison. "These cats know their Blues and they know how to dress it up," said Keith Richards of The Rolling Stones, in one of the few non-rambling comments he made during his introduction of the Texas trio. (Twelve years earlier, ZZ Top had formally introduced Cream into the Rock and Roll Hall of Fame with sincerity, grace, and admiration.)

Besides his musical endeavors, Dusty Hill made a few appearances on television. On September 30, 1998, Hill showed up on *The Drew Carey Show*. In the episode, "In Ramada da Vida," Drew and two of his buddies attempt to quickly put a band together by offering potential guitarists the pricey sum of $10. In the next scene, a host of Rock musicians audition for Carey. One by one, each is rejected – first former Guns N' Roses guitarist Slash and then ax-man Rick Nielsen of Cheap Trick. Next, Dusty Hill, dressed in a long black leather coat and wearing sunglasses and a reversed baseball cap, delivers a short bass run. Carey asks him: "Are you real attached to the beard?" "It's a Texas goatee," replied Hill. Carey and his friends immediately dismiss Hill with a characteristic ZZ Top windmill arm "goodbye." It was a very humorous bit. Years later, Hill and his bandmates were featured in the "Hank Gets Dusted" episode of *King of the Hill* in 2007.

When Gibbons wasn't performing with Hill and Beard, he would pop up at various venues adding tasty roadhouse guitar licks to a host of other musicians' recordings and performances. Over the years, Gibbons made appearances with the likes of B. B. King, Sammy Hagar, Kid Rock, and Jeff Beck, among others.

Gibbons also did some acting on television, primarily as Angela's Dad in a recurring role from 2005-2011 on *Bones*, the forensic anthropology comedy-drama.

Nearly a decade passed without a ZZ Top studio album, although two live DVD performances were released: *Live From Texas* in 2008 and *Double Down Live: 1980 & 2008* in 2009.

I contacted Hill in 2010 after I learned that he had seen *For God and Texas*, a painting by Richard Luce that graced the cover of my 1997 book, *Alamo Almanac & Book of Lists* (ZZ Top was actually the last listing in the book's alphabetical section). Luce, a fellow member of The Alamo Society, told me that Hill had a great interest in history and the Battle of the Alamo.

"I guess my initial interest in American History came in elementary school in Dallas," said Hill, who recalled the Davy Crockett Craze of the 1950s. "Every kid was a fan of Fess Parker and Davy Crockett. I assumed that we were all related! I had a coonskin cap, of course. We were taught Texas History first and U.S. History later. Of course, over the years I've traveled to different parts of the country and the world. Once, somewhere, some guy asked me why I was taught Texas history first. I just replied that it was taught to me first. It's our history. We didn't tour Europe until 1980, but when we got over there the people were just as interested in Texas as they were interested in the band."

Hill explained his friendship with Billy Bob Thornton, who played Crockett in *The Alamo* in 2004. "Billy Bob Thornton invited me to *The Alamo* movie set in 2003. He was particularly nervous because he was playing Davy and he wanted to see what I thought about his performance. I said to him: 'It looks good to me.' But as a result of being on the movie set I wanted have some Alamo art. I went to a few galleries to look for something. I went to San Antonio and didn't find anything - not even a good poster. No framed art, nothing. I mean, you travel to Washington D.C. and you can get anything on the Washington monument. I was frustrated by the whole experience. Well, I went to a gallery in Austin and saw Richard Luce's *For God and Texas*. I wanted something like that! Word got out and Richard Luce contacted me."

"It was a thrilling experience to meet Dusty," said Luce. "But I laughed when he told me that he had experienced some *mild* success as a musician. Dusty is a great guy."

"He first created a large 40" x 60" sketch," explained Hill. "I approved and he went ahead with the painting."

Hill was pleased with Luce's completed canvas. "The painting, *The Price of Freedom*, turned out better than I expected," he said. "It's breathtaking; I'm proud of it. I actually loaned it to the Alamo a few years ago. To have a painting I possess – I don't like to say that I *own* it – placed on display at the Alamo was a big compliment."

Hill paused for a moment. "I have a reverence for the Alamo," he said "I like the idea of having no photography inside; it helps give you that feeling."

Hill is annoyed by the tasteless commercialism that faces the Alamo on the other side of the street in downtown San Antonio. He seemed to echo the similar comments that Gibbons made to me about the Alamo back in 1980. "You can't abuse an historical area like that," he stated. "It's a crying shame. Something has to be done."

Although the band's decades-old appeal to perform on the U.S. space shuttle never materialized, one unfinished new tune, "Flyin' High," actually ended up in space after Houston-based astronaut Michael Fossum, a friend of the band, played the track while aboard a Russian rocket that was headed to the International Space Station in 2011. Three years earlier, Fossum played ZZ Top's "Got Me Under Pressure," a track from *Eliminator*, while aboard the space shuttle *Discovery*.

The band eventually finished "Flyin' High" and packaged it in a new studio album in 2012: *La Futura*, a surprisingly strong assortment of classic-sounding ZZ Top compositions. Primarily written by Gibbons, the ten-song collection recalled the straight-forward, stripped-down power of the roadhouse Rock trio from its early years, although some twentieth century studio tech embellishments garnished the project. Surprising, some of the albums best tracks are such restrained Blues rockers as "Over You" and "Heartache in Blue," which display Gibbons' passionate road-worn vocals.

In support of the album, ZZ Top visited large music outlets in select cities, where the band members autographed copies of the new CD for fans. *La Futura* was the trio's biggest success in years. It rose to #6 on *Billboard's* album chart and reaffirmed the band's viability and relevance.

ZZ Top also devoted time and effort to a number of causes that were dedicated to assist less fortunate members of society. At the same time the *La Futura* was released, the band participated in the 60,000

Soldiers Housed campaign, which attempted to secure housing for the large number of homeless veterans.

"According to HUD [United States Department of Housing and Urban Development], over 60,000 American veterans sleep abandoned and forgotten on our nation's streets – our streets, where they've been beaten, robbed, even killed," said Hill in a public service message. "Yet if this happened behind enemy lines, we wouldn't stand for it. Veterans matter. We must take care of our own."

ZZ Top provided additional information about the veterans' campaign on its website.

Beard also supported the Texas BigBeat charity event, which raised funds for Cherish Our Children International, an organization dedicated to "changing lives of the world's most vulnerable children living in the most desperate situations." The drummer also contributed his time to the Mr. Holland's Opus Foundation, which helps raise funds to purchase musical instruments for Houston-area school children.

In 2014, ZZ Top geared up for another year's worth of concerts. Before the band hit the road, Gibbons showed up at Nashville's Municipal Auditorium, where he helped welcome the new inductees at the Musicians Hall of Fame and Museum event on January 28. Among those honored were Stevie Ray Vaughan and Double Trouble.

The Texas trio kicked off its 2014 concert tour on March 5 in Las Vegas, and then performed a few dates in Colorado and Nebraska before heading to Canada. After a brief return to the United States in April, the band's schedule included dates in Norway and Germany.

With every passing year, ZZ Top re-establishes its record as the band that has played together the longest with its original members; as a matter of fact, 2014 marked the 45th Anniversary for Billy Gibbons, Dusty Hill, and Frank Beard as members of the "little 'ol band from Texas"

In 2014, all the band members turned sixty-five years old.

ZZ Top and Medicare. It just doesn't sound right.

Chapter 17

Notes and Quotes

The Beatles

Although I saw The Beatles in concert three times (Atlantic City's Convention Hall in 1964, New York's Shea Stadium in 1965, and Philadelphia's John F. Kennedy Stadium in 1966), John, Paul, George, and Ringo were too far away from me to say hello. I had tried to get closer, though, in 1965, when the band was rehearsing for *The Ed Sullivan Show* in Manhattan.

I had a plan.

Since all the fans were barricaded on West 53rd Street, across from the theater's side entrance, I temporarily abandoned my girlfriend at the time and walked down the block to Eighth Avenue. Then I crossed to the other side and strolled back up 53rd Street towards the theater. Surprisingly, security wasn't that tight on the theater side of the street since all the police were concentrating on the mob of screaming girls on the opposite side of the roadway.

I casually walked into the side entrance and entered a small anteroom, which I saw once again on Feb. 9, 2014, when David Letterman escorted Paul McCartney and Ringo Starr through the same entrance during a segment of the TV special *The Night That Changed America:*

A Grammy Salute to The Beatles. The adjacent stage area was jammed with reporters and photographers. I edged my way in closer to the side of the stage and saw a mass of humanity around The Beatles. Unfortunately, the only band member I could see clearly was Ringo, who was sitting on his elevated drum kit. A security person stopped me and asked who I was – and I paused. Here was my moment, and I was prepared to distort the truth. I first considered identifying myself as a young relative of one of the network's producers, either Bill Todman or Mark Goodson, but I thought that the guard would have probably known all of their sons and nephews. I decided against it and paused again for what seemed like an eternity. It seemed an even longer wait for the guard whose questioning frown was growing with each passing second. Instead, I gave my own name. What was I thinking? He checked a list of names on a clip board and noticed that mine wasn't on it. What a surprise. He promptly threw me out. As I turned away from the stage, I saw Ringo – but he didn't see me.

So close yet so far.

Rich Blake

"Mine is the story of a journeyman guitarist," explained Rich Blake following a gig with veteran keyboardist Paul ("Pauly D") DeLorenzo at Serpico's Restauarant in Barnegat, New Jersey in 2014.

However, Blake was more than just a "journeyman."

He started playing professionally in the late 1950s. His uncanny ability ability to replicate guitar solos from hit Pop, Rock, and Jazz records caught the attention of New York booking agents, who teamed him up with various touring acts. Blake backed scores of hit making artists including The Dovells, The Duprees, Linda Scott, The Essex, The Earls, Freddie Cannon, The Belmonts, The Echoes, Bobby Rydell, and many more.

"Although most of them were polite, some were ego-maniacs," remarked Blake. "So many acts just came in and depended on on-site musicians like myself. Most of the time it was a five minute 'talk over rehearsal.'" As a result, many elaborate instrumental parts or solos that were featured on recordings were eliminated from live performances because the artists feared that their songs could be negatively compromised by the hired musicians.

Blake, though, wasn't in the compromise business.

"I got to play with Connie Francis once," he recalled. "She was going to skip 'Lipstick on Your Collar' because every guitar player she had given the solo to messed it up. So I said, 'listen to this,' and played her the solo – and in several keys. So the song was put back in and she thanked me."

Blake later studied under Jazz guitarist Chuck Wayne and became an accomplished Jazz player, performing in New York area clubs for decades. Although he never achieved major acclaim, Blake remains comfortable in his musical role. "I'm a lounge lizard," he noted. "A *respectful* lounge lizard."

Rick Nielsen of Cheap Trick

Rick Nielsen, the quirky-looking, baseball cap-wearing guitarist of Cheap Trick, was concerned that his on-stage persona got in the way of his creative side.

To some, Nielsen's professional appearance conjured up comparative images of Huntz Hall, the zany gang member of East Side Kids and Bowery Boys fame. Hall's movie characters weren't exactly prototypes that one associated with intelligence and sophisticated creativity.

"I am what I am," stated Nielsen, who wrote Cheap Trick's most identifiable songs: "I Want You to Want Me," "Surrender," and "Dream Police."

"But to me, my songs are just as good as anyone's," he said. "Yet rarely do people think about the real talent in me. Most of the time it's just, 'Oh, he's the crazy one,' and "Oh, there's [lead singer] Robin [Zander]; he's the good looking one.' I'm just as proud of certain things that I've written about – you know, the creating of images and things like that. I guess you could call our music avant-garde, melodic Rock and Roll with unsubtle lyrics. Well, most of the time."

Phil Collen of Def Leppard

In the 1980s, guitarist Phil Collen of Def Leppard viewed the band's early success from a rather humble point of view.

"You can never be too confident about anything, especially in this business," said Collen, who joined the band in 1982 after the departure of original member Pete Willis. "But right now, we seem to have the best of both worlds right now: we're young, and that's an advantage, and we still have the hunger; it's still there."

The band's youthful enthusiasm was evident on such videos as "Bringin' on the Heartache" and the chart-topping "Photograph," but the guitarist was surprisingly frank when it came to assessing the band members' dramatic posturing in their popular audio-visual productions.

"Look, after all, we are just a Rock band," he said. "We're not actors in a Spielberg film."

Jerry Garcia

Jerry Garcia was the centerpiece of the Grateful Dead. Within the protective confines of the band, Garcia casually weaved his extended guitar jams and vocals with relaxed joy. The bearded musician always seemed confidently laid back, even when he was performing in front of tens of thousands of people.

However, it was a different matter when he was alone onstage.

On April 10, 1982 at the Capitol Theater in Passaic, New Jersey, Garcia was going to play his first solo acoustic concert. Before the show, he paced backstage like a jungle cat in a cage. In fact, Garcia looked concerned and somewhat nervous. In an effort to calm him down, I walked up to him and asked him how he was doing. "I'm scared shitless!" he told me, with an anxious look on his face.

For a moment, I was speechless; I didn't know what to say to him. "Good luck, Jerry," I remarked. Then he began pacing again. Garcia seemed unable to shake off his bad case of the jitters, and showtime was rapidly approaching.

Minutes later, the houselights dimmed and the curtain opened. Jerry walked out with his guitar and stopped at the microphone stand and kicked off the concert with "Deep Elem Blues." The crowd immediately went wild and embraced him with cheers and applause. The confident, calm, and relaxed Jerry Garcia was back – just as the audience expected.

Garcia and The Grateful Dead were inducted into the Rock and Roll Hall of Fame in 1994. Sadly, Garcia died on August 9, 1995.

Larry Graham

Larry Graham, the incredibly inventive Funk bassist, wanted the world to know about his musical origins – from the womb.

"I started singing and playing guitar and organ long before I learned how to play bass," he explained. "As a matter of fact, I started performing – well, at least I was on the stage – before I was born! My mom was pregnant with me at the time, but she was still playing the piano in clubs around the San Francisco Bay area. She managed to keep performing until just a few days before I was born. That's how it all started for me; I just went on from there."

Graham "went on" to join the experimental Soul-Funk group Sly and the Family Stone in the 1960s. The band, of course, was a major act that scored with such best-selling albums as *Stand!* and *There's a Riot Goin' On*. He later fronted his own band, Graham Central Station, in the 1970s, and worked with a number of artists on other projects. Graham established himself as a solo artist and scored a Top 10 hit with "One in a Million You" in 1980. In the following years, he continued to perform with other artists, notably Prince, in concert halls around the world.

As a member of Sly and the Family Stone, Graham was inducted into the Rock and Roll Hall of Fame in 1993.

Steve Howe of Yes

In 1980, I interviewed the members of Yes, the progressive Rock band noted for their musical complexities and elaborate compositions. The band – Steve Howe (guitar and vocals), Geoff Downes (keyboards), Alan White (drums and vocals), Chris Squire (bass and vocals), and Trevor Horn (vocals) – marked the decade with its tenth studio album, *Drama*.

At the time, Howe was the reigning "Overall Best Guitarist" according to *Guitar Player* magazine, but he was not content to shift his instrument into cruise control. Howe explained that he still was a student of the instrument.

"Although I was amazed by receiving *Guitar Player's* award, I must say that I won't stop studying the guitar," said Howe. "After twenty-one years of playing, I still enjoy listening to other guitarists. Andres Segovia, Les Paul, Chet Atkins, James Burton, Jeff Beck, and Frank Zappa – they're all talented individuals."

Howe explained that the most remarkable guitarists separate themselves from the rest of the pack in a certain way.

"The great guitarists make their guitars talk in a totally dexterous way," he said. "That's the style of play I really appreciate."

Jermaine Jackson

Jermaine Jackson, like his famous younger brother, Michael, struck out from the Jackson 5 to pursue a solo career. Jermaine had his first taste of individual success with his self-titled debut album, which included the Top 10 hit "Daddy's Home," a remake of Shep and the Limelites' classic, in 1972. Other albums and singles followed.

However, a decade later, Jermaine was concerned about other issues besides new musical offerings.

When Jackson released his solo album, *Let Me Tickle Your Fancy*, in 1982, he was eager to talk about the recording and the music business, but he also stressed the need for entertainers to help solve some of the nation's social problems. His reply still seems very appropriate today.

"People are struggling to get jobs and fighting to keep them, and those who are working are paying more and more taxes," he said, during an interview with him at his Manhattan hotel room. "These forces, of course, have a great impact on the family. One result of these conditions is the increase of street people of all ages and a rise of drug abuse. Drugs are ruining careers and destroying lives. Musicians should get active in something; you just can't keep playing music and ignore the world around you."

As a member of the Jackson 5, Jermaine was inducted into the Rock and Roll Hall of Fame in 1997.

Joan Jett

Is Joan Jett as tough as she looks?

I wanted to find out – and I did.

When she was a member of the Runaways, the all-girl Rock band, Jett maintained a rough-edged, no-nonsense look that almost seemed menacing at times.

"I like being physical," explained Joan Jett, who told me in 1980 that she once knocked out her producer, Kenny Laguna, during a boxing match.

"Boxing gloves, individual mouthpieces, the whole thing," noted Laguna.

"I guess it's because I was a tomboy when I was small," explained Jett. "While the other little girls were playing with their dolls, I was playing with G. I. Joe and watching *Combat* on television." [*Combat* was a World War II drama that starred Vic Morrow and Rick Jason and ran from 1962 to 1967.]

"Oh, and I just broke my foot playing softball," remarked Jett. "But it's not gonna keep me from the stage."

During our interview, I noticed that Jett had a knife placed in a sheath that was tucked into her belt.

"Yeah, I carry a knife most of the time," she quipped. "So what?"

Despite the tough girl posture, Jett was a romantic of sorts.

In February 1981, she sent me a homemade greeting card. It was made of black construction paper and included a white-note page pasted in its interior which read: "Dear Bill: Happy Valentine's Day," and she signed her name to it. Stuck to the cover of the card was red pinback button that featured a black heart.

Tough yet romantic.

Brian Johnson of AC/DC

It's a difficult act to replace the lead vocalist in a successful band, especially when the singer had such a distinctive sound and style.

I asked Brian Johnson what it was like to replace AC/DC's powerful front man, Bon Scott, who died in 1980, and what would the fans think?

"I wasn't too concerned about them liking me or accepting me," said Johnson. "Hell, I was too busy trying to remember the lyrics to all the songs! But I knew that the fans were putting me on some sort of trial period for a while. You couldn't blame them. After all, I respected Bon so much, too."

After the success of Johnson's first AC/DC album, *Back in Black*, he felt more at ease with his fellow band members and the fans.

"It made me feel a lot more relaxed after the LP did so well," he said. "Really, it was smashing!"

Numerous hit albums followed – from *For Those About to Rock We Salute You* and *Razors Edge* to *Ballbreaker* and *Black Ice*.

As a member of AC/DC, Johnson was inducted into the Rock and Roll Hall of Fame in 2003.

Kentucky Headhunters

In 1991, the Kentucky Headhunters caused quite a stir among Baby Boomers when the band released of "The Ballad of Davy Crockett," the multi-covered tune that dominated the music charts in 1955, on the eve of the Rock and Roll era.

Bill Hayes, "Tennessee" Ernie Ford, and Fess Parker, who starred in Walt Disney's TV mini-series, *Davy Crockett*, all had Top 10 hits with the song. The Crockett Craze, symbolized by the frontier hero's ubiquitous coonskin cap, was the 1950s most memorable cultural event for kids.

"We needed to come out with 'Davy Crockett,' make it fast, make it rock," explained Fred Young, the group's drummer, to me in an *Alamo Journal* interview.

The band appeared in a slap-stick video that featured an amazing "bear" and a room filled with coonskin cap-wearing fans.

"We geared the video to be real funny for the kids of today, and invite them to find out more about Davy Crockett," added guitarist Richard Young. "If we came up there all serious like, they would never have taken an interest in it."

The song reached #56 on the Country charts.

Phil Lynott of Thin Lizzy

Phil Lynott, the vocalist, bassist, and chief song writer of Thin Lizzy, helped crank out such classic rockers as "The Boys Are Back in Town" and "Jailbreak," among others.

I met him when he was promoting his solo album, *Solo in Soho*, which contained "Ode To A Black Man," a rocking Rhythm and Blues tune about the Black experience. Lynott was in the business of Rock and Roll, but he was also concerned about race and his legacy.

"I'm Black and I'm very proud to be Black, but I'm very angry about the state of the Black man in the world today," stated Lynott, who grew up in Dublin with his White mother and Black father. "Unlike the sixties, when there was a spirit of great unification, all you have today is a worsening of the whole situation. Africa, the home of all Black men, is dying. If the Third World is not saved, there's not going to be any world."

Lynott was determined to do his part through song.

"I'd like to be remembered for making a few statements that were valid," he said. Lynott, though, died in 1986.

John Mellencamp

I interviewed John Mellencamp back in the days when his management thrust the awkward name John Cougar on him. The Midwest rocker was bold, up front, and honest; as a matter of fact, he still is.

I first met him when he performed an energetic set at the Bottom Line in New York City in 1980. He set the tone that he was not about to be restricted to the confines of the stage when he danced around the entire club during the lengthy instrumental introduction of "I Need a Lover," which had become his first hit the year before.

The singer-songwriter displayed keen lyrical insights about the American heartland on his early albums but he didn't think too much of them.

"I don't consider myself a writer," he confessed. "Tennessee Williams was a writer. Personally, I ain't got shit to say. Look, after ten years of performing, all I try to do is take something insignificant and do something with it."

And he did. Mellencamp was inducted into the Rock and Roll Hall of Fame in 2008.

The Righteous Brothers

The Righteous Brothers – Bill Medley and Bobby Hatfield – defined blue-eyed Soul in the 1960s with the epic "You've Lost That Lovin' Feeling," but the duo decided to hang it up in 1968. Although the pair joined forces a few times over the years, the singers kicked off an official reunion in 1985.

"We didn't plan on a twenty-year reunion but it happened and it was successful and, even more so, enjoyable," noted Hatfield in 1983.

"Ultimately, I'd like to see the Righteous Brothers continue to have a lot of fun musically while turning on a lot of people to good music," added Medley.

In the years that followed, the Medley and Hatfield concentrated on their solo careers while occasionally teaming up in concert. Medley, of course, had a more successful solo career with songs like "(I've Had) The Time of My Life," which was the signature song of the film *Dirty Dancing*, in 1987. The song topped the *Billboard* Hot 100 and earned a Best Original Song Oscar.

The Righteous Brothers were inducted into the Rock and Roll Hall of Fame on March 10, 2003. Unfortunately, Hatfield died eight months later

Dee Snider of Twisted Sister

Dee Snider, the outspoken member of the neo-glitter megawatt-powered Twisted Sister, once told me that getting a record deal was as easy as "getting a Twinkie." However, he pointed out that getting the *right* deal was much more difficult. In fact, Snider was not fond of how the music business operated.

"What gets passed off in the United States as the next big thing – and it's usually from England – is just the result of corporate conniving and exploitation of the market place," said Snider. "The corporate biggies, who know little or nothing about Rock and Roll, say to themselves, 'well, we've shoved this shit down their throats, but *now* what can we invent?'"

After performing hundred of shows in the greater New York metro area, Twisted Sister eventually secured a major record deal with Atlantic Records, and in 1983 released *You Can't Stop Rock 'n' Roll*. A year later, the band delivered *Stay Hungry*, which contained "We're Not Gonna Take It" and "I Wanna Rock." Both tunes were immortalized in goofy fun-filled videos that received heavy rotation airings on MTV.

The fun was put on hold when Tipper Gore and the Parents Music Resource Center (PMRC) placed "We're Not Gonna Take It" on a list of the "Filthy Fifteen" most offensive songs. However, in 1984, Snider stood up for his music when he testified before a U.S. Senate committee that was investigating PMRC's allegations.

"It is my job as a parent to monitor what my children see, hear, and read during their pre-teen years," said Snider in his concluding remarks to the committee. "The full responsibility for this falls on the shoulders of my wife and I because there is no one else capable of making these judgments for us. Parents can thank the PMRC for reminding them that there is no substitute for parental guidance, but that is where the PMRC's job ends."

Ian Stewart of The Rolling Stones

Although I never interviewed The Rolling Stones, I crossed the paths of a few band members over the years, notably Mick Jagger, who was wearing a *Satanic Majesties Request*-like cape, in Manhattan's Hotel Americana in 1968, and Keith Richards, who was shopping with Anita Pallenberg, in London's Harrods department store in 1974.

However, the most interesting band member was Ian Stewart, an original Rolling Stone, whom I saw in May of 1965 when he was unloading the band's equipment behind New York City's Academy of Music where the band was performing. Stewart, who added the Johnnie Johnson and Lafayette Leak-flavored piano lines on the Stones' early recordings, had assumed the duties of road manager after being removed from the band's onstage lineup by manager Andrew Loog Oldham.

It was hard to believe that all of the band's equipment – guitars, a drum kit, and amplifiers – were carried in a rented 1964 Chevrolet station wagon that Stewart drove. The band utilized the venue's sound system, so there was no need to transport anything except the instruments and the amps. Stewart, who looked like a rugged dock worker, handled all the heavy lifting.

Once he unloaded the equipment, Stewart's next task was wiping the lipstick messages – "I Love Mick," "Keith," "Rolling Stones Forever," and so much more – from the windshield; as a matter of fact, the entire car was covered in lipstick! Stewart didn't even grumble at the task, although he always had a stern look about him.

As the years passed, Stewart gave up his duties as the hands-on road manager but occasionally contributed keyboard licks to the band's albums.

Stewart died in 1985 at the age of forty-seven, and the band dedicated its *Dirty Work* album in 1986 to him. Four years later, The Rolling Stones were inducted into the Rock and Roll Hall of Fame. Jagger and company insisted that Stewart be inducted with them. And he was.

Edgar Winter

When Edgar Winter, the Texas Blues rocker, released *The Edgar Winter Album* in 1979, the LP included a number of danceable tunes, such as "It's Your Life to Live" and "Please Don't Stop," which seemed to reflect the Disco craze that had swept the nation. Had the multi-talented musician who once cranked out "Keep Playin' That Rock and Roll" gone Disco?

"I'm not a Disco artist," he stated during an interview in his Manhattan apartment. "But I'm not anti-Disco. There's a lot of confusion out there. People tend to categorize too much these days. Like all musical artists, I've been categorized to a certain extent, but I'm sure the new album will catch a lot of people off guard."

Winter, who topped the charts with the instrumental rocker "Frankenstein" in 1973, saw no reason to join the anti-Disco bandwagon. Instead, he diplomatically explained the dance music style within the context of his own career.

"Essentially, Disco springs from Rhythm and Blues and Gospel," he said. "And that's where my musical background is rooted."

The Edgar Winter Album failed to chart.

In 1986, Winter's fans were caught off guard again when he recorded *Mission to Earth*, an awkward collection of tunes written by Scientology founder L. Ron Hubbard. Following the crash landing of *Mission to Earth*, he returned to more familiar Rock and Blues territory.

"Rock And Roll Is Here to Stay"

Danny and the Juniors, 1958

Index

A Different Kind of Truth 200
"A Girl Like You" 239
"A Groovy Kind of Love" 41
A Hard Day's Night 37
"A Quick One, While He's Away" 222, 226
A Little Bit of This – A Little Bit of That 30
"A Man in a Purple Dress" 232
"A Place to Rest My Head" 20
"A Tale of Two Springfields" 231
A Taste of Colorado 139
A Touch of Evil: Live 98
AARP 30
Abacab 38
Abba 30, 42, 56
ABC-Paramount Records 66, 67, 69, 73
ABC-TV 16, 244
Abstractions 227
Academy Awards 39, 42, 146
Academy of Music 273
"Ace of Spades" 119
Ace of Spades 121
AC/DC 268, 269
Acid Eaters 173
Adams, Jonathan 102
Adane, Tommy 71
Aday, Marvin Lee (see Meat Loaf) 101
Adele 47

¡*Adios Amigos!* 174
Aerosmith 57, 182
Afterburner 254, 255
Aftershock 126, 127
Against All Odds 39
"Ain't Talkin' Bout Love" 180, 196
"Ain't That a Shame" 67
Aladdin 133
Alamo 15, 19, 28, 29, 35, 37, 38, 40, 43-47, 252, 257, 258
Alamo Defenders Descendants Association 43
Alamo, Siege and Battle of 252, 256
Alamo, The (1960 film) 36, 40, 252
Alamo, The (2004 film) 257
Alamo Almanac & Book of Lists 256
Alamo and Beyond: A Collector's Journey, The 35, 45
Alamo Journal, The 44, 269
Alamo Plaza 43
Alamo Society, The 35, 43, 44, 256
Alamo Village 252
Alan Parsons Project 135
Albany (NY) 153
Alcoholics Anonymous 211
Alive! 49, 50
Alive II 50

Alive II Tour 51
Alpine Valley Music Theatre 212
"Also sprach Zarathustra" 157
Alston, John 143, 145, 146
"All Around the World" 69
All Summer Long 3
All the Best Cowboys Have Chinese Eyes 231
"All The Way" 93
Allen, Theresa 104
Allman, Gregg 247
A&M Records 207
Ambassador East Hotel 39
American Bandstand 64, 65, 68, 73, 83
American Graffiti 78
American Blues 250
American Cancer Society 57
American Gigolo 179
American Hot Wax 80
American Idol 111, 138
American Music Award 41
Americathon 106
An Evening with Sister Sledge – Live at the Roxy 158
"And the Cradle Will Rock" 181
...And Then There Were Three 38
Anderson, Ed 183
Anderson, Drexel 159, 160
Andre the Giant 199
Angel of Retribution 97
Angela's Dad 256
"Angels are Crying Heaven, The" 138
Animal Boy 172
Animals 136, 220
Anka, Paul 70, 79
"Another Day in Paradise" 41
"Another One Bites the Dust" 198
Another Perfect Day 121
Antenna 255
Anthrax 122
Apple Records 20

"Anna Lee, the Healer" 7
"Anyway, Anyhow, Anywhere" 219, 220
Anthony, Michael 185, 188, 189, 193, 196, 200, 201
Apollo 156
Apollo Hammersmith 124
"April Love" 67
Aquarian Weekly, The 104, 120, 230
Aragon Ballroom 18
Are You Experienced 207
Arista Records 109
Ark 2 37
Arnold, Eddy 139
Arsenio Hall Show, The 212
Artists United Against Apartheid 172
"As Time Goes By" 53, 255
Asbury Park (NJ) 87, 130, 131, 181, 203, 204, 210, 223, 231, 232, 250
Ashburn, Benny 143, 147, 151, 152, 154, 155, 159
Associated Press 59
"At The Hop" 65-67, 69, 70, 73, 77-79, 82, 83, 85
"Athena" 230
Atkins, Al 88
Atkins, Chet 266
Atlanta (GA) 194
Atlantic Records 37, 45, 109, 139, 237, 241, 242, 244, 272
Atlantic City (NJ) 73, 82, 261
Atlantic Ocean 36, 92, 166, 221, 223
"Atomic Punk" 181
Attila the Hun 116
Auditorium Shores 213
Augusta (GA) 21
Austin (TX) 207, 205
Austin City Limits 212, 214
Austin Music Awards 209-211, 213
Australia 2, 27-29, 32, 73, 110, 111, 125, 169
Australian Boys Choir 111
Austria 127

Index

Avalon, Frankie 84
Aykroyd, Dan 244

"Baba O'Reilly" 229
Babbitt, Bob 45-47
"Baby Baby Please" 150
Baby Boom 49, 51, 269
"Baby, I Love You" 167, 168
"Baby You Come Rolling Cross My Mind" 16
Back in Black 269
Back to the Beach 212
Back to the Future III 255
"Back to the Hop" 75
Back to the Hop 83
Bad Attitude 109
Badfinger 103
Bain, Rodger 88
Baker, Arthur 173
Baker, Ginger 136
Balance 200
Ballbreaker 269
"Ballad of Davy Crockett, The" 15, 43, 269
Ballard, Hank 211
Banditos 152
Banks, Jim 41
Banks, Tony 37, 43
"Banjo Man" 20
"Bang to Rights" 120
"Barbara Ann" 3, 220
Barclay's Center 60
Bare Bones 29
Barge 236
Barigian, Warren 105
Barkeys 148
Barnegat (NJ) 262
Barr, Byron 204
Barry, Len 76
Baryshnikov 180
Basie, Count 37

Basile, Frank 30
Bastard, The 118
Bastards 126
Bastards 123
Bat Out of Hell 102, 103-107, 110-112
Bat Out of Hell: Live with the Melbourne Symphony Orchestra 111
Bat Out of Hell II: Back into Hell 109
Bat Out of Hell III: The Monster is Loose 111
Battin, Skip 24
BBC-TV 219
"Be My Girl" 64
"Be True to Your School" 2, 11
Beach Boys 1-13, 134, 135, 199, 220
Beach Boys Concert 3
Beach Boys Party! 3
Beach Boys Today! 3
Beacon Theater 80
Beat Room, The 219
Beard, Frank 249-253, 256, 259
Beatlefest 140
Beatles 3, 5, 7, 20, 22, 37, 38, 76, 117, 129, 132, 138, 149, 166, 218, 220, 229, 235, 236, 261, 262
Beatles Stories 139
Beau Brummels 4
Beautiful Boy 110
Beck, Jeff 13, 256, 266
Belgium 223
Belknap, Raymond 95
Bell, Marc 167
Bellamy Brothers 15, 21, 26, 28
Belmonts 80, 262
Benatar, Pat 199
Berlin Wall 173
Bernstein, Sid 236, 237
Berry, Chuck 2, 8, 78, 79, 116, 135, 218
Berte, Loredana 158
Bertinelli, Valerie 190, 196
Bertorelli, Andrea 38

Best, Pete 117
Best of Both Worlds 200
Best of Herman's Hermits 130
Best of Herman's Hermits, Vol. 2 130
Best of Herman's Hermits, Vol. 3 132
Best of the Beach Boys 3
Best of the Beach Boys Vol. 2 7
Best of the Beach Boys Vol. 3 7
"Beth" 50, 51, 53, 56
Bethel (NY) 77
"Better By You, Better Than Me" 96
Beverly Hills (CA) 139
Big Brother and the Holding Company 4
Big Guitars – Vol. I 29
Big Guitars – Vol. II 29
Billboard 3, 6, 11, 18, 20, 25, 50, 51, 55-57, 66, 68, 69, 74-76, 78, 83, 102, 109, 112, 119, 130, 132, 135, 165, 167, 172-174, 181, 191, 208, 210-212, 221, 222, 228, 229, 237-240, 251, 255, 258, 271
Billy and the Essentials 76
Billy J. Kramer and the Dakotas 133
Binks, Les 89
"Birthday Party" 76
Bitburg (Germany) 173
Bittan, Roy 106
"Bittersweet" 155
Black Dog 110
Black Sabbath 88, 94, 98, 99, 133
"Black Diamond" 50
Black Ice 269
Blackbird 207
Blackpool (UK) 218
Blackwell, Robert 69
Blackwell, Dewayne 29
Blake, Rich 236, 262-263
Blast 162
Blind Before I Stop 109
"Blitzkrieg Bop" 166, 176
Blondie 172, 175, 184
Blood, Sweat & Tears 152
Bloomfield College 217
"Blue and Broken Hearted Me" 25
Blue Magoos 130, 223-227
Blue Öyster Cult 118
Blues Brothers Band 106
Blues Explosion 211
Blues Project 222
BMI 139
BMI Icon Award 139
"Bohemian Rhapsody" 198
Bomber 119
Bonds, Gary U. S. 168
Bones 256
Bon Jovi 168
"Bonzo Goes to Bitburg" 173
Boone, Pat 67
Boonton (NJ) 245
Bop 64, 65
"Boris the Spider" 225, 231
Borisoff, Leonard 76
"Born to Die in Berlin" 174
Born To Run 103, 230
Boston (MA) 72, 82, 213
Boston Arena 72
Both Sides 41
"Both Sides of the Story" 41
Bottom Line 270
Bowen, Jimmy 27
Bowery Boys 263
Bowie, David 133, 206, 208-210, 230
Bowie, Jim 35
"Boys Are Back in Town, The" 120, 121, 270
Brackettville (TX) 252
Brady Bunch, The 16
Brain Drain 173
Brandenberg, Cutter 204
Brazil 54
"Breaking the Law" 87, 90, 96, 98
Brennan, Kathleen 174
Brescia, Vance 137, 138

Index

Brickman, Marc 246
Brigati, Dave 237, 239, 242, 245
Brigati, Eddie 235-242, 244-246
"Bringin' On the Heartache" 264
Brisbane (Australia) 29
Bristol (UK) 133
Bristol Hippodrome 133
British Blues Explosion 139
British Invasion 3, 4, 22, 49, 76, 140, 220, 241
British Phonographic Industry 125
British Steel 87, 90
Broadway 39, 78, 190, 246
Broas, Hillary 197
Brockenback Winery 125
Bronx (NY) 82
Brooklyn (NY) 49, 58-62, 82
Brooks, Garth 15, 26
Brooks, Terron 46
Bronze Records 118
"Brothers" 212
Brown, James 148, 149, 181, 218, 219
Brown, Jim 152
Brown, Larry 65
Brown, P. R. 111
Brown, W. Earl 119
Brown, Warrick 160
Browne, Jackson 105, 206, 208, 255
Browne, Mark 134
Brubaker 21
Bruce, Jack 183
Brunswick Records 219
Brütal Legend 123
Bryson, Wally 241
Buckinghams 1, 6
Budnitz, Roy 106
Bulldog 241
Bundy, Al 137
Bundy, Axel 137
Burgess, John 219
Burke, Clem 172

Burke, Solomon 152, 237
Burlage, Jim "J. B." 204
Burrito Works 28
Burston, Michael "Würzel" 122
Burton, James 16, 21, 22, 266
Bus Stop Records 134
Busey, Gary 112
Buslowe, Steve 108, 109
Buster 41
...But Seriously 41
"By Myself" 54
Byrds 18
Byrne, Mike 227

Cadd, Brian 29
Cadillac 87
California 1, 2, 6, 16, 27, 102, 111, 112, 136, 138, 139, 150, 181, 183, 185, 194, 228
"California Girls" 3, 6, 199
California Jukebox 27
Campbell, Glen 2
Campbell, Phil "Wizzo" 122, 127
Canada 29, 63, 75, 111, 117, 125, 151-153, 159, 160, 185, 212, 243, 259
Cancer Support Community 57, 59
"Candy Cane, Sugary Plum" 75
Cannon, Freddie 85, 262
"Can't Stop Loving You" 42
Capitol Records 3, 12, 13
Capitol Theatre 156, 265
Carey, Drew 174, 255
Caribbean Sea 85
Carnegie Hall 156, 210
Carlucci, Bill 75, 78
Carnes, Kim 15, 21
Carson, Johnny 40
Carr, Eric 54, 190
"Carry Me Back" 240
Casablanca 53
Casablanca Records 50, 53, 134

Cassidy, David 133
Cassidy, Hopalong 51
Cash, Johnny 15
Cashbox 83
Cast You Fate to the Wind 29
Castles in the Air 242, 243
CATV 162
Caulton, Mel 143, 145
Cavalcade of Stars 148
Cavaliere, Felix 235-237, 240-247
Cavern Club 117
CBGB 166
CBS Records 22-24, 134
Celebrity Apprentice 112
Cellar 154, 162
Central Park 239
Cevey, Orianne 42
Change 161
Chairmen of the Board 135
Cheap Trick 169, 174, 175, 256, 263
Checker, Chubby 76, 84
Cheetah 146, 147
Chelsea 49
Chemerka, Debbie 40, 46, 98, 136
Cher 10, 105, 106
Cherish Our Children Int'l 259
Cherone, Gary 200
Chevrolet 70, 273
Chicago (IL) 6, 18, 39, 40, 68, 120, 213
China 27
Chiswick Records 118
Chosen Few, The 98
Choo Choo Club 59
Christmas 59, 75, 95
Christmas at Baxters 29
Cincinnati (OH) 156, 230
"City Life" 155
Civil War 245
Clapton, Eric 135, 206, 212-214
Clark, Dave 135

Clark, Dick 65, 66, 69, 73, 83
Clark, Petula 220
Clarke, "Fast" Eddie 118, 120
Clarke, Stanley 230
Clash, 230
Clinton, George 161
"Closer to You" 25
Cobra 5
Cobras 207
Cocktail 10
Cohen, Leonard 56
Cole, Natalie 42
"Cold Gin" 50
Cold War 77
Collections 238
Collen, Phil 264
Collins, Albert 206
Collins, Lilly 39
Collins, Mathew 42
Collins, Nicholas 42
Collins, Phil 29, 35-47
Collins, Simon 38
Colorado 259
Columbia Pictures 70
Columbia Records 89
Columbia World of Sports: Rodeo Daredevils 72
Colvin, Douglas 165
Combat 268
"Come On Up" 238
Commodores 55, 143, 146, 147, 155, 156, 158
Communism 77
Concert For Sandy Relief 232
Concorde 40
Conner, George 134
Convention Hall 87, 90-92, 130, 131, 181, 203, 223-227, 232, 250
Conway, Lee 28
Conway Recording Studios 158
Coolidge, Rita 20

Index

Cordell, Richie 171
Corley, Robin David 151, 154, 159, 161, 162
Corman, Roger 167
Cornish, Gene 235-237, 240-242, 244-246
Coronation Street 132
Corpus Christi (TX) 206
Costello, Elvis 190
Cougar, John [see John Mellencamp] 270
Couldn't Have Said it Better 110
"Could This be Magic" 183
Couldn't Stand the Weather 210, 212
Courtenay, Tom 130
Covay, Don 237
Cowap, Peter 133
"Cowboy Beat" 26
Cray, Robert 212, 214
Crazy in Alabama 110
Crazy From the Heat 199
Cream 88, 181, 183, 222, 238, 255
Crenshaw, Marshall 203
Crickets 67, 70, 73
Criscuola, Peter 49
Criss, Gigi 59
Criss, Peter 49-61
Criss, Jenilee 52
"Crocodile Rock" 198
Crockett, Davy 15, 35, 36, 38, 43, 44, 257
Crockett, Davy (TV) 36, 43, 269
Crockett Hotel 20
Crosby, David 36
"Cry For a Shadow" 29
Crystal Mansion 78
CSI 160
Cummings, John 165
Curb Records 24, 25, 27, 28
Curtis, King 237
Cutner, Bernard 150
Cutner, Paul 149, 150

"Daddy's Home" 267
Daily News (NY) 246
Daking, Geoff 224
Dalce, Jerry 159
Dallas (TX) 26, 40, 206, 213, 214, 257
Dalton, Dan 16
Dalton, David 110
Daltrey, Roger 191, 218-221, 225-227, 230-232
Damned 175
Dance Into the Night 42
"Dance the Night Away" 191
"Dancing in the Street" 191
"Dancing on Your Grave" 122
"Dandy" 131
Danelli, Dino 235, 236, 239-242, 244, 245
Daniels, Charles 145
Daniels, Stephen 143-163
Danny and the Juniors 63-85
Daughters of the Republic of Texas 38, 43
Dave Clark Five 135, 220
Dave Edmunds Band 203
Davis, Mac 21
Davis, Spencer 137
Davis, Tommy 149
"Davy Crockett at the Alamo" 36
Davy Crockett Craze 15, 257, 269
"Daydreamer" 75
"Dawn of Correction" 77
Dazz Band 159
Dead Ringer 106, 107, 109
Decca Records 49, 219
Dee, Joey 235, 237
Dee, Mikkey 123
"Deep Elem Blues" 265
Deep Purple 133, 181
Def Leppard 171, 264
Defenders of the Faith 95
DeFore, John 124
Deguello 252, 254
Dells 255

DeLorenzo, Paul 262
Delphonics 148, 149
Demolition 97
Denmark 29, 185
Deodato, Eumir 157
Derringer, Rick 109
DeRosa, Ed 227
Destroyer 49, 50
"Deuce" 50
Detours 218
"Devil's Child" 93
DeVito, Karla 104
Di Leonardo, Lydia 49
"Diamonds and Rust" 89
Dick Clark Show 69, 73, 74
Dick, Nigel 111
Dick Whittington 133
Diddley, Bo 118, 161, 219
"Different Drum" 18, 19
"Die You Bastard" 122
Dillinger, John 52
Dillon, Matt 190
Diltz, Henry 17
Dio, Ronnie James 98
Dion, Céline 111
Dion and the Belmonts 73
Dirty Dancing 271
Dirty Work 273
Discovery 258
Disney, Walt 15, 36, 42, 43, 269
"Dissident Aggressor" 98
Diver Down 191
Dixieland 168
"D. O. A." 181
"Does She Wish She Was Single Again" 25
"Do The Bop" 64, 83
"Do You Love Me" 73
"Do You Remember Rock 'n' Roll Radio?" 167
Dokken, Don 123
Dolenz, Micky 140

Domino, Fats 67, 71, 78
Donovan 131, 136
"Don't" 67
"Don't Go" 93
"Don't Leave Me Girl" 145, 161
"Don't Lose My Number" 40
"Don't You Care" 6
"Don't' Worry Baby" 2, 3, 11
Doo-Wop Shop 77
Doobie Brothers 230
Doors 4, 137
Doremi Fasol Latido 117
Dot Records 16, 67
"Dottie" 73
Double Down Live: 1980 & 2008 256
Double Fantasy 107
Double Platinum 50
Double Trouble 203-205, 207, 210-214, 259
Douglas, Robert 154, 161
Dourdan, Gary 160
Dovells 82, 262
Down Town 208
Downes, Geoff 266
Downey, Mort 20
Downing, K. K. 87-93, 96, 98
Doyle, Mark 107
Dozier, Lamont 45
Dr. John 22, 214
Drama 266
Drama Desk Awards 78
Drayton, Clarence 149, 150
"Dream Lover" 23
"Dream Police" 263
Dressed To Kill 50
Drew Carey Show, The 174, 256
Drifters 80, 237
Dublin (Ireland) 7, 270
Duprees 262
Durdin, Bob 160
Duryea, Dick 5, 6

Index

Dylan, Bob 208
Dynamics 218
Dynasty 52

E Street Band 106, 109
Eagle Oaks Country Club 59
Eagles 16, 19, 32, 55
"Eagles Are (Unbelievable), The " 85
Earls 262
"East Meets West"
East Orange (NJ) 150
East Rutherford (NJ) 191
East Side Kids 263
East Troy (MI) 212
Easy To Be Free: The Songs of Rick Nelson 29
Eat 'Em And Smile 200
Ebony 144
Echoes 262
Ecstasy Paradise 157
Ed Sullivan Show, The 72, 73, 237, 261
Edgar Winter Album 274
"Eddie" 102
Eddy D Orchestra 162
Edison (NJ) 58
Electric Comic Book 224
"Electric Eye" 93
Electric Factory 46
Eliminator 254
"Eliminator" 254, 255, 258
Elizabeth II 44
El Loco 254
Emerson, Keith 247
EMI Records 219
"Eminence Front" 230
Emmy Award 44
End of the Century 167, 170
End of the Century: The Story of the Ramones 176
Endless Summer 8
Endless Wire 232

England 7, 20, 92, 129, 133, 166, 221, 222, 272
Eno, Brian 150
Entertainment Spectrum 104, 241
Entwistle, John 218-220, 225, 230-232
Epic Records 109, 209
Epitaph World Tour 98
Epstein, Brian 60
Erdelyi, Thomas 165
"Eruption" 180
Escalator 117
Esposito, Mike 224
Essex County (NJ) 143
Ethiopia 40
Ethridge, Chris 24
Europe 6, 7, 73
"Eve of Destruction" 77
"Every Breath You Take" 40, 41
"Everybody Needs Somebody To Love" 152
"Everybody Wants Some" 181, 196
Everly Brothers 17, 67, 73
Everything Louder than Everyone Else 123
"Evil Fantasies" 96
"Exciter" 99
Extreme 200
Extreme Dating 110
"Eye of the Hurricane" 26

Fabulous Thunderbirds 206
Face Dances 230
Face Value 229
Facebook 31
Faces 229
Fair Warning 185, 186, 196
Fairclough, Stanley 132
Family Style 212
Famous Monsters of Filmland 169
Fandango 251
Farm Aid '86 212
Farmingdale (NJ) 59
Farner, Mark 26

285

Fat Larry's Band 156
Faulkner, Richie 98
Feeling Nice: A Collection of Super Rare and Super Heavy Funk 45s From The Late 60s & Early 70s Vol. I 162
Felix Cavaliere's Rascals 244, 247
Felt Forum 78
Fender 146, 204, 207
Ferraro's Club Choo Choo (see Choo Choo Club) 236
Festival For Peace 240
15 Big Ones 8
Fifty Big Ones 12
50s & 60s Party Songs (My Music) 85
5150 200
Fight 97
Fight Club 110
Fillmore East 228
Fillmore West 19
"(Finale): Once Upon A Dream" 239
Finland 127, 223
"First Kiss to the Last" 83
Fischer, Bobby 29
Five Satins 80
Flaming Youth 37
Flash Cadillac and the Continental Kids 78
Fleetwood Mac 230
Floating Circus 102
Florida 30
Flower Power concerts 139
"Fly, The" 76
"Flyin' High" 258
Flying Burrito Brothers 15, 23-29, 32
The Flying Burrito Brothers: Encore – Live in Europe in 1990, The 26
Foles, Nick 85
Foley, Ellen 102-104
"Fools Rush In" 23
For God and Texas 256
For Those About to Rock We Salute You 269
For Unlawful Carnal Knowledge 200
Ford 70, 104, 254
Ford, "Tennessee" Ernie 269
Ford, William "Stag" 143, 149
Fort Lee (NJ) 159
Fort Leonard Wood 149
Fortune, Sonny 150
41 Original Hits from the Soundtrack of American Graffiti 78
Fossum, Michael 258
Foster, Harry 71
Foster the People 12
Fotomaker 241, 242
Four Coins 63
Four Lads 63
Four Seasons 3, 9, 10
Four Tops 144
Fox, Lucas 118
Frampton, Peter 230
France 134
Francis, Connie 263
"Frankenstein" 274
Franklin, Aretha 161, 208
Frederic 136
Fredericks of Hollywood 196
Freed, Alan 72, 73, 80, 167
Freedom Suite 239
Freddie and the Dreamers 130, 220
Frehley, Ace 49, 50, 52, 55-59, 190, 241
Freight 88
Frey, Glenn 17, 32
Friends 7
Fulstone, Suellen 96
"Fun, Fun, Fun" 2, 13
Funk Brothers 45
Funky Hot Pants: 14 Super Rare Original Funk Monsters from the Late 60's to the Early 70's 148

Index

G. C. Dangerous 242
G. I. Joe 268
Gabriel, Peter 37, 38, 60
Galfas, Stephan 106
Gallup Poll 51
"Game of Love" 130
Garcia, Jerry 264, 265
Garden State Parkway 226
"Garden Party" 22
Garfield (NJ) 236
Gates, Walter 65, 66
Gaye, Marvin 156, 157
G-Clefs 224
Geffen Records 232
General Artists Corporation 73
Genesis 37, 38, 41, 42, 43, 47
Genesis 38
"Genocide" 96
Gere, Richard 179
Georgia 194
Germany 20, 120, 123, 125, 127, 162, 211, 222, 259
Gerry and the Pacemakers 133
Gibbons, Billy 249-256, 258, 259
Gibson 206
Gilbert, Michael 147
Gilbert, Ron 224
Gill, Pete 122
Gilmore, Ray 77
"Gimme All Your Lovin'" 254
"Girl Can't Help It, The" 69
"Girl Gone Bad" 196
Girlschool 119, 124
"Give Me Just a Little More Time" 135, 136
Glee 110
Glitter, Gary 133
"Glory Glory" 241
"God Only Knows" 4, 6
"God Speaks of Marty Robbins" 232
Goffin, Gerry 129
Go Go Mania 132

Going Back 45
"Going to Brazil" 123
Golden Gods Awards 126
Golden Nugget 20
Golden Years, The 119
"Good Lovin'" 237, 238, 244, 246
Good Lovin' Tour 244
Good Morning Vietnam 10
"Good Timin'" 9
"Good Vibrations" 4, 10, 12
Goodson, Mark 262
Gordy, Berry 143
Gordon, Flash 51
Gore, Tipper 272
Gore, Leslie 76, 85
Gossert, Gus 77, 78
"Got Me Under Pressure" 258
"Got to Get You Off My Mind" 152
Graham Central Station 266
Graham, Larry 265, 266
Grammy Award 12, 40, 44, 47, 97, 98, 123, 124, 130, 208, 211-214
Grand Canyon 37
Grand Funk Railroad 103
Grand Ole Opry 19
Grateful Dead 4, 102, 264
Gray, Paul 126
Grease (play) 78
Grease (film) 80
Great Britain 5, 12, 26, 40, 79, 90, 109, 119, 120, 129, 133, 166, 168, 219-223, 228, 231, 238, 243
Great Train Robbery 41
Greece 185, 217
Green, Al 230
Green, Karl 129, 137
Green Day 176
Greenburg, Florence 20
Greeenberg, Mark "Twig" 217, 221
Greenwich United Way 140
Greenwood Cemetery 245

287

Greenwich Village 226
Greiner Middle School 214
"Groovin'" 238, 239
Groovin' 239, 244
"Groovy Little Hippy Pad" 254
Grossi, Nancy 119
Guilbeau, Gib 19, 24-28
Guilbeau, Ronnie 25
Guiness 44
Gull Records 88, 89
Gumbs, Mavis 160, 161
Guns N' Roses 174, 256
Guitar Hero: Metallica 123
Guitar Player 180, 266
Guitar World 213
Guntersville (AL) 26
Guthrie, Arlo 19
Guy, Buddy 205, 213, 214
Guyden Records 75
GWR Records 122

Hair 102
Hackett, Steve 38
Hagar, Sammy 200, 256
Haggard, Merle 15, 28
Haiti 159
Haizlip, Ellis 148
Halford, Rob 87-89, 91-99
Halfway to Sanity 172
Hall, Huntz 263
Hall and Oates 60, 103, 107
Hall of the Mountain Grill 117
Halloween 57, 152
Halloween 167
Ham, Bill 250, 254
Hammered 124
Hammerstein Ballroom 175
Hammond B-3 235, 237, 247
Hammond Hall of Fame 247
Hammond, John 208
Hand Sown ... Home Grown 19

Hang Cool Teddy Bear 112
Hang Cool Tour 112
"Hank Gets Dusted" 256
Happy Birthday 229
Happy Days 79
"Happy Jack" 221, 222
Happy Jack 222, 226
"Happy Trails" 196
"Hard Luck Woman" 51, 56
Hard Rock Café 59, 97, 138
Harley Davidson 91
Harpo, Slim 218
Harris, Carl 150
Harris, Emmy Lou 21, 30
Harrison, George 7, 255, 261
Harrison, Pattie 7
Harrod's 273
Hassles 145
Hatfield, Bobby 271
Havens, Richie 137
Hawaii 2, 185, 228
Hawkins, Dale 16
Hawkwind 117, 118
Hayes, Bill 269
Hayes, Isaac 175
Headgirl 120
"Heading Out to the Highway" 93, 99
"Heard It on the X" 254
"Heart of Glass" 184
Hearts on the Line 25
"Heartache in Blue" 258
"Heartbreaker" 127
Heineken 115
Hell Bent For Leather 89
Hell in a Handbasket 112
Hello, I Must Be Going 39
"Hello It's Me" 103
"Hello Mary Lou" 23
Helmick, Ralph 213
"Help Me Rhonda" 2, 3

Index

Henderson, Jocko 63
Hendrix, Jimi 88, 148, 149, 181, 206, 207, 209, 212, 213, 239
Herman's Hermits 129-134, 136-139, 220, 223, 234, 227
High Numbers 218, 219
Highway Records 147, 162
Hill, Dusty 249, 250, 252-254, 256-259
Hill, Ian 87, 88, 91, 96, 98
Hill, Jesse 218
"Hillbillies from Outerspace" 212
Hillman, Chris 24
Hilton Hotel 20
History Shop 43
Hit Parader 217
...Hits 42
Hodges, Kenny 17, 18
Hoffman, Sylvia 153
Holland, Dave 87, 89, 91, 95
Holland, Eddie 218
"Hold Me Tight" 146
Hold On! 132
"Hold On" (Rascals) 240
"Hold On" (Wilson Phillips) 10
"Hold On I'm Comin'" 145
Holiday, Billie 208
Hollies 18, 218
Holly, Buddy 67, 70, 73
"Hooligan" 59
Hollywood (CA) 16, 124, 173, 193
Hollywood Bowl 19, 228
Hollywood Reporter 16, 124
Hometown (IL) 15
Honky 19
Hopkins, Charles 245
Hopkins, Nicky 106
Hopwood, Keith 129, 137
Horn, Trevor 266
"Hot For Teacher" 196
"Hot Fun in the Summertime" 11
"Hot Line" 155

Hot Springs (AR) 37
Hotel Americana 273
Hotter Than Hell 50
House of Blues 82, 125
House of Music 106
Houston (TX) 250, 252, 258, 259
Houston, Thelma 155
Hovis, Guy 19
"How Can I Be Sure" 239
Howard Stern Show, The 174
Howdy Doody 51
Howe, Steve 266
Hubbard, L. Ron 274
HUD 259
Hullabaloo 137, 167, 237
Humble Pie 250
Humperdink, Englebert 19
Hunter, Ian 107
Huthmacher, Ned 30
Hyatt 156
Hyman, Charlotte 175
Hyman, Jeffrey 165, 175

I Am 229
"I Ain't Gonna Eat Out My Heart Anymore" 237
"I Beg of You" 67
"I Can Hear Music" 8
"I Can See For Miles" 228
"I Can Take or Leave Your Loving" 131, 132
"I Can't Explain" 221
"I Can't Help Myself (Sugar Pie Honey Bunch)" 144
"I Don't Mind" 219
"I Don't Want to Grow Up" 174
"I Get Around" 2, 3, 6, 11, 13
"I Gotta Dance to Keep from Crying" 218
"I Just Called To Say I Love You" 39
"I Need a Lover" 271

"I Saw the Light" 103
"I Screamed Annie" 135
"I Thank You" 254
"I Understand (Just How You Feel)" 224
"I Walk the Line" 160
"I Wanna Be Sedated" 167
"I Wanna Be Your Boyfriend" 167
"I Wanna Rock" 272
"I Want to Hold Your Hand" 76
"I Want You to Want Me" 263
"I Was Made for Lovin' You" 52
"Ice Cream Man" 180
"I'd Do Anything for Love (But I Won't Do That)" 110
"I'd Rather Be Lonely" 138
"If Something Should Come Between Us (Let it be Love)" 25
"I'll Be Taking Her Out Tonight" 135
"I'll Be Your Sister" 119
"I'll Take My Chances" 161
"I'll Wait" 196
Illinois 15, 16, 18, 31
"I'm a Man" 219
"I'm Drinking Canada Dry" 25
"I'm Free" 229
"I'm Henry VIII, I Am" 129, 130, 132, 140
"I'm Into Something Good" 129, 132, 136, 139
"I'm Making Monsters for My Friends" 174
"I'm Telling You Now" 130
"I'm the Face" 218
"In My Life" 138
"In My Lonely Room" 45
"In Ramada da Vida" 174, 256
In Search of Space 117
In Step 212
In The Beginning 213
"In the Air Tonight" 38
"In The Midnight Hour" 237

India 7
"Indian Giver" 172
Indianapolis Colts 232
Inferno 124
Ingram, Elisha "Skip" 154
Inhofer, Greg 134
Intruders 144
Iowa 8
International Space Station 258
"Into the Void" 56
Invisible Touch 38
Iron Fist 120
"Iron Fist" 120, 121
Iron Maiden 93, 118
Island of Real, The 241
Isley Brothers 181
Italy 158, 185, 221
"It's a Beautiful Morning" 239
"It's All Coming Back to me Now" 111
It's Hard 230
It's Time 156, 157
iTunes 97
"It's Your Life to Live" 274
"I've Been Lonely Too Long" 238
"I've Got Love if You Want It" 218
"(I've Had) The Time of My Life" 271

Jack Daniels 125
Jacobs, Paul 107, 108
Jackson 5 267
Jackson, Hal 145
Jackson, Jermaine 155, 267
Jackson, Johnny 152, 154
Jackson, Michael 46, 157, 267
Jagger, Mick 230, 273
"Jailbreak" 270
Jamaica 153
James Vance et al v. Judas Priest 96
"Jamie's Cryin'" 196
Japan 51, 169, 185, 244

Index

Jardine, Adam 11
Jardine, Al 2, 5, 8, 11, 12
Jardine, Matt 11
Jason, Rick 268
Jasper, Kevin 156
Jefferson Airplane 4
"Jellyfish" 145, 147
Jensen, Debra 52, 54
Jersey City (NJ) 146
Jett, Joan 267, 268
Jesus Christ Superstar 108
Joel, Billy 56, 145
Johansen, David 168
John, Elton 108, 150, 198
John Beland: The Flying Burrito Brothers Years 29
John Bartram High School 63, 67
John Edward Beland 20
John F. Kennedy Stadium 40, 261
Johnny Casino and the Gamblers 80
Johnson, Brian 268, 269
Johnson, Buddy 238
Johnson, Jimmy 147
Johnson, Johnnie 273
Johnson, Kelly 120
Johnston, Bruce 2, 5, 6, 11, 12
Johnston Records 134
Johnstone, Davey 106, 108
Jolson, Al 186
Jones, Booker T. 247
Jones, John Paul 130, 183
Jones, Kenny 229, 230
Jones, Quincy 19, 157
Jones, Thelma 148
Jones, Victor 154, 156, 159, 161
Joplin, Janis 240
Joshua Tree (CA) 24
Journey 181
Judas Priest 87-99
Jugulator 97
Julian 179

"Jump" 194, 106, 198, 201
"Just a Gigolo/I Ain't Got Nobody," 199
Juvenaires 63, 64

K. C. and the Sunshine Band 181
Kalamazoo County Fair 212
Kansas 228
"Keep Playin' That Rock and Roll" 274
Keith, Toby 11
Kellehear, Tamika 28
Kelly, Chip 85
Kendricks, Eddie 46
Kentucky Headhunters 269, 270
Kessel, Barney 207
Keystone Cops 70
Kid Rock 256
Kids Are Alright Tour 231
Kill Master 123
Killing Machine 89, 96
Kilmister, Lemmy 115-127
"Kind of a Drag" 1, 6
King, Albert 205, 206, 250
King B. B. 205, 206, 209, 214, 250, 256
King, Ben E. 237
King, Carole 129, 139
King, Freddie 250
King, Tony 20
King Creole 72
King Diamond 123
King of the Hill 256
King Records 19
"Kings of Speed" 118
Kingsmen 119
Kinks 131, 191, 218
Kirmayer, Tobias 162
Kiss 49, 50-60, 134, 169, 181, 190, 241
Kiss 50-53
Kiss of Death 124
Kiss Army 53, 56, 59
Kiss Expo 58

Kiss 40 60
Kiss Symphony: Alive IV 57
"KKK Took My Baby away, The" 170
Kleinow, Sneaky Pete 24-26
"Kokomo" 10
Kool and the Flames 146
Kool and the Gang 146, 156
Kool Jazz Festival 156
Kooper, Al 22
Koster, Iren 135
Krackerjack 207
Krauss, Alison 28
Krebs, Kaye (McCool) 76, 84
Krieger, Robby 137
Kristiansand, Norway 30
Kristofferson, Kris 15, 20, 21
Krupa, Gene 49

La Futura 258
Ladies' Night 156
Lads, The 130
Lady Bird Lake Trail 213
"La Grange" 251, 254
La Rosa, Julius 70-72
Laguna, Kenny 268
Lambert, Kit 218, 219, 225, 226
"Lament" 251
Lane, Ronnie 229, 230
Larson, Nicolette 26, 183
Las Vegas (NV) 20, 139, 247, 259
Las Vegas Hilton 139
Last Command, The 16
Lauper, Cyndi 42, 168
Laverne & Shirley 136
Lawrence Welk Show 19
Layton, Chris "Whipper" 204, 205, 207
Leadon, Bernie 16, 24
Leak, Lafayette 273
Leave Home 166
"Leaving Here" 218
Leckenby, Derek "Lek" 129, 137

Le Coq Dor 152
Led Zeppelin 39, 130, 133, 183, 191
Lee Andrews and the Hearts 67, 84
Lee, Brenda 175
Left Banke 239
"Legs" 254
Leisure Lads 73
Lemmy 124
Lennon, Cynthia 7
Lennon, John 7, 107, 261
"Lenny" 209
Let Me Rock You 55
Let Me Tickle Your Fancy 267
Let The Good Times Roll 78
"Let Your Love Flow" 21
"Let's Dance" 166, 206
Let's Dance 208, 209
Let's Rock 70, 72
Lethal Weapon 2 10
Letterman, David 40, 261
Lewis, Jerry Lee 64, 71, 116
Lewis, Will 156
Liberace 132
Lick It Up 55
Life 144
Lima (Peru) 194
Lindsay, Mark 137, 140
Link Belt 73
Lips 49
"Lipstick on Your Collar" 263
Little Anthony and the Imperials 66, 80
"Little Bit O' Soul" 172
"Little Deuce Coup" 2
"Little Doll" 68
Little Dream Foundation 42
"Little Lover" 135,
Little Richard 67-69, 78, 79, 116
Little Theater 69
"Little Wing" 213
Live Aid 40, 95, 231

Index

Live Alive 211
Live – The 50th Anniversary Tour 13
Live at Brixton 123
Live at Carnegie Hall 213
Live at Hull 232
Live at Leeds 229
Live at Montreux 1982 & 1985 213
Live From Texas 256
Live From Toronto 232
Live in Las Vegas 11
Live in London 97
Liverpool (UK) 117, 129
"Living After Midnight" 90
Lloyd, Ian 108
Lloyd, Michael 25, 27, 28
Lofgren, Nils 181
London 9, 188, 124, 133, 138, 221, 273
London Symphony Orchestra 9
London Records 250
Longbranch Pennywhistle 17
Long Island (NY) 79, 156, 228, 236
"Look Out Little Sister" 211, 212
Los Angeles (CA) 10, 16-18, 21, 32, 55, 98, 102, 123-125, 156, 158, 181, 208
Los Angeles International Airport 24
Los Globos Club 152
Lost in the Wilderness 242
"Lost Woman Blues" 127
"Lotta Love" 183
Loudwire 99
"Louie Louie" 119
Louisiana 24
Love, Mike 2, 3, 6-9, 12, 13
"Love is a Battlefield" 199
"(Love Is Like A) Heatwave" 45
Love Gun 49, 50, 59
"Love Makes Me Feel Good" 156
"Love Struck Baby" 205
Love You 8
Luce, Richard 256
Lulu 138

Lyngstad, Frida 42
Lynott, Phil 270
Lynyrd Skynyrd 109

M-80 175
M&Ms 189
McAuliffe, Kim 119
McBride, Jim 110
McCartney, Paul 3, 4, 46, 56, 190, 261
McCool, Kaye (see Kaye Krebs)
McDonald, Greg 22, 23
McDonald, Michael 22
McGuire, Barry 77
McPhee, Katherine 111
Mack, Lonnie 207, 211
Madara, John (see John Medora) 63-65, 73, 75-77, 81, 83, 84
Made In Italy 158
Madison Square Garden 78, 93, 189, 190, 230, 232, 244
Madonna 161
Maffei, Bob 68, 73, 81, 82
Maffei, Frank 63, 64, 66, 68, 70 73, 78-82, 84, 85
Magic Sam 206
Maharishi Mahesh Yogi 7, 8
Maharishi International University 8
Makeup to Breakup: My Life in and out of Kiss 57
Making Strides 3K 57
Malone, Tom 106
Mamas and the Papas 8
"Mama's Hungry Eyes" 28
Mammoth 181
Man on the Silver Mountain award 98
Manchester (UK) 129, 130
Mandal (Norway) 30
Manfred Mann 220
Manhattan Transfer 78
Mangione, Chuck 161
Mann, Kal 73

Mansfield, Ken 27
"March of the Damned" 99
March or Die 123
Marchesi, Lex 241
"Marching Off to War" 122
Marina del Ray 10
Marini, Lou 106
Marks, David 2, 12
Maroon 5 12
Marquis Theatre 246
Married With Children 137
Martha and the Vandellas 191
Marx, Groucho 68
"Mary Had a Little Lamb" 212
"May I Have a Talk With You" 212
Mayfield, Curtis 56
Mayhew, Phil 41
Mazda 21
MCA Records 109
Meaden, Peter 218, 229
Meadowlands Arena 191
"Mean Street" 185, 187
Meat Loaf 101-113
Meat Loaf Soul 102
Meat Loaf: To Hell and Back 110
Medal of Honor 108, 110, 245
Medley, Bill 271
Medora, John [see also John Madara] 63
Medicare 259
Mediterranean Riviera 151
"Meet Me Down on the Corner at Joe's Café" 134
Megaforce Records 57
Meher Baba 230
Melanie 145
Melbourne Symphony Orchestra 57, 111
Mellencamp, John 270, 271
Melody Maker 217
Memphis (TN) 23, 25, 211, 255
"Memphis" 207
Memphis Sessions, The 23, 25

Mercedes-Benz 198
Mercenaries of Metal Tour 95
Mercury Records 76, 121
Mescalero 255
Metal Works '73-'93 97
Metallica 122, 124
Mexican Army 35, 37
Mexico 151, 152, 252
MGM 132
Miami (FL) 232
Miami Vice 41
Mickey Mouse 51
"Mickey's Monkey" 238
Midler, Bette 105
Midnight at the Lost and Found 109
Millet, McKinley 69
Mills, Stephanie 156
Milwaukee (WI) 94
Mindbenders 41, 130, 133, 220
Miracles 218
"Misery" 218
Mission to Earth 274
Missouri 149
M.I.U. Album 8
Moby Grape 4
Moments 148
"Moments to Remember" 63
Mondo Bizarro 173
"Monday Without You" 11
Monette, Ray 45
Monk 110
Monkees 140, 168
Monmouth County (NJ) 59
Montclair (NJ) 150
Monterey International Pop Music Festival 223
Monterey Pop 223
Montez, Chris 166
Montreal (Canada) 152, 154, 160
Montreaux Jazz Festival 208, 211
Montrose 181

Index

Moon, Keith 218-220, 222, 224, 225, 227-232
Moore, Pam 108
More Than You Deserve 102
Morello, Tom 60
Morgan, Lorrie 11
Morning Show, The 244
Morrow, Vic 268
Most, Mickie 129, 136
"Motorhead" 118
Motörhead 115-127
Motörhead (album) 118
Motörhead (video game) 123
Motörhead: The Complete Early Years 126
Motörizer 124
Motown 22, 37, 39, 45, 46, 102, 143-145, 150, 154, 155, 157, 158, 238
Moving Sideways 250
Mr. Holland's Opus Foundation 259
"Mrs. Brown, You've Got a Lovely Daughter" 129-132, 140
Mrs. Brown, You've Got a Lovely Daughter [album] 132
Mrs. Brown, You've Got a Lovely Daughter [film] 132
MTV 55, 107, 192, 193, 199, 230, 249, 254
MTV Unplugged 56
Murphy, Audie 110
Murphy, Cheryl 102
Murray, Bill 244
Murray, Larry 29
Murray the K 167, 221-223, 238
"Murray the K's Music in the Fifth Dimension" 221, 222, 238
"Museum" 131
Music Explosion 172
Music of the Alamo 43
Musicians Hall of Fame and Museum 259
"Mustang Sally" 237
"My Brain is Hanging Upside Down (Bonzo Goes to Bitburg)" 173

"My Generation" 130, 131, 218, 219, 221-224
My Generation (TV show) 136
My Music: '60s Pop, Rock & Soul 139
"My Sentimental Friend" 132
My Two Dads 136
"My Way" 54
Myer, George 107
Myers, Michael 167

Nader, Richard 78, 79
Napa (CA) 29
Naked Gun: From the Files of Police Squad 136
Napoleon 193
NASA 252, 253
Nairn (Scotland) 228
Nash, Johnny 145, 146, 148
Nashville (TN) 21, 26, 29, 138, 259
"Nashville Lady" 19
Nashville Municipal Auditorium 259
Nashville Teens 226, 247
Nassau Coliseum 156
Natalie Noone and the Maybes 138, 139
National Association of Music Merchants 247
National Breast Cancer Awareness Month 57
National Football League 84, 152
National Guard 150
National Lampoon Show 102
NBC-TV 51, 146, 168, 237
Nazario, Joe 64
Nebraska 259
Neeley, Ted 107-109
Neil, Bobby 25
Nelson, Baby Face 52
Nelson, Gunnar 29
Nelson, Matthew 29
Nelson, Rick 15, 22, 25, 26, 29
Nesbitt, Glynn 143-146, 149-151

Nesbitt, Richard 143, 150
Netherlands 181
Neville, Art 214
New Haven (CT) 170, 187
New Jersey 3, 57-59, 82, 87, 92, 103, 106, 130, 140, 143-147, 150, 156, 159, 162, 181, 191, 203, 223, 228, 231, 235, 236, 241, 244, 245, 250, 262, 265
New Musical Express 5
New Orleans Saints 240
New Rascals 244
New South Wales (Australia) 125
New York City 44, 54, 59, 70, 71, 80, 97, 98, 102, 103, 115, 123, 134, 138, 145, 146, 154, 166, 175, 185, 187, 189, 210, 222, 232, 235, 261
New York State 93, 154, 226
New York Dolls 103, 165
New York Illustrated 146
New York Post 246
New York Pro Sports and Entertainment League 106
New York Symphony Orchestra 9
New York Yankees 103
New Zealand 169, 254
Newark (NJ) 1, 2, 4, 136, 144-146, 151, 156, 162
Newark Evening News 221, 223, 225
Newark International Airport 136
Newcastle upon Tyne (UK) 111
Newell, Norman 219
Newton, Wayne 78
Nielsen, Rick 174, 256, 263, 264
Nightcrawlers 207
Night Cruiser 157
Night Owl 226
The Night That Changed America: A Grammy Salute to the Beatles, The 261-262
Nine Tonight 108
19 47

"99th Floor" 250
1910 Fruitgum Company 172
1916 123
1984 194, 196, 201
Nippon Budokon 51
Nirvana 60
No Jacket Required 39
"No Milk Today" 131, 138
"No, Not Much" 63
Nö Sleep at All 123
No Sleep 'til Hammersmith 120
"Noise Boom" 146
Noone, Natalie 136
Noone, Peter 129-140, 224, 228
North Carolina 73
Norway 29, 32, 223, 259
Nostradamus 97
"Nothin' to Lose" 50, 56
Nothin' to Lose: The Making of Kiss, 1972-1975 58
"Nothing Left to Lose" 135
"Now and Then" 75
"Now I Wanna Sniff Some Glue" 166
Nugent, Ted 206
Nursery Cryme 37

"Objects in the Rear View Mirror May Appear Closer than They Are" 110
Ocean First Theater 82
"Ode to a Black Man" 270
"Of Love" 73
Off-Broadway 101
Ognedal, Bright Owe 32
"(Oh) Pretty Woman" 181, 182, 196
"Oh! You Pretty Things" 133
Ohio Players 181, 198
Oldham, Andrew Loog 60, 273
Oliver, Greg 124
Omni Arena 194
"On Fire" 196
On Parole 119

Index

"On The Record" 221
"On The Run" 93
One Day at a Time 190
One For All 57
"One In a Million You" 266
One Man's Family 17, 18
"One More Night" 39
"One of the Boys" 134
One of the Glory Boys 135
"1-2-3" 76
Once Upon a Dream 239
"Once Upon a Time" 102
O'Neill, Ed 137
"Only a Lonely Heart Sees" 243
"Oo-La-La Limbo" 75
"Ooh Poo Pah Doo" 218
Opal Butterfly 117
"Open Up Your Door" 217
Opus Collection: Rockaway Beach 176
Orange (NJ) 144
Orbison, Roy 191
Orgasmatron 122
Orshowski, Wes 124
Oscar [see also Academy Awards] 39, 42, 44
Osmond, Donny 133
OU812 200
"Our Love" 76
Our Roots Are Country Music 25
"Out in the Street" 221
Out Of Control 52, 54, 55
Outlaws 27
Outside The Alamo: Songs of Ned Huthmacher 30
"Over You" 258
Overkill 119
Overnight Sensation 123
Owens, Buck 28, 29
Owens, Tim "Ripper" 97
Oxford (UK) 133
Oxford New Theatre 133

Ozark Mountain Daredevils 242

Padgham, Hugh 39
Page, Jimmy 130
Painted Turtle 112
Painkiller 97
Palace Theatre 140
Palisades Amusement Park 145, 146, 148
Pallenberg, Anita 273
"Panama" 196
Pandora's Box 111
"Papa Was a Rolling Stone" 45
"Paradise by the Dashboard Light" 101, 103, 108
Paramount Theater 71
Parents Music Resource Center (PMRC) 272
Parkway North 150-152
Paris 78, 252
Parker, Fess 36, 44, 257, 269
Parkinson's Disease 30, 31
Parrish, Paul 16, 29
Parsons, Gram 24, 25
Parton, Dolly 15, 21, 22, 30
Passaic (NJ) 156, 265
Pastorius, Jaco 183
Pat Boone Show, The 68
Patti Page Show, The 68
Patton, Larry 28-30
Patton & Beland: Reach For The Sky! 29
Paul, Les 266
Paul Revere and the Raiders 134, 137, 140
PBS 85, 148
Peaceful World 241
Peaches and Herb 156
Peacock, Trevor 130
Pearl Jam 175
"Pearl Necklace" 254
Peart, Neil 188
Pennebaker, D. A. 223
"People Got To Be Free" 239, 243, 244

Penridge, Stan 59
Peppermint Trolley Company 16
"Peppermint Twist" 235
"Perfidia" 29
Peru 194
Pet Sounds 4, 12
Peter and Gordon 220
Petillo, Johnny 82
Petty, Tom 175
Petagno, Joe 118, 126
Phil Collins Big Band 42
"Phil the Shill" 41
Philadelphia (PA) 10, 40, 45, 46, 63, 75, 83-85, 156, 179, 184, 185, 261
Philadelphia Music Alliance's Walk of Fame 83
Philadelphia Eagles 84, 85
Philbin, Regis 244
Phillips. Chynna 8
Phillips, John 8
Phillips, Michelle 8
Phoenix (AZ) 80
"Photograph" 264
Pickett, Wilson 222, 237, 238
Pickering, Nigel 17, 18
Pictures at Eleven 29
"Pinball Wizard" 229
Pink Floyd 133
Pirates of Penzance 136
Pitney, Gene 175
Pixies Three 76, 84
Plain & Fancy 21
Plant, Robert 39
Plasmatics 120
Platinum Hook 143, 151, 154-158, 160-162
Platinum Hook 155
Pleasant Dreams 169, 170
"Please Don't Stop" 274
"Please Don't Touch" 124
"Please, Please, Please" 219, 221

Playboy 52
Plowboy Records 139
Poco 32
"Poetry in Motion" 20
Point of Entry 93
Point Pleasant (NJ) 57, 59
Point Tapatio Resort 80
Poitier, Sidney 146
Police 40
PolyGram Records 115, 116, 118
Pontiac 66
"Popeye the Sailor Man" 190
Portland Coliseum 3
"Playing Hard to Get" 73
Plymouth 81, 91
Poco 31
Police 40
"Pony Express" 75
"Poor Little Fool" 22
Pop Gear 132
Portland (OR) 3
Portland Coliseum 3
Prelude 157
Prep Records 64
Presley, Elvis 16, 21, 67, 68, 77, 116
Preston, Billy 247
Price, Lloyd 148
Price of Freedom, The 257
"Pride and Joy" 205
Priest...Live! 95
Prima, Louis 168
Prince 255, 266
Principle of Moments, The 39
Prof. LaPlano and the Planotones 80
Providence (RI) 51, 170
Psychedelic Lollipop 224
Psycho Circus 56
"Psychotherapy" 172
Pure Prairie League 242

Index

Quadrophenia 229, 231
Quartzsite (AZ) 80, 81
Queen 198
Queens (NY) 165, 176

"R.A.M.O.N.E.S" 123
"Rag Doll" 3
Rage Against the Machine 60
Rainbow 98
Rainbow Bar & Grill 124
Raitt, Bonnie 213, 214
Ram It Down 95
Ramone, C. J. 173, 175, 176
Ramone, Dee Dee 165, 169, 173, 176
Ramone, Elvis 172
Ramone, Johnny 165, 169, 173, 176
Ramone, Joey 165, 166, 168-175
Ramone, Marky 167, 174-176
Ramone, Richie 172
Ramone, Tommy 165, 166, 175, 176
Ramones 165-176
Ramones 166
Randell, Riff 167
Ranwood Records 16, 17
Rapp, Danny 63-66, 69-71, 73, 75, 78-80
Rasberries 241
Rascals [see also Young Rascals] 53, 222, 237-247
Rascals: Once Upon A Dream 246
Raven, Marion 111
Rays 67
Razors Edge 269
RCA Records 19, 158, 159, 255
"Reach Out I'll Be There" 144
Ready Steady Go 238
Reagan, Ronald 173
Reco-Art Studio 65
Record World 25
Recording Industry Association of America (RIAA) 10, 12, 69, 83, 89, 124, 173, 208, 251

Recycler 255
Redfish, Travis W. 106
Reed, Jimmy 250
Regents 3, 220
Reinhardt, Richie 172
Reinking, Ann 39
"Release Me" 10
"Remember (Walking in the Sand)" 11
Reno (NV) 96
Republic of Texas 213
Resorts Hotel and Casino 139
Restless Heart 139
Return to Vienna 22
Reuters 57
Revolver 126
Rhode Island 51
Rhythmeen 255
Richard and the Young Lions 217
Richard Rodgers Theatre 246
Richards, Ann 213
Richards, Keith 255, 272
Richie, Lionel 147
Ricky Nelson Story, The 26
"Right On" 240
Righteous Brothers 237, 272
Ringo Starr's All-Starr Band 231, 244
Rio Grande Mud 250
Rizzuto, Phil 103, 108
RKO Theater 222
Roadie 106
Robertson, Brian 116, 120, 122
Roberts, Austin 29
Robinson, Smokey 157
Rochester (NY) 67
"Rock and Roll All Nite" 50, 59
Rock and Roll Hall of Fame 10, 32, 35, 56, 59, 60, 175, 176, 231, 244, 245, 255, 265-267, 269, 271, 273
"Rock And Roll Is Here To Stay" 68, 69, 77, 80, 81, 85

Rock and Roll is Here to Stay: The Radio Show 82
"Rock And Roll Music" 8
Rock And Roll Over 50, 51
"Rock and Roll Revival" 78
"Rock of Ages" 137
Rock, Roll & Remember 65
Rocka Rolla 88
"Rockaway Beach" 167, 176
Rock 'n' Roll 122, 123
Rock 'n' Roll High School 167
Rockhead's Paradise 153
Rocket to Russia 166
Rockin' Vickers 117
Rockpile 107
Rocky Horror Show, The 102
Rocky Horror Picture Show, The 102
Rocksimus Maximus Tour 57
Rodgers, Jimmie 67
Rodgers, Nile 212
Rogers, Cee Cee 159
Rogers, Larry 22
Rolling Stone 59, 79
Rolling Stones 60, 206, 213, 219, 220, 229, 230, 255, 273
Romance Dance 21
Rome 217
Ronettes 167
Ronnie James Dio Stand Up and Shout Cancer Fund 98
Ronnie Speeks and the Elrods 236
Ronstadt, Linda 15, 17-19, 22, 30, 31, 60
Ronson, Mick 106
Rosé 125
"Rosebud" 173
Rossington, Gary 109
Roth, David Lee 179-201
Rotor Clip Company 162
"Rough Boy" 254, 255
Rough Mix 230
Roxy Music 133

Royal Victorian Order 44
Rubber Soul 5
Rubin, Alan 106
"Rude Mood" 208
Runaways 267
Rundgren, Todd 103
"Runnin' with the Devil" 180, 196
Rush 188
Rush, Otis 206, 207
Rushen, Patrice 150
Rutgers-Newark 151
Rutherford, Mike 37, 43
Rydell, Bobby 84, 262
Ryder, Mitch 222

Sacrifice 123
Sad Wings of Destiny 89
Sahara Hotel 20
Sailin' 21
Sam and Dave 145, 148, 254
Sam the Sham and the Pharoahs 132
Sam Gopal 117
San Antonio (TX) 19, 45, 252, 257, 258
San Francisco Bay 265
San Jacinto, Battle of 44
Sanctuary Records 126
Sandy 232
Santa Anna, Gen. Antonio López de 35
Santa Barbara (CA) 136, 138, 190
Santana 181
Satanic Majesties Request 273
Saturday Night Live 23, 212
Sawyer Brown 11
Scala, Ralph 223
Scandanavia 29, 32, 120
Scepter Records 20
"School Boy Romance" 70
Scientology 274
Scotese, Artie 64
Scotland 7, 127
Scott, Bon 268, 269

Index

Scott, Dr. Everett 102
Scott, Linda 262
Screaming For Vengeance 93
Screen Gems 21
Scruggs, Randy 25, 27, 28
Search and Nearness 240, 241
Searchers 133
Sebastian, John 137
Second City 18
Secrets 76, 84
See 240
Seger, Bob 55, 108, 181, 255
Seize the Night Tour 111
Segovia, Andres 266
Serious Moonlight 209
Serpico's 262
Shack 154
Shaffer, Paul 244
Shahan, Happy 252
Sha-Na-Na 77, 80
Shannon, Del 20, 56
Shannon, Tommy 204, 206, 207
Share The Wealth 161
Sharp, Ken 58
Shaw Junior High School 64
"She Belongs to Everyone But Me" 25
Shea Stadium 148, 149, 235, 237, 240, 261
"Sheena Is a Punk Rocker" 166, 167
Shelburne Hotel 73
Shep and the Limelites 267
Shilo 22
Shindig 167
Shiraz 125
Shirelles 80
Showboat Hotel 82
"Shut Down" 2
"Silhouettes" 138
"Silly Love Songs" 134
Silverado Morning 29
Silver Lining Lounge 80

Simmons, Gene 49, 50, 52, 57-60, 181
Simon, Paul 168
Simple Dreams 30
Simpson, Bart 98
Simpsons, The 98, 173, 231
Sin After Sin 89, 96
Sinatra, Frank 54, 55
"Since I Fell for You" 238
Singer, Artie 65, 66, 73
Singer, Eric 57, 60
Singular Records 65
"Sinner" 89
Sire Records 166, 173
Sirius-XM Radio 139
Sister Sledge 158
"Six Strings Down" 214
16 217
"60,000 Soldiers Housed" 258, 259
Skaggs, Ricky 28, 29
Sklar, Leland 39, 47
Sky is Crying, The 213
Skyscraper 200
Slade 133
Slash 125, 174, 256
Slaughter 152
Slayer 122
"Sleepy Joe" 132
"Sleeping Bag" 254
Slipknot 127
Sloman, Larry 57
"Sloop John B" 3
Sly and the Family Stone 265, 266
Smile 5, 12
Smile Sessions, The 12
Smiley Smile 5
Smith, Jimmy 247
Smith, John W. 44, 45
Smith, Patti 56
Snake Bite Love 123
Snaggletooth 118
Snider, Dee 272

Snyder, Tom 52, 55
So Far 139
"So This is Love" 185
Soles, P. J. 167
Solo in Soho 270
Somerset (NJ) 162
"(Somebody Else Been) Shakin' Your Tree" 250
"Something About You" 45
Something Good With Peter Noone 139
"Sometimes (When I'm All Alone)" 65, 78, 82
"Somehow I Can't Forget" 73
"Something Old, Something New (Something Borrowed & Blue)" 134, 139
Sons of the Golden West 27
Soul 148
Soul Dukes 143-154, 161, 162
"Soul Man" 145
Soul Patrol records 148
"Soul-69" 147, 148
Soul to Soul 211
South Africa 173
South Carolina 83
South Mountain Arena 241
South Pacific 72
Souther, J. D. 17
Southern Girls 30
Southside Johnny and the Asbury Jukes 91
Soviet Red Army Choir 9
Spain 185
Spanky and Our Gang 16, 18
Sparks (NV) 95
Sparky J's 156
Spector, Phil 103, 167, 175
Spectrum 179, 185, 188, 190
Spencer David Group 218
Spielberg, Steven 264
Spiral Starecase 78
Spokesmen 77
Spooky Lady's Sideshow 21

Spooky Tooth 96
Springfield (MA) 147
Springfield, Dusty 56
Springsteen, Bruce 56, 91, 103, 106, 230, 246
Squire, Chris 266
St. Johns University 58
St. Louis (MO) 156
St. Valentine's Day Massacre 120
St. Valentine's Day Massacre 120, 124
St. Vincent's Court 21
Stadium Hilton Hotel 185
Stamp, Chris 218
"Standing in the Shadows of Love" 45
Stafford (NJ) 82
Stained Class 89, 96
Stamford (CT) 140
Stand! 266
Stand By Your Man 120
"Standing on the Verge (Of Getting It On)" 155
Stanford, Tina Renee 154, 155
Stanley, Paul 49, 50, 57, 58, 60, 108
Stable Records 117
Staple Singers 56
Star Trek 117
Starr, Ringo 20, 231, 244, 261, 262
Stars and Stripes Vol. 1 11
Stax 37
Stay Hungry 272
"Steal This Episode" 98
Steel Pier 73
Steinman, Jim 101-103, 105, 106, 109, 111, 112
Steppenwolf 18
Stern, Howard 174
Stevens, Cat 60
Stevie Ray Vaughan Day 213
Stevie Ray Vaughan Memorial Scholarship Fund 214

Index

Stevie Ray Vaughan Remembrance Ride & Concert 214
Stewart, Ian 273
Still Cruisin' 10
Sting 40, 41
Stone Canyon Band 22, 23
Stone Poneys 18
Stoney & Meat Loaf 102
Strasser, Mireille 132
Strauss, Richard 157
Strawberry Alarm Clock 4
Streatham Odeon 133
"Strutter" 50
Studio 54 156
Stuermer, Daryl 38
Subterranean Jungle 172
Sullivan, Ed 167
Summer, Donna 134
Summer Days (And Summer Nights!!) 3
Summer in Paradise 11
Suncoast Hotel and Casino 84, 247
"Sun City" 173
"Sunday Will Never Be the Same" 16
Sunset Sundown 25
Super Bowl 232
Supremes 39, 155
"Surfer Girl" 6
"Surfin'" 2, 11
"Surfin' Surfari" 2
"Surfin' U. S. A." 2
"Surrender" 263
"Susan" 6
"Susie-Q" 16
"Suspicious Minds" 77
"Sussudio" 39
Swampwater 19, 20
Swan Records 73, 75
Sweat, Keith 161
Sweden 125, 127
Sweet, Matthew 174

"Sweet Little Sixteen" 2
Switzerland 44, 127, 208
Symphony Hall 1, 5, 6, 145, 146, 156

T-Rex 133
Table Tennis Topnotchers 72
Tahiti 194
"Take on the World" 89
"Tale of Two Springfields" 231
Talking Heads 175
Talmy, Shel 219
Tarrytown (NY) 108
Tate, Howard 148
Tarzan 193
Tarzan (film) 42
Tarzan (musical) 42
Taylor, Phil 116, 118, 119, 123
Tavelman, Jill 39
"Teardrops" 67
"Teenage Lobotomy" 166, 176
Tejas 251
Temple University 73
Templeman, Ted 181
Temptations, The 46
Tennessee 146
Terrace Ballroom 145
Terranova, Joe [Joe Terry] 63-66, 69-73, 75-85
Testify 42
Tex, Joe 148, 237
Texas 30, 40, 92, 110, 206, 209, 214, 249, 250, 252, 254, 255, 257, 259
Texas BigBeat charity 259
Texas Flood 204, 205, 208, 209
Texas Revolution 35, 47
That Lucky Old Sun 13
That Metal Show 5, 60, 89, 125, 126
That's Why God Made the Radio 12
Thayer, Tommy 57
The Chosen Few 98

303

"The Fly" 76
The Night That Changed America: A Grammy Salute to the Beatles 261, 262
"The Thought of Loving You" 78
The Tonight Show with Jay Leno 162
Theatre World Award 78
"There's a Kind of Hush" 131, 138, 140
There's a Riot Goin' On 266
Thielhelm, Emil "Peppy" 224, 226
Thin Lizzy 120, 270
33rd New Jersey Volunteer Infantry 245
Thomas, Carla 237
Thomas, David Clayton 152
Thomas, Joe 11
Thomas, John Charles 68
Thomas, Rufus 237
Thoreau, Henry David 245
Thornton, Billy Bob 257
Three Stooges 168
"Til I Die" 11
Tillotson, Johnny 20, 85
Tilt-A-Whirl Band 214
Time 130
"Time" 156
Time Peace: The Rascals Greatest Hits 239
Tiny Tim 228
Tipton, Glen 87-91, 96
To Hell and Back 110
To Hell and Back: The Meat Loaf Story 110
"To Sir, with Love" 138
"Tobacco Road" 226
Todd, Nick 67
Todman, Bill 262
Tokyo 51
"Tomorrrow Never Knows" 38
Tomorrow with Tom Snyder 51, 52, 55
Tommy 226, 229
Tony Awards 78
"Too Many Fish in the Sea" 238
Too Tough to Die 172
Toorish, John B. 63

"Toot Toot Tootsie! Goodbye" 186
Topanga Canyon 17
Top of the Pops 238
Tork, Peter 168
Toronto (Canada) 152
Townshend, Pete 218-221, 224-227, 229-232
Tramp Records 162
Transcendental Meditation 7
"Transcendental Meditation" 8
Transfer Station 242
Travis, Scott 97
Travis, William B. 35
"Travelin' Man" 22, 23
Treasure 241
Tremblers 134-135
Tres Hombres 251
Triple Threat 207
Troop Beverly Hills 10
Troubador 16, 17, 31
Trouble Walkin' 55
Troyer, Eric 107
"True Colors" 42
Trump, Donald 112
Trunk, Eddie 56, 59, 89, 98, 126
Truth In Music 82
"Tube Snake Boogie" 254
Turbo 95
"Tush" 251, 254
20/20 8
21 47
24th Street Band 243
Twice Nightly 134, 135
Twisted Sister 272
"Twistin' Germany" 75
"Twistin' Italy" 75
"Twistin' U. S. A." 73
"Two Hearts" 41
"Two Out of Three Ain't Bad" 103
"Tutti Frutti" 67
Tyler, Dana 44, 46, 47

Index

UFO 181
"Unchained" 185, 196
Uncle Floyd Show 168
UNICEF 7
United Nations 8
Unleased in the East 89
United Artists 118, 119
United Negro College Fund 148
Unity Shoppe 138
Unity Telathon 138
Universal Music Group 127
Universal-International 110
University High School 162
University of Texas 250
Upbeat 167
Urban Cowboy 253
Urban Decay 110
U. S. Senate 272
US Festival 194
USA Today 30
Utterbach, Joel 149

Vagrants 228
Valentine, Kevin 56
Valentine's Day 82
Valli, Frankie 10
Van Halen 171, 179-201
Van Halen 180, 186
Van Halen Best Of Vol. I 200
Van Halen II 181, 186
Van Halen, Eddie 135, 179-185, 188, 189, 193, 195, 196, 199-201
Van Halen, Alex 179, 181, 183-185, 188, 189, 193-196, 201
Van Halen, Wolfgang 200
Van Zandt, Steven 150, 173, 244, 246
Vance, James 95, 96
Vance, Kenny 80
Vaughan, Jimmie 212-214
Vaughan, Leonora 209
Vaughan, Martha 214

Vaughan, Stevie Ray 203-214, 259
Vandross, Luther 161
Vedder, Eddie 175, 176
Vee, Bobby 20
"Velcro Fly" 255
Very Best of John Beland, The 29
VH1 56, 125, 136
Victim of Changes 89
Video Report Card 230
Vietnam 7, 77, 102
Village People 134, 162
Vincent, Vinnie 241
Vinci, Frankie 241
Virgin Islands 40, 252
Virginia Beach (VA) 170
Vis-à-vis 242
Vivino, Floyd 168, 170, 175
Vocal Bio Matrix 105
Vocal Group Hall of Fame 82
"Voodoo Child (Slight Return)" 210, 212
Volkswagon 147, 225

WCBS-FM 77, 78
WCBS-TV 44
W. C. Handy Award 211
Waits, Tom 174
"Wake Up Call" 42
Waldorf Astoria 175
"Walk Away Renée" 239
Walker, T-Bone 250
Wall Township (NJ) 59
Wallace, Glenn 154
Wallis, Larry 118
Walt Disney World 139
Wanders, Daniel 162
War 150
War of Words 97
Ward, C. J. 173
Warner Bros. Records 180, 181, 183, 252, 255
Warrior on the Edge of Time 117

305

Warwick, Dionne 240
Washington D.C. 257
Washington, Booker T. 247
Washington, Grover 161
Watching You 158, 159
Waters, Muddy 250
Wayne, Chuck 263
Wayne, John 36, 40, 204, 252
Wayne Fontana and the Mindbenders 130, 133, 220
"(We Ain't Got) Nothing Yet" 224
"We Are Family" 158
We Are Motörhead 124
We Can't Dance 41
"We Want the Airwaves" 170
Webb, Cameron 124, 127
Weinberg, Max 106, 109
Weissman, Mitch 190
Welch, Lenny 238
Welcome to the Neighbourhood 110
Welk, Lawrence 16
Weller, Freddy 29
Weller, Michael 102
Wembley Stadium 40
"We're Not Gonna Take It" 272
West, Leslie 228
West Orange (NJ) 106, 241
Westchester Premier Theatre 108
Westhampton Beach (NY) 236
Weston, Kim 148, 208
Wexler, Jerry 208
"Wham" 207
What's Words Worth 122
"What You See is What You Get"
"What You Want" 158
When the Boys Meet the Girls 132
"When Will I Be Loved" 17
"Whiplash" 124
Whiskey A Go Go 123
White, Alan 266
White, Clarence 18, 24

White, Dave 63-66, 68-71, 73, 75-78, 80, 81, 84
White, Sandra 84
Whites 26
Whitwam, Barry 129, 137, 138
Who 88, 102, 130, 131, 136, 191, 217-232, 238
Who Are You 229
Who By The Numbers 229
Who Sell Out, The 228, 229
Who Sings My Generation, The 221
Who's Next 229
"Whole Lotta Shakin' Going On" 64
Wicked Lester 50
Wild Bill's 206
Wild Honey 7
Wildwood (NJ) 73
Wiener, Allen 43
Williams, Milan 147
Williams, Tennessee 271
Williams, Terry 107
Winwood, Steve 247
Williams, Larry 147, 149
Williams, Robert 134
Williams, Romeo 150
Williams, Wendy O. 120
Willis, Eddie 45
Willis, Ian 117
Willis, Pete 264
Wilson, Brian 1-7, 10-13
Wilson, Carl 2, 3, 5, 6, 11
Wilson, Carnie 7
Wilson, Dennis 2, 5, 6, 10
Wilson, Marilyn 7
Wilson, Timothy 150
Wilson, Wendy 7
Wilson Phillips 8, 10
Wilsons, The 11
"Wind Cries Mary, The" 209
Winter, Edgar 107, 274
Winter, Johnny 240

Index

With Love 229
Woman in Red 39
Women and Children First 181, 186
Wonder Bar 225, 226, 232
Wonder, Stevie 39, 213
"Wonderful World" (Herman's Hermits) 138
"Wonderful World" (Platinum Hook) 158
"Won't Get Fooled Again" 229, 231
Wood, Randy 16
Woodstock 77, 105, 229
Woodstock (film) 229
"Words of Love" 157
Wörld is Yours, The 124
World Vengeance Tour 95
World War II 49, 124, 268
World Wide Blitz Tour 93
"Wouldn't It Be Nice" 4, 6
Wright, Greg 155-157
Wyman, Bill 219
Wynans, Reese 211

XXX 255

Yacht Club Motel 80
Yardbirds 218
Yes 266
You Bet Your Life 68
"You Better Run" 52, 238
"You Better You Bet" 230
"You Can't Do That" 135

"You Can't Hurry Love" 39
You Can't Stop Rock 'n' Roll 272
You Don't Know Me: Rediscovering Eddie Arnold 139
"You Don't Own Me" 76
"You Really Got Me" 191, 196
"You Say Yes" 93
"You Took the Words Right Out of My Mouth (Hot Summer Night)" 103
"You'll Be in My Heart" 42, 44
Young, Richard 269, 270
Young Rascals (see Rascals) 53, 222, 235-247
"You're in Love" 10
"(You're) Having My Baby" 79
"(You're My) Soul and Inspiration" 237
"You've Got Another Thing Comin'" 93
"You've Lost That Lovin' Feeling" 271

Zacherley 169
Zander, Robin 264
Zappa, Frank 266
Zombie 169
"Zoot Suit" 218
Zucker, David 136
ZZ Top 118, 174, 213, 249-259
ZZ Top's First Album 250
ZZ Top's First Annual Texas Size Rompin' Stompin' Barn Dance and Bar B. Q. 250

www.ingramcontent.com/pod-product-compliance
Lightning Source LLC
Chambersburg PA
CBHW071652160426
43195CB00012B/1438